TWO STORY
HOME PLANS

A collection of 300 of our finest two-story
residential designs culled from the portfolios of
award-winning architects and designers across the country.

the
Garlinghouse
company

Two Story Home Plans, 4th Edition

James D. McNair III, *CEO & Publisher*
Steve Culpepper, *Editorial Director*
Debbie Cochran, *Managing Editor*
Christopher Berrien, *Art Director*
Debra Novitch, *Assistant Art Director*
Andrew Russell and Melani Gonzalez, *Production Artists*

Submit all Canadian plan orders
to the following address:

Garlinghouse Company, 102 Ellis Street, Penticton, BC V2A 4L5

Library of Congress: 97-77624
ISBN: 1-893536-00-9

10   9   8   7   6   5   4

Cover Plan # 24567 p.22

Table of Contents

Photography provided by Frank Betz and Associates, Inc.

design 60138 | The Perfect Family Home

Versatile Spaces Make Room for Young and Old

Imagine never having to worry about having enough room. With more than 3,000 square feet of living space, this home can provide that peace of mind.

From its ample two-story family room to its tandem three-car garage with optional sunroom, this plan delivers a huge return on the investment.

Designer Eric Taylor said a variety of versions of this home have been built all across the country. It started its life as a model home. Everywhere it's built, it wins the hearts of families, thanks to its amazing versatility.

"It has a big, wide two-story family room and a lot of people still like that. And the stacked (lined up in a row) living and dining rooms, often people will put French doors between the two," according to Taylor. This allows the open floor plan to be divided for use in com-

pletely different functions, such as turning the living room into a media room or home office.

"Some people take the rear portion of the garage and turn that into a sunroom. In fact, these photographs show the sunroom. And we've also had people take this plan and turn that optional sunroom into a bedroom downstairs with a small bath, which is great for a child or as a guestroom."

Taylor likes the fact that sightlines are clear throughout the house. "You see everything. And thanks to the sightlines, where you can see from one room, through another and to the outdoors, even though the house is just over 3,000 square feet, that openness makes it feel much bigger."

One line of site is obstructed, he said; but that's purposeful. Looking into the kitchen, the island and triangular coat closet/pantry structure combine to block views of the messy part of the kitchen, which mothers will love."

Taylor said the versatility of this design will allow it to work well on a narrow infill lot in an old neighborhood. "There's just a lot of flexibility to it."

OPPOSITE: Pleasant and comfortable, this great family home presents a welcoming face to the neighborhood.

RIGHT: Elegant wainscoting, crown molding and a bank of tall windows add grace and style to the formal dining room.

BELOW: This optional sunroom looks through French doors into the two-story family room. This room could either remain as part of the garage or could also become a small bedroom suite for a child or guests.

TOP LEFT: A large room with tray ceiling and adjacent sitting area, the master bedroom enjoys its own half of the upstairs, ensuring privacy and quiet.

TOP: The deep tray ceiling in the master bath adds a dramatic sense of depth and scale to the room, which includes an oversized tub, separate shower and enclosed water closet.

LEFT: A two-story wall of windows adds plenty of natural light and visual warmth to the family room. Notice the built-in niche to the left of the fireplace.

RIGHT: The kitchen area combines the best of form with function in a well-organized space that serves as breakfast area, cooking area and butler's pantry.

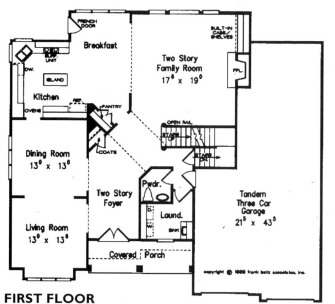

FIRST FLOOR

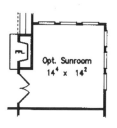

Opt. Sunroom
14⁴ x 14²

design 60138

Units	Single
Price Code	H
Total Finished	3,068 sq. ft.
First Finished	1,473 sq. ft.
Second Finished	1,595 sq. ft.
Bonus Unfinished	197 sq. ft.
Dimensions	53'x49'
Foundation	Basement
	Crawl space
Bedrooms	4
Full Baths	3
Half Baths	1
First Ceiling	9'
Second Ceiling	8'
Max Ridge Height	32'6"

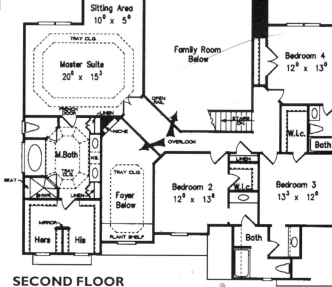

SECOND FLOOR

Photography provided by John Ehrenclou

design 10396 | Fit For a Wooded Hillside

High Windows and Broad Decks Take in the View

What a lifestyle. The cool shade of a quiet forest right out your door. And inside, all the pleasures of home. This completely outfitted home contains all the elements you want, from a private upstairs master suite to a recreation room and a large shop space. Sometimes a home in the woods can be dark inside. But thanks to large walls of windows, numerous skylights and a bank of clerestory windows, light and views spill throughout the home.

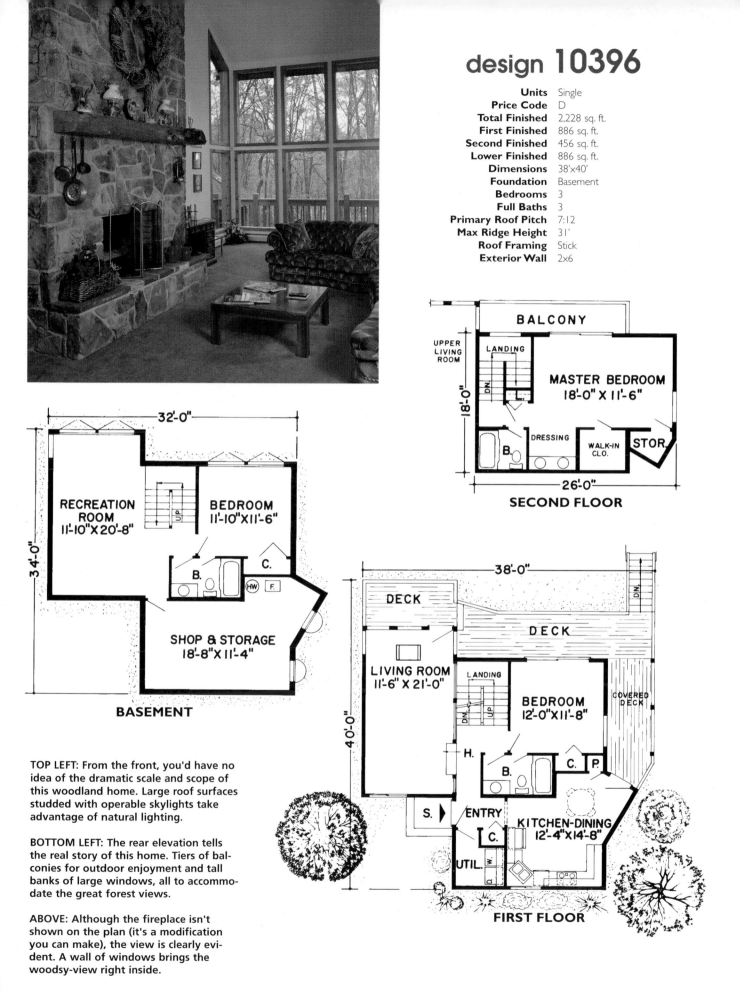

design 10396

Units	Single
Price Code	D
Total Finished	2,228 sq. ft.
First Finished	886 sq. ft.
Second Finished	456 sq. ft.
Lower Finished	886 sq. ft.
Dimensions	38'x40'
Foundation	Basement
Bedrooms	3
Full Baths	3
Primary Roof Pitch	7:12
Max Ridge Height	31'
Roof Framing	Stick
Exterior Wall	2x6

BALCONY

UPPER LIVING ROOM

LANDING

DN.

MASTER BEDROOM
18'-0" X 11'-6"

18'-0"

B.

DRESSING

WALK-IN CLO.

STOR.

26'-0"

SECOND FLOOR

32'-0"

34'-0"

RECREATION ROOM
11'-10" X 20'-8"

UP

BEDROOM
11'-10"X11'-6"

C.

B.

HW F.

SHOP & STORAGE
18'-8"X11'-4"

BASEMENT

38'-0"

DECK

DECK

DN.

LIVING ROOM
11'-6" X 21'-0"

LANDING

DN. UP

BEDROOM
12'-0"X11'-8"

COVERED DECK

40'-0"

H.

B.

C. P.

S.

ENTRY

C.

KITCHEN-DINING
12'-4"X14'-8"

UTIL. W.

FIRST FLOOR

TOP LEFT: From the front, you'd have no idea of the dramatic scale and scope of this woodland home. Large roof surfaces studded with operable skylights take advantage of natural lighting.

BOTTOM LEFT: The rear elevation tells the real story of this home. Tiers of balconies for outdoor enjoyment and tall banks of large windows, all to accommodate the great forest views.

ABOVE: Although the fireplace isn't shown on the plan (it's a modification you can make), the view is clearly evident. A wall of windows brings the woodsy-view right inside.

Photography provided by Alan Mascord Design Associates, Inc.

design 91595 | Arts & Crafts Comfort

TOP: Low eaves, earthy colors, natural siding and exposed rafter tails are trademark elements of Arts and Crafts designs, all displayed here in this beautiful reproduction.

BOTTOM: Just inside the foyer this gorgeous built-in bench awaits family and visitors alike. Sit down, unburden yourself of packages, coats and boots, and enjoy the result of first-class carpentry, woodworking and careful attention to detail.

Authentic Details and Great Craftsmanship Create a Stunner

Take a look at this home with its beautiful mix of natural siding, including shingles and local stone, its low, sheltering eaves, broad gables and inviting front steps and get a sense of what Arts and Crafts, or Craftsman style, was meant to be.

Inside, the careful craftsmanship and attention to detail carry through. For instance, just inside the foyer is a beautifully made built-in bench flanked by see-through display cabinets with leaded-glass doors. Note how the piece ends well below the ceiling, creating a dramatic partial view of the adjoining dining room and allowing light to flow through.

In the secluded downstairs study is a built-in window-seat and daybed. Notice a few of the particular features of the daybed and surroundings: Built-in shelving, a small cabinet below the shelves, drawers below the

LEFT: The Craftsman tradition of natural wood finishes reaches a contemporary zenith in this large gourmet kitchen, exemplified by the pot rack made of clear western fir. RIGHT: Box beams, built-in china cabinets with leaded-glass doors, stenciling and lots of natural wood clearly define this dining room as an heir to the Arts and Crafts tradition.

daybed, a picture rail with meticulously detailed support brackets running around the room, chair rail and clear douglas fir wainscoting.

While the dining room is rich in traditional Craftsman touches, such as the built-in china cabinets, box-beams, stenciling, and rich natural wood tones, straight across the hall the great room is an altogether different story.

The great room features the same level of care as the rest of the house, and the same sense of Craftsman tradition, but it's somehow more contemporary. Some of the explanation for the difference can be seen in the woodwork and trim: It's all painted as opposed to the heavy woodsy presence in the rest of the home's woodwork.

Another difference the designer brought to the great room was the scale. At two stories, this room is probably unlike any other Arts and Crafts room of its kind. The large number of windows really lets the light pour into the room. But despite the airy quality of the space, it's all kept grounded in traditional Craftsman sensibility by the massive stone fireplace.

Although box beams and columns set the spaces apart, this home still manages to feel quite open. Subtle stylistic differences from space to space become clearer as one walks from the great room into the kitchen.

Abundant outdoor-indoor spaces grace the home, such as the front porch with three built-in benches, and the decks and porches around the rest of the home. A deck awaits outside the master suite upstairs and forms the roof of the private deck off the study below. Also on the first floor, a small porch out back lets onto the breakfast nook and sunroom.

Two Story Home Plans 11

TOP LEFT: Although the woodwork in the great room is painted, unlike the more traditional natural woodwork in the rest of the home, the flavor of Arts and Crafts remains strongly anchored by the massive hand-laid stone fireplace and Craftsman mantle.

TOP RIGHT and BOTTOM LEFT: Secluded even though it's in the front of the home, this private study and library brings out the best of Craftsman design. A few elements of note: natural woodwork, built-ins like the shelving and daybed, earthy colors like the mossy green of the walls and tiles, and beautiful details, as displayed in the woodwork throughout the space.

Details clearly make a lot of difference in this home: From left to right beginning with the top row: a natural wood picture rail with hand-crafted support brackets in the study; Craftsman details in the study mantle; inlaid wood and more Craftsman detailing in the great room fireplace; leaded-glass see-through doors flank the built in bench in the foyer; painted box beams with stenciling in the dining room; a beautifully made natural wood range hood and cabinetry in the kitchen.

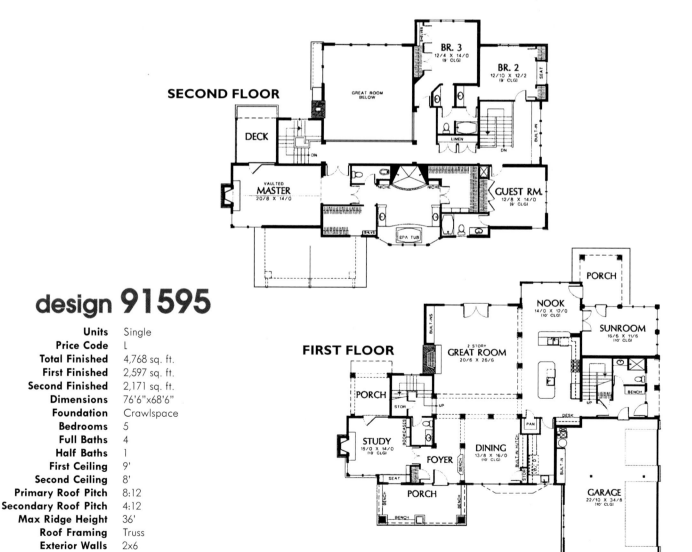

SECOND FLOOR

BR. 3
12/4 X 14/0
(9' CLG)

BR. 2
12/10 X 12/2
(9' CLG)

GREAT ROOM BELOW

DECK

LINEN

VAULTED
MASTER
20/8 X 14/0

GUEST RM.
12/8 X 14/0
(9' CLG)

SPA TUB

FIRST FLOOR

PORCH

NOOK
14/0 X 12/0
(10' CLG)

SUNROOM
16/6 X 11/6
(10' CLG)

2-STORY
GREAT ROOM
20/6 X 26/6

PORCH

BENCH

STUDY
15/0 X 14/0
(10' CLG)

FOYER

DINING
13/8 X 16/0
(10' CLG)

SEAT

PORCH

GARAGE
22/10 X 34/8
(10' CLG)

design 91595

Units	Single
Price Code	L
Total Finished	4,768 sq. ft.
First Finished	2,597 sq. ft.
Second Finished	2,171 sq. ft.
Dimensions	76'6"x68'6"
Foundation	Crawlspace
Bedrooms	5
Full Baths	4
Half Baths	1
First Ceiling	9'
Second Ceiling	8'
Primary Roof Pitch	8:12
Secondary Roof Pitch	4:12
Max Ridge Height	36'
Roof Framing	Truss
Exterior Walls	2x6

LEFT: Traditional details highlight the exterior of this thoroughly modern home which features the open floor plan that's so popular with families today.

BELOW: The use of a different siding material (in this case shingle-siding instead of clapboard) and a change of color scheme can help personalize a home.

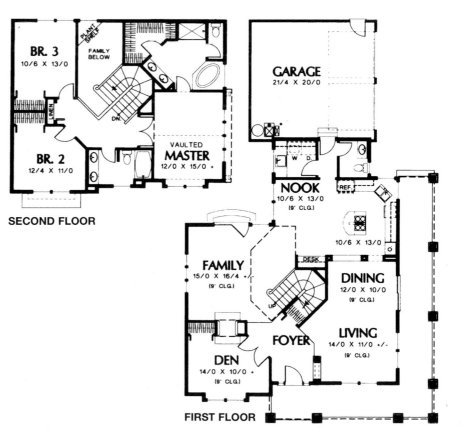

Photography provided by
Alan Mascord Design Associates, Inc.

design 91592 | Classic Update

Price Code: E

■ This plan features:

— Three bedrooms

— Two full and one half baths

■ A full wrap-around porch graces the exterior of this home

■ The open, central staircase defines the living spaces and anchors the home, offering equal access to all the rooms

■ The family room and den share a fireplace

■ This home is designed with a crawl-space foundation

■ The dimensions of this home are 43' x 69'

First floor — 1,317 sq. ft.
Second Floor — 916 sq. ft.
Garage — 427 sq. ft.

Total living area:
2,287 sq. ft.

SECOND FLOOR

BR. 3
10/6 X 13/0

FAMILY BELOW

PLANT SHELF

LINEN

DN

BR. 2
12/4 X 11/0

VAULTED
MASTER
12/0 X 15/0

FIRST FLOOR

GARAGE
21/4 X 20/0

W D

NOOK
10/6 X 13/0
(9' CLG.)

REF.

10/6 X 13/0

FAMILY
15/0 X 16/4
(9' CLG.)

DESK

DINING
12/0 X 10/0
(9' CLG.)

UP

FOYER

LIVING
14/0 X 11/0 +/-
(9' CLG.)

DEN
14/0 X 10/0
(9' CLG.)

Photography provided by Frank Betz and Associates, Inc.

design 60137 | Comfortable Country Appeal

An Efficient Plan
Puts Every Inch to Use

Originally designed for a local home show, this spacious but cost-effective design has found broad appeal.

"This home is much more cost effective than its size would suggest, but it has all the bells and whistles that people want today," according to Eric Taylor, designer with Frank Betz Associates.

"It has a nice sitting room in the master suite; it has a bedroom downstairs, which people really want now. It has a large family room, elegant dining room, an ample kitchen with plenty of storage, a big front porch and front and rear stairs."

Although its particular style is hard to peg, Taylor calls it a hybrid. "I can't say it's Colonial, or Georgian—it's a nice mix of many favorite styles. This house simply goes back to our country traditions."

What makes this nearly 4,500 square-foot house so efficient is its basic rectangular shape, which has been enlivened by carefully placed front gables, a wide porch with attached octagonal gazebo and generous rooms full of elegant detailing.

"The master suite is very open," according to Taylor. "And we use the fireplace peninsula (a three-sided fireplace) to delineate between the bedroom and sitting area." An octagonal tray ceiling enriches the master bedroom, further visually separating it from the vaulted sitting room within the open plan.

"This house builds a lot more efficiently and cost effectively than some others because it makes use of every square foot," Taylor said. "It makes very efficient use of space."

TOP: This traditional design offers a comfortable country lifestyle and lots of space for every member of the family. Especially appealing are its well-designed front gables, wide porch and attached gazebo.

TOP LEFT: With its recessed sideboard niche, wainscoting, arched entry and deep crown molding, the dining room represents all that's most elegant about the traditional country home, in which formal spaces are balanced against the informal.

TOP RIGHT: With its traditional standing-seam metal roof, hand-crafted Chippendale rail and octagonal form, this gazebo attached to the front porch provides a quiet, separate outdoor space for individual relaxation or small group privacy.

MIDDLE LEFT: The large kitchen island with double sink does a great job of visually separating the kitchen from the adjoining breakfast area and family room. Banks of tall windows flood the kitchen with natural light.

BOTTOM LEFT: A full retreat is available in the master bedroom suite, which includes a spacious bedroom with adjoining sitting room and three-sided peninsula fireplace.

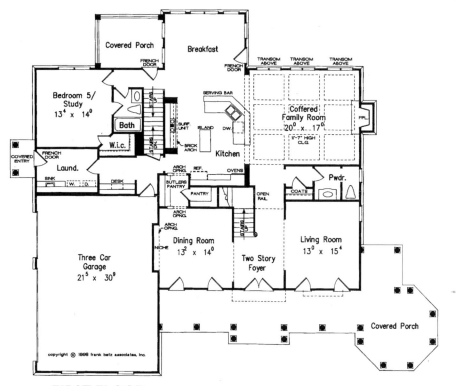

FIRST FLOOR

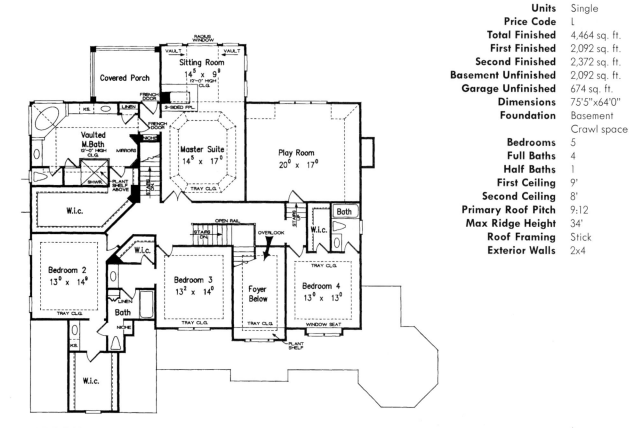

SECOND FLOOR

design 60137

Units	Single
Price Code	L
Total Finished	4,464 sq. ft.
First Finished	2,092 sq. ft.
Second Finished	2,372 sq. ft.
Basement Unfinished	2,092 sq. ft.
Garage Unfinished	674 sq. ft.
Dimensions	75'5"x64'0"
Foundation	Basement
	Crawl space
Bedrooms	5
Full Baths	4
Half Baths	1
First Ceiling	9'
Second Ceiling	8'
Primary Roof Pitch	9:12
Max Ridge Height	34'
Roof Framing	Stick
Exterior Walls	2x4

Photography provided by John Ehrenclou

design 24802 | Life On a Grand Scale

Lots of Natural Light Complements This Open Floor plan

Fully-equipped with the latest amenities, yet true to its classic inspiration, this home provides all the modern family requires for a life of real luxury. From its spacious master suite with adjoining study and room-sized walk-in closet to its home theater, recreation room, hearth room and large open kitchen with breakfast area; this is the place you want to call home. And throughout the home, thoughtful added storage allows you to clear out the clutter and enjoy life at its best.

TOP: An interesting composition of gables and varying window shapes, stucco siding and a brick base course work to make a visually appealing home.

LEFT: Graceful columns frame the sunny elegance of the vaulted dining room.

TOP: Beautiful, classic built-ins surround this Federal-style mantle, echoing the curved theme throughout the living room. BOTTOM LEFT: Spacious and serene, the master suite offers room for a private sitting area. BOTTOM RIGHT: A free-standing, clear-glass shower and windowed whirlpool tub create a bright and airy master bath.

TOP: Dual island workstations provide ample space for more than one chef to prepare dinner in this spacious kitchen.

LEFT: With lots of windows on two sides, this clean, bright hearth room, furnished with a table and chairs, provides a very pleasant place to enjoy your morning coffee.

OPPOSITE BOTTOM: With the right orientation, the rear elevation can provide this home with nearly all the light it needs during daylight hours, filling the home with soft natural light.

design 24802

Units	Single
Price Code	L
Total Finished	4,064 sq. ft.
Main Finished	2,466 sq. ft.
Lower Finished	1,598 sq. ft.
Basement Unfinished	876 sq. ft.
Garage Unfinished	665 sq. ft.
Deck Unfinished	144 sq. ft.
Dimensions	78'x52'4''
Foundation	Basement
Bedrooms	4
Full Baths	3
Main Ceiling	9'-11'
Primary Roof Pitch	8:12
Secondary Roof Pitch	10:12
Max Ridge Height	32'
Roof Framing	Stick
Exterior Walls	2x6

LOWER FLOOR

MAIN FLOOR

Photography provided by Susan Gilmore

design 24567 | Modern Traditional

Beautiful Mix of Styles Blends with Any Neighborhood

The exterior of this attractive home successfully blends contemporary features with a traditional sensibility in an original-looking hybrid style. Pretty details like the double columns of the front porch and the thoughtful mix of siding styles give this modern home a traditional feel that will make it blend beautifully with existing neighborhoods while standing out as an original, contemporary design with great details.

The two-story foyer and open staircase lead you into an efficient floor plan that makes great use of space while providing all the comforts. From the well-proportioned formal spaces to the well-appointed master suite, this home offers all the best of two-story design.

OPPOSITE TOP: A simple yet effective color scheme highlights the beautiful mix of siding and exterior details of this well designed home.

OPPOSITE LEFT: The simple beauty of this home's fine details is highlighted in the view through the arched opening of the family room into the breakfast room and the thoughtfully laid-out kitchen beyond.

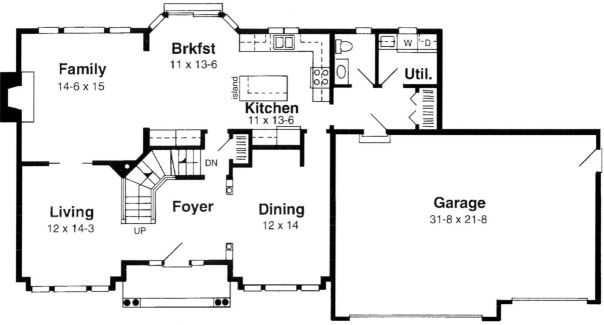

FIRST FLOOR

design 24567

Units	Single
Price Code	E
Total Finished	2,432 sq. ft.
First Finished	1,332 sq. ft.
Second Finished	1,100 sq. ft.
Basement Unfinished	1,293 sq. ft.
Garage Unfinished	686 sq. ft.
Dimensions	72'x36'8''
Foundation	Basement
	Crawlspace
	Slab
Bedrooms	3
Full Baths	2
Half Baths	1
First Ceiling	9'
Second Ceiling	8'
Primary Roof Pitch	8:12
Secondary Roof Pitch	12:12
Max Ridge Height	31'
Roof Framing	Stick
Exterior Walls	2x6

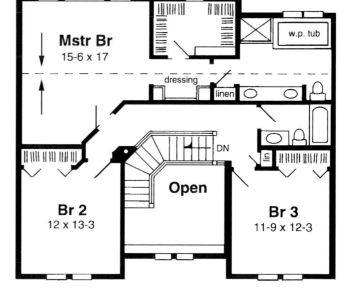

SECOND FLOOR

design 99491 | Cul-de-Sac Favorite

Price Code: C

■ This plan features:

— Four bedrooms

— Two full and one half baths

■ Efficient floor plan packs a lot of living into this compact design

■ Inviting wrap-around porch leads into large foyer with big closet and views of the fireplaced great room

■ Second floor master bedroom suite offers the serenity of a whirlpool tub and ample closet space

■ This home comes with a basement or slab foundation

■ The dimensions of this home are 44' x 40'

First floor — 919 sq. ft.
Second Floor — 927 sq. ft.
Garage — 414 sq. ft.

Total living area:
1,846 sq. ft.

FIRST FLOOR

SECOND FLOOR

RIGHT: This modern interpretation of the classic Victorian style features an eye-catching turret with wrap-around porch.

Photography provided by John Ehrenclou

design 20093 | Victorian Charmer

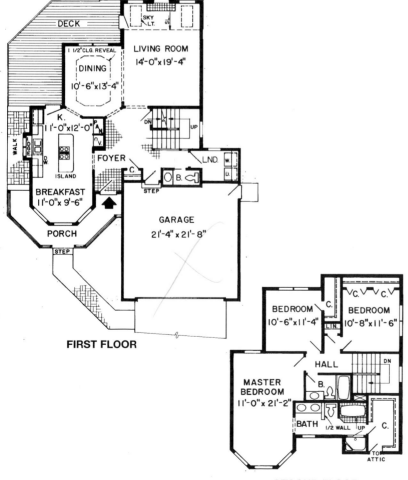

FIRST FLOOR

DECK

1 1/2" CLG. REVEAL

DINING
10'-6"x13'-4"

LIVING ROOM
14'-0"x19'-4"

SKY LT.

K.
11'-0"x12'-0"

WALK

ISLAND

FOYER

BREAKFAST
11'-0"x 9'-6"

PORCH

STEP

GARAGE
21'-4" x 21'-8"

DN / UP

LND. W. D.

STEP

B.

SECOND FLOOR

BEDROOM
10'-6"x11'-4"

BEDROOM
10'-8"x11'-6"

C.

HALL

DN

MASTER BEDROOM
11'-0"x 21'-2"

B.

BATH

1/2 WALL UP

C.

TO ATTIC

Price Code: D

■ This plan features:

— Three bedrooms

— Two full and one half baths

■ A modern, flowing floor plan distinguishes this graceful home

■ The fireplaced living room with its skylights and access to a rear deck opens to the tray-ceilinged dining room and the spacious foyer

■ The breakfast nook features a bay window looking out onto the wrap-around front porch

■ This home is designed with a basement foundation

■ The dimensions of this home are 43' x 56'

First floor — 1,027 sq. ft.
Second Floor — 974 sq. ft.
Garage — 476 sq. ft.

Total living area:
2,001 sq. ft.

Photography provided by Design Basics, Inc.

design 94904 | Fabulous Farmhouse

Price Code: C

■ This plan features:

— Three bedrooms

— Two full and one half baths

■ Covered porch leads into two-story foyer in this lovely center-hall plan

■ French doors lead from the bay-windowed living room into the fireplaced family room

■ Mud room entrance, accessible from the rear and the garage, is perfect for kids' coats and muddy boots

■ Spacious master suite features a cathedral ceiling, a whirlpool with a view and an enormous closet

■ This home comes with a crawlspace foundation

■ The dimensions of this home are 55' 4" x 37' 8"

First floor — 1,093 sq. ft.
Second Floor — 905 sq. ft.
Garage — 527 sq. ft.

Total living area:
1,998 sq. ft.

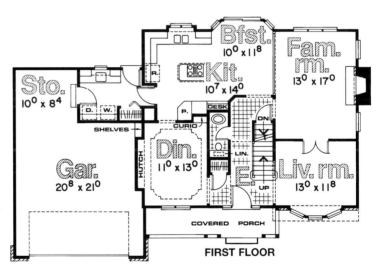

FIRST FLOOR

SECOND FLOOR

Photography provided by Alan Mascord Design Associates, Inc.

design 91526 | Family Flair

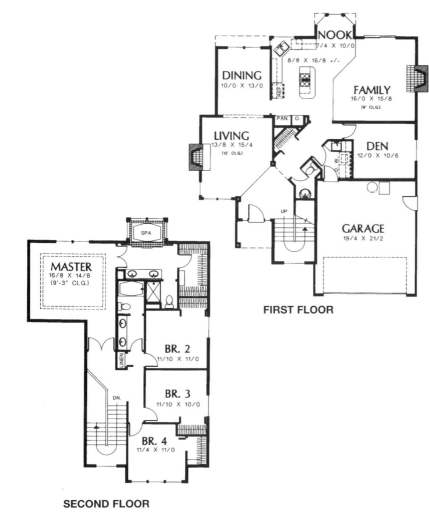

FIRST FLOOR

SECOND FLOOR

Price Code: E

■ This plan features:

— Four bedrooms

— Two full and one half baths

■ Striking modern design offers ample space for any family

■ Both the living room and the family room feature fireplaces

■ A nice size den tucked away from the main public rooms offers a cozy retreat

■ Large master suite plus three bedrooms and two full baths on the second floor make this home ideal for a growing family

■ This home comes with a crawlspace foundation

■ The dimensions of this home are 42' x 53' 4"

First floor — 1,321 sq. ft.
Second Floor — 1,155 sq. ft.
Garage — 420 sq. ft.

Total living area:
2,476 sq. ft.

design **64128** | **Timeless Classic**

Price Code: H

- This plan features:

— Three bedrooms

— Three full baths

- Thoughtful cabinetry highlight the kitchen with its center island and pass-through bar to the great room

- Elegant columns define the formal living areas

- The first floor master suite features access to a rear porch, ample walk-in closet space and a bath with whirlpool tub, walk-in shower and double vanity

- This home is designed with a slab foundation*

- The dimensions of this home are 47' x 50'

First floor — 1,716 sq. ft.
Second Floor — 618 sq. ft.

Total living area:
2,334 sq. ft.

* Alternate foundation options available at an additional charge. Please call 1-800-235-5700 for more information.

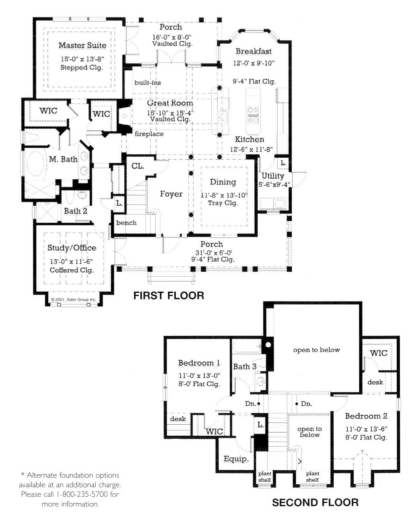

design 64170 | Sumptuous French Country

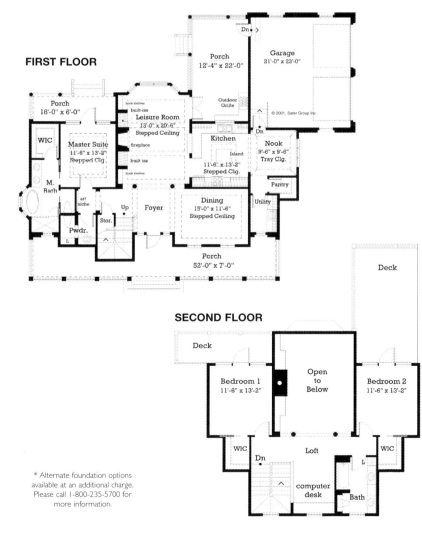

FIRST FLOOR

- Porch 18'-0" x 6'-0"
- WIC
- Master Suite 11'-6" x 13'-2" Stepped Clg.
- M. Bath
- art niche
- Pwdr.
- Stor.
- Up
- Foyer
- Porch 12'-4" x 22'-0"
- Garage 21'-0" x 23'-0"
- Dn
- book shelves / built-ins
- Leisure Room 13'-0" x 20'-6" Stepped Ceiling
- fireplace
- built ins
- book shelves
- Outdoor Grille
- © 2001, Sater Group Inc.
- Kitchen
- Island
- 11'-6" x 13'-2" Stepped Clg.
- Dn
- Nook 9'-6" x 9'-6" Tray Clg.
- Pantry
- Dining 15'-0" x 11'-6" Stepped Ceiling
- Utility
- Porch 52'-0" x 7'-0"

SECOND FLOOR

- Deck
- Deck
- Bedroom 1 11'-6" x 13'-2"
- Open to Below
- Bedroom 2 11'-6" x 13'-2"
- WIC
- Dn
- Loft
- WIC
- computer desk
- Bath

* Alternate foundation options available at an additional charge. Please call 1-800-235-5700 for more information.

Price Code: I

■ This plan features:

— Three bedrooms

— Three full and one half baths

■ The leisure room offers inviting spaciousness with its grand scale, stepped ceiling, built-ins and fireplace

■ The first floor master suite features access to a private rear porch and a luxurious bath with bay-window whirlpool tub

■ Two second floor bedrooms feature private decks and walk-in closets

■ This home is designed with a crawl-space foundation*

■ The dimensions of this home are 70' x 55' 8"

First floor — 1,493 sq. ft.
Second Floor — 723 sq. ft.

Total living area:
2,216 sq. ft.

design 64177 | Graceful Victorian

Price Code: I

■ This plan features:

— Three bedrooms

— Three full baths

■ The grand room features columns, coffered ceilings, built-ins and three sets of French doors that lead onto a rear porch

■ The first floor master suite features a stepped ceiling, bay window, his and her walk-in closets and a large, private bath

■ Two second floor bedrooms feature built-ins and walk-in closets

■ This home is designed with a crawl-space foundation*

■ The dimensions of this home are 76' 4" x 69' 10"

First floor — 2,215 sq. ft.
Second Floor — 708 sq. ft.

Total living area:
2,923 sq. ft.

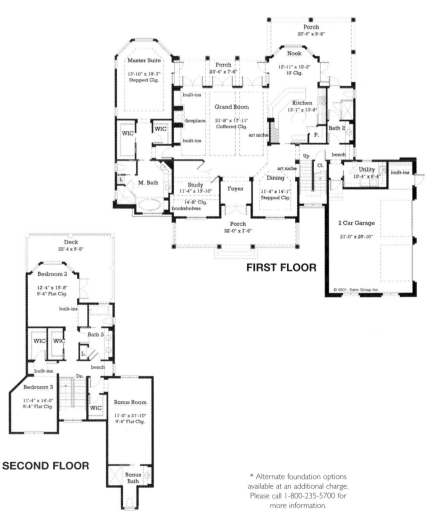

* Alternate foundation options available at an additional charge. Please call 1-800-235-5700 for more information.

design 65001 | Open and Airy

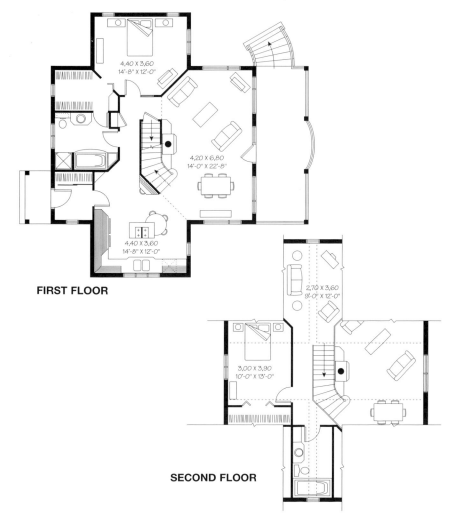

FIRST FLOOR

4,40 X 3,60
14'-8" X 12'-0"

4,20 X 6,80
14'-0" X 22'-8"

4,40 X 3,60
14'-8" X 12'-0"

SECOND FLOOR

2,70 X 3,60
9'-0" X 12'-0"

3,00 X 3,90
10'-0" X 13'-0"

Price Code: A

■ This plan features:

— Three bedrooms

— Two full baths

■ The two-story great room features a woodstove and open staircase

■ An upper-level loft can serve as a third bedroom or create a private sitting area or lounge

■ The first floor bathroom can be accessed both from the hall and from the master bedroom

■ This home is designed with a basement foundation

■ The dimensions of this home are 32' x 40'

First floor — 1,024 sq. ft.
Second Floor — 456 sq. ft.

Total living area:
1,480 sq. ft.

design 65003 | Charming Cottage

Price Code: A

■ This plan features:

— Two bedrooms

— Two full baths

■ This cozy design packs a lot of living into its efficient use of space with ample storage and volume ceilings

■ The great room has a cathedral ceiling and a fireplace

■ An upper-level loft creates a private sitting area off the master bedroom

■ This home is designed with a crawlspace foundation.

■ The dimensions of this home are 22'8" x 26' 8"

First floor — 593 sq. ft.
Second Floor — 383 sq. ft.

Total living area:
976 sq. ft.

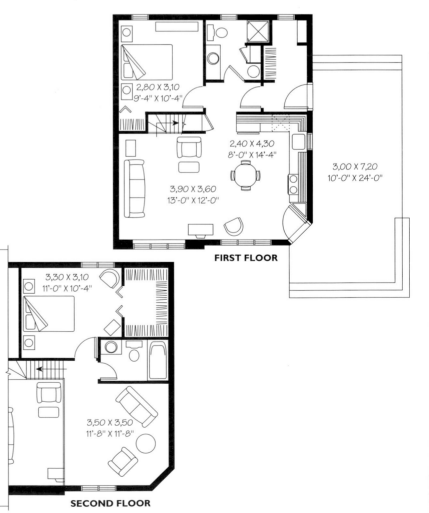

2,80 X 3,10
9'-4" X 10'-4"

2,40 X 4,30
8'-0" X 14'-4"

3,90 X 3,60
13'-0" X 12'-0"

3,00 X 7,20
10'-0" X 24'-0"

FIRST FLOOR

3,30 X 3,10
11'-0" X 10'-4"

3,50 X 3,50
11'-8" X 11'-8"

SECOND FLOOR

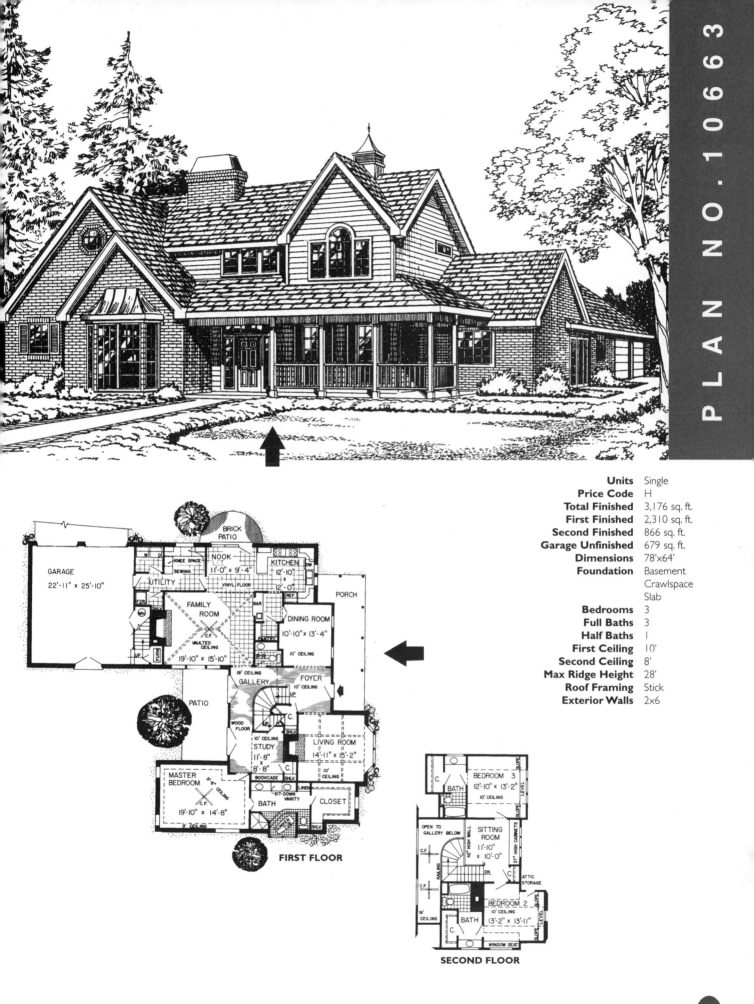

FIRST FLOOR

GARAGE
22'-11" x 25'-10"

BRICK PATIO

NOOK
11'-0" x 9'-4"

KITCHEN
12'-10" x 12'-0"

UTILITY

FAMILY ROOM
19'-10" x 15'-10"
VAULTED CEILING

DINING ROOM
10'-10" x 13'-4"

PORCH

PATIO

GALLERY

FOYER

WOOD FLOOR

STUDY
11'-8" x 8'-8"

LIVING ROOM
14'-11" x 15'-2"

MASTER BEDROOM
19'-10" x 14'-8"

BATH

CLOSET

SECOND FLOOR

BEDROOM 3
12'-10" x 13'-2"

BATH

OPEN TO GALLERY BELOW

SITTING ROOM
11'-10" x 10'-0"

ATTIC STORAGE

BEDROOM 2
13'-2" x 13'-11"

BATH

WINDOW SEAT

Units	Single
Price Code	H
Total Finished	3,176 sq. ft.
First Finished	2,310 sq. ft.
Second Finished	866 sq. ft.
Garage Unfinished	679 sq. ft.
Dimensions	78'x64'
Foundation	Basement Crawlspace Slab
Bedrooms	3
Full Baths	3
Half Baths	1
First Ceiling	10'
Second Ceiling	8'
Max Ridge Height	28'
Roof Framing	Stick
Exterior Walls	2x6

Units	Single
Price Code	E
Total Finished	2,495 sq. ft.
First Finished	1,142 sq. ft.
Second Finished	1,353 sq. ft.
Basement Unfinished	1,142 sq. ft.
Garage Unfinished	512 sq. ft.
Dimensions	57'4''x43'
Foundation	Basement
	Crawlspace
Bedrooms	4
Full Baths	2
Half Baths	1
First Ceiling	9'
Second Ceiling	8'
Max Ridge Height	31'6''
Roof Framing	Stick
Exterior Walls	2x4

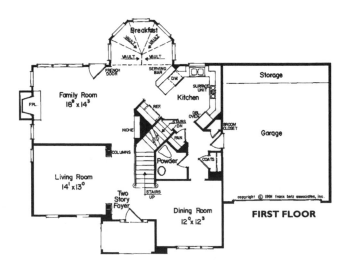

To order your Blueprints, call 1-800-235-5700

Units	Single
Price Code	K
Total Finished	3,895 sq. ft.
First Finished	2,727 sq. ft.
Second Finished	1,168 sq. ft.
Bonus Unfinished	213 sq. ft.
Basement Unfinished	2,250 sq. ft.
Garage Unfinished	984 sq. ft.
Porch Unfinished	402 sq. ft.
Dimensions	73'8"x72'2"
Foundation	Basement
Bedrooms	4
Full Baths	4
Half Baths	1
First Ceiling	9'
Second Ceiling	8'
Vaulted Ceiling	22'
Max Ridge Height	43'
Roof Framing	Stick
Exterior Walls	2x6

Photography supplied by the Meredith Corporation

FIRST FLOOR

PATIO

FAMILY 15x19

DECK

BRKFST 12x10

PORCH

MASTER BEDROOM 15x18

CLOS

KIT 18x14

GREAT-ROOM 18x16

UP

DN

O R

W D P

BATH

CLOS

LDRY

DINING 12x17

ENTRY

GUEST/STUDY 14x11

GARAGE 20x14

UP

PORCH

SECOND FLOOR

OPEN TO FAMILY

OFFICE 10x13

OPEN TO GREAT-ROOM

BEDROOM 12x12

DN

BRIDGE

DN

BEDROOM 12x18

CLOS

BEDROOM 12x14

OPEN TO ENTRY

BONUS ROOM 10x19

Units	Single
Price Code	F
Total Finished	2,582 sq. ft.
First Finished	2,003 sq. ft.
Second Finished	579 sq. ft.
Bonus Unfinished	262 sq. ft.
Basement Unfinished	2,003 sq. ft.
Garage Unfinished	400 sq. ft.
Dimensions	54'x60'
Foundation	Basement Crawlspace
Bedrooms	4
Full Baths	3
First Ceiling	9'
Second Ceiling	8'
Max Ridge Height	31'
Roof Framing	Stick
Exterior Walls	2x4

FIRST FLOOR

54'-0"

Sunroom/Keeping 13'⁹ x 13'⁹

Breakfast

Bedroom 4/Study 11'⁹ x 11'⁰

Vaulted M.Bath

Vaulted Great Room 15'⁰ x 19'⁹

Kitchen

Bath

Her's

His

60'-0"

Master Suite 13'⁰ x 21'⁵

Two Story Foyer

Dining Room 12'⁰ x 13'³

Laund.

Garage 19'⁵ x 19'⁹

Sitting

© Frank Betz Associates, Inc.

SECOND FLOOR

Great Room Below

Bath

Bedroom 3 12'⁰ x 13'⁰

Foyer Below

Bedroom 2 12'⁰ x 13'³

W.i.c.

W.I.C.

Opt. Bonus Rm. 11'⁵ x 19'⁹

Units	Single
Price Code	E
Total Finished	2,345 sq. ft.
First Finished	1,395 sq. ft.
Second Finished	950 sq. ft.
Basement Unfinished	1,395 sq. ft.
Garage Unfinished	396 sq. ft.
Dimensions	48'6''×47'
Foundation	Basement
	Crawlspace
	Slab
Bedrooms	3
Full Baths	2
Half Baths	I
First Ceiling	9'
Second Ceiling	9'
Max Ridge Height	30'9''
Roof Framing	Truss
Exterior Walls	2x4

FIRST FLOOR

Nook 10-2 x 10-2

Kitchen 14'5 x 14'0

Great Room 20-2 x 19-9

Sunroom 10-1 x 10-5

Hall

Dining Room 11-9 x 14-9

Foyer

Two Car Garage 20-0 x 20-0

Porch

SECOND FLOOR

Master Bedroom 12-0 x 17-0

Bedroom #3 12-0 x 12-0

Bedroom #2 11-8 x 14-9

OPTIONAL CRAWLSPACE/SLAB

To order your Blueprints, call 1-800-235-5700

Units	Single
Price Code	D
Total Finished	2,119 sq. ft.
First Finished	1,132 sq. ft.
Second Finished	987 sq. ft.
Basement Unfinished	1,132 sq. ft.
Garage Unfinished	556 sq. ft.
Dimensions	56'x38'
Bedrooms	3
Full Baths	2
Half Baths	1
First Ceiling	9'
Max Ridge Height	32'

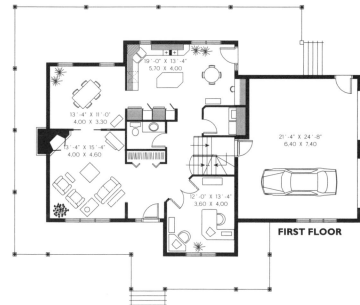

FIRST FLOOR

SECOND FLOOR

To order your Blueprints, call 1-800-235-5700

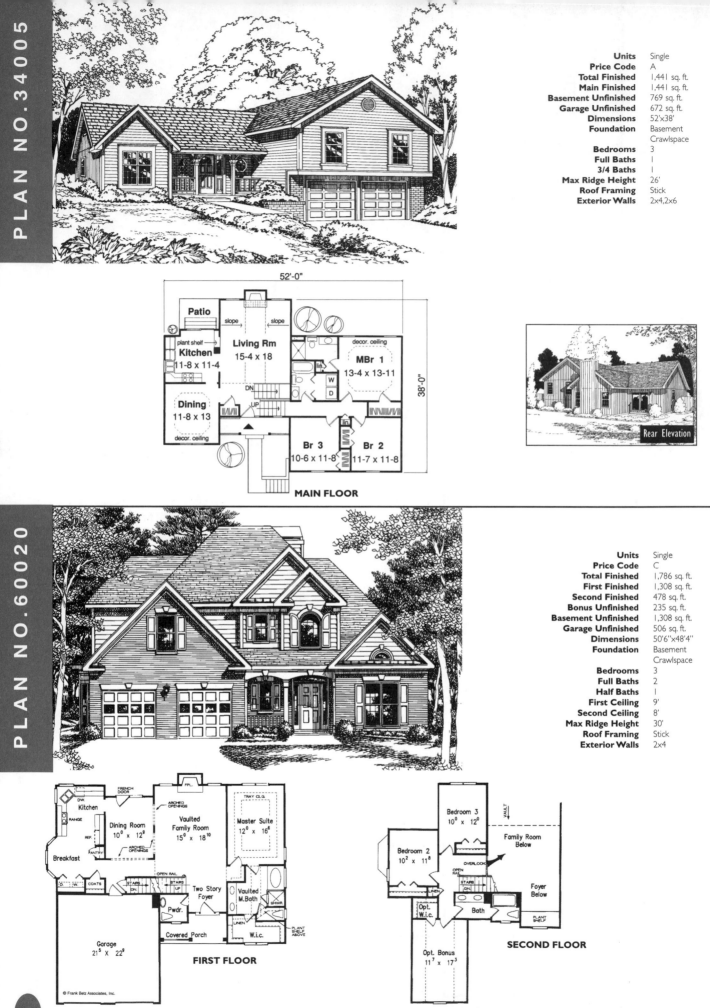

Units	Single
Price Code	A
Total Finished	1,441 sq. ft.
Main Finished	1,441 sq. ft.
Basement Unfinished	769 sq. ft.
Garage Unfinished	672 sq. ft.
Dimensions	52'x38'
Foundation	Basement
	Crawlspace
Bedrooms	3
Full Baths	1
3/4 Baths	1
Max Ridge Height	26'
Roof Framing	Stick
Exterior Walls	2x4,2x6

52'-0"

Patio

plant shelf

Kitchen
11-8 x 11-4

slope   slope

Living Rm
15-4 x 18

decor. ceiling

MBr 1
13-4 x 13-11

38'-0"

Dining
11-8 x 13

decor. ceiling

DN

UP

W
D

Br 3
10-6 x 11-8

Br 2
11-7 x 11-8

MAIN FLOOR

Rear Elevation

Units	Single
Price Code	C
Total Finished	1,786 sq. ft.
First Finished	1,308 sq. ft.
Second Finished	478 sq. ft.
Bonus Unfinished	235 sq. ft.
Basement Unfinished	1,308 sq. ft.
Garage Unfinished	506 sq. ft.
Dimensions	50'6''x48'4''
Foundation	Basement
	Crawlspace
Bedrooms	3
Full Baths	2
Half Baths	1
First Ceiling	9'
Second Ceiling	8'
Max Ridge Height	30'
Roof Framing	Stick
Exterior Walls	2x4

Kitchen

FRENCH DOOR

DW.

RANGE

Dining Room
10' x 12'

REF.

PANTRY

ARCHED OPENINGS

FPL.

Vaulted Family Room
15' x 18'10

ARCHED OPENINGS

TRAY CLG.

Master Suite
12' x 16'6

Breakfast

D.   W.

COATS

STAIRS DN

OPEN RAIL

STAIRS UP

Two Story Foyer

Pwdr.

Covered Porch

Vaulted M.Bath

SHWR.

LINEN

PLANT SHELF ABOVE

W.i.c.

Garage
21'5 x 22'8

FIRST FLOOR

© Frank Betz Associates, Inc.

VAULT

Bedroom 3
10' x 12'0

Family Room Below

Bedroom 2
10'2 x 11'8

OPEN RAIL

OVERLOOK

LINEN

OPEN RAIL

STAIRS DN

Foyer Below

Bath

Opt. W.i.c.

PLANT SHELF

Opt. Bonus
11'7 x 17'3

SECOND FLOOR

To order your Blueprints, call 1-800-235-5700

REAR ELEVATION

SECOND FLOOR

BR. 2
10/0 X 12/2

ATTIC STORAGE

OPEN TO BELOW

LINEN

BONUS
20/2 X 23/0 +/-

DN.

ATTIC STORAGE

OPEN TO BELOW

BR. 3
10/6 X 12/0

Units	Single
Price Code	D
Total Finished	2,196 sq. ft.
Dimensions	56'x50'
Foundation	Crawlspace
Bedrooms	3
Full Baths	2
Half Baths	1

FIRST FLOOR

VAULTED
MASTER
13/6 X 16/6

NOOK
10/0 X 12/6
(9' CLG.)

VAULTED
GREAT RM.
17/6 X 17/10

3RD CAR /SHOP
11/0 X 15/6

REF.

W D

UP

STOR.

BUILT-IN

GARAGE
20/0 X 19/6

VAULTED
FOYER

DINING
10/6 X 12/0
(9' CLG.)

DEN/BR. 4
11/0 X 10/6
(9' CLG.)

© Alan Mascord Design Associates, Inc.

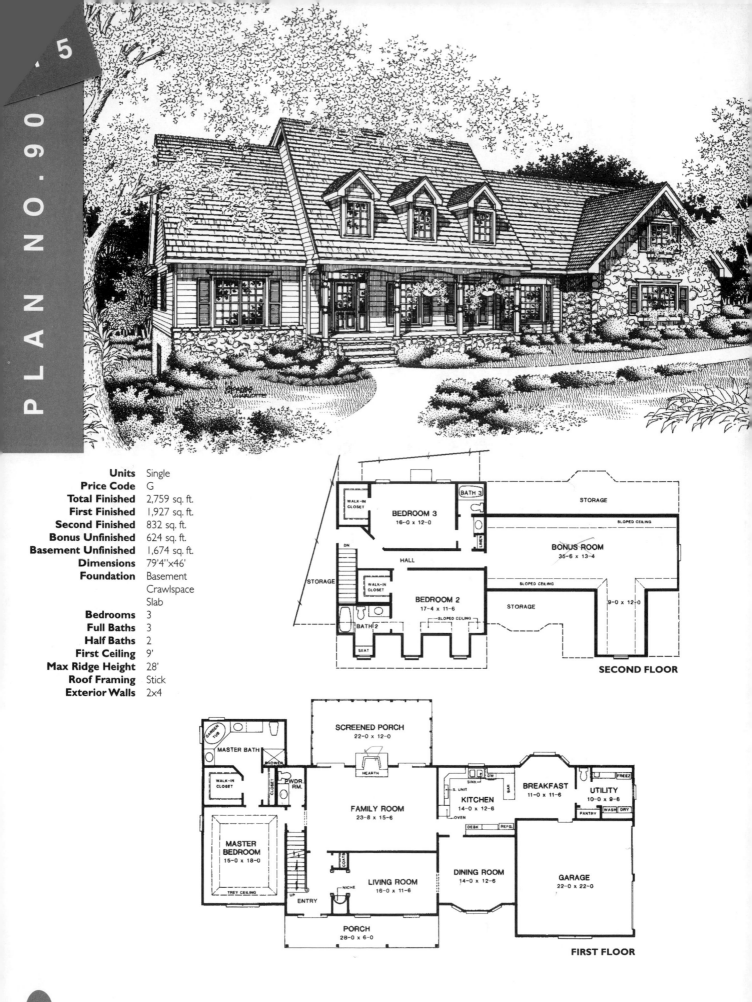

Units	Single
Price Code	G
Total Finished	2,759 sq. ft.
First Finished	1,927 sq. ft.
Second Finished	832 sq. ft.
Bonus Unfinished	624 sq. ft.
Basement Unfinished	1,674 sq. ft.
Dimensions	79'4"x46'
Foundation	Basement
	Crawlspace
	Slab
Bedrooms	3
Full Baths	3
Half Baths	2
First Ceiling	9'
Max Ridge Height	28'
Roof Framing	Stick
Exterior Walls	2x4

SECOND FLOOR

WALK-IN CLOSET

BEDROOM 3
16-0 x 12-0

BATH 3

STORAGE

SLOPED CEILING

BONUS ROOM
35-6 x 13-4

DN

HALL

LINEN

STORAGE

WALK-IN CLOSET

SLOPED CEILING

9-0 x 12-0

BEDROOM 2
17-4 x 11-6

STORAGE

BATH 2

SLOPED CEILING

SEAT

FIRST FLOOR

GARDEN TUB

MASTER BATH

SHOWER

SCREENED PORCH
22-0 x 12-0

HEARTH

S. UNIT

SINK

DW

BAR

FREEZ.

BREAKFAST
11-0 x 11-6

UTILITY
10-0 x 9-6

WALK-IN CLOSET

PWDR. RM.

CLOSET

KITCHEN
14-0 x 12-6

WASH DRY

FAMILY ROOM
23-8 x 15-6

OVEN

PANTRY

DESK

REFG.

MASTER BEDROOM
15-0 x 18-0

UP

COATS

LIVING ROOM
16-0 x 11-6

DINING ROOM
14-0 x 12-6

GARAGE
22-0 x 22-0

TREY CEILING

ENTRY

NICHE

PORCH
28-0 x 6-0

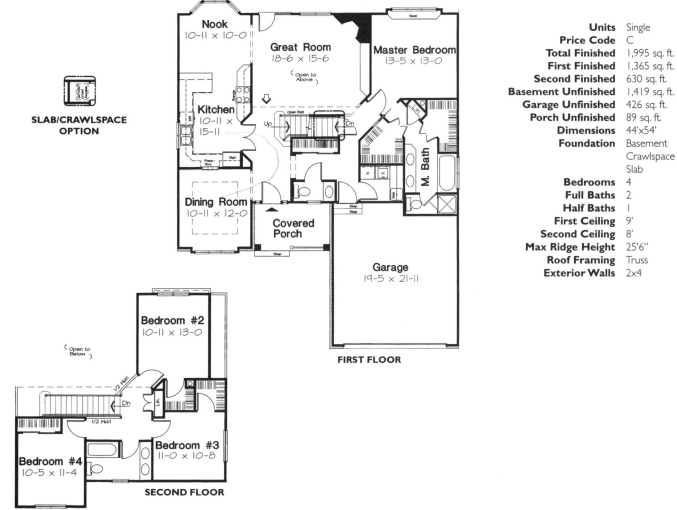

SLAB/CRAWLSPACE OPTION

Nook 10-11 × 10-0

Great Room 18-6 × 15-6

(Open to Above)

Master Bedroom 13-5 × 13-0

Kitchen 10-11 × 15-11

Open Rail

Up

Dn

M. Bath

Dining Room 10-11 × 12-0

Step

Step

Covered Porch

Garage 19-5 × 21-11

FIRST FLOOR

Bedroom #2 10-11 × 13-0

(Open to Below)

1/2 Wall

Dn

1/2 Wall

Bedroom #3 11-0 × 10-8

Bedroom #4 10-5 × 11-4

SECOND FLOOR

Units	Single
Price Code	C
Total Finished	1,995 sq. ft.
First Finished	1,365 sq. ft.
Second Finished	630 sq. ft.
Basement Unfinished	1,419 sq. ft.
Garage Unfinished	426 sq. ft.
Porch Unfinished	89 sq. ft.
Dimensions	44'x54'
Foundation	Basement Crawlspace Slab
Bedrooms	4
Full Baths	2
Half Baths	1
First Ceiling	9'
Second Ceiling	8'
Max Ridge Height	25'6''
Roof Framing	Truss
Exterior Walls	2x4

Units	Single
Price Code	F
Total Finished	2,701 sq. ft.
First Finished	2,352 sq. ft.
Second Finished	349 sq. ft.
Garage Unfinished	697 sq. ft.
Porch Unfinished	724 sq. ft.
Dimensions	69'x69'10''
Foundation	Basement
	Crawlspace
	Slab
Bedrooms	3
Full Baths	2
Half Baths	1
3/4 Baths	2
First Ceiling	9'
Second Ceiling	8'
Roof Framing	Stick
Exterior Walls	2x4

FIRST FLOOR

SECOND FLOOR

To order your Blueprints, call 1-800-235-5700

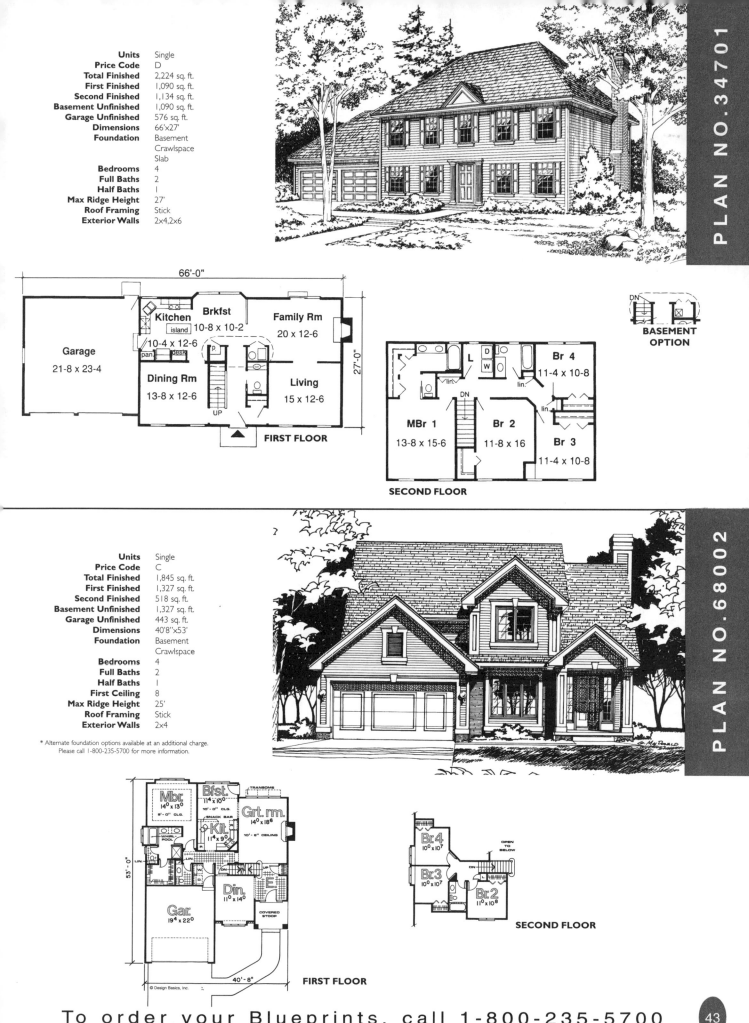

Units	Single
Price Code	D
Total Finished	2,224 sq. ft.
First Finished	1,090 sq. ft.
Second Finished	1,134 sq. ft.
Basement Unfinished	1,090 sq. ft.
Garage Unfinished	576 sq. ft.
Dimensions	66'x27'
Foundation	Basement
	Crawlspace
	Slab
Bedrooms	4
Full Baths	2
Half Baths	1
Max Ridge Height	27'
Roof Framing	Stick
Exterior Walls	2x4,2x6

66'-0"

Garage
21-8 x 23-4

Kitchen
island
10-4 x 12-6
pan. desk

Brkfst
10-8 x 10-2

Family Rm
20 x 12-6

Dining Rm
13-8 x 12-6

Living
15 x 12-6

UP

27'-0"

FIRST FLOOR

L
D W

MBr 1
13-8 x 15-6

DN

Br 2
11-8 x 16

Br 4
11-4 x 10-8

Br 3
11-4 x 10-8

SECOND FLOOR

DN

BASEMENT OPTION

Units	Single
Price Code	C
Total Finished	1,845 sq. ft.
First Finished	1,327 sq. ft.
Second Finished	518 sq. ft.
Basement Unfinished	1,327 sq. ft.
Garage Unfinished	443 sq. ft.
Dimensions	40'8"x53'
Foundation	Basement
	Crawlspace
Bedrooms	4
Full Baths	2
Half Baths	1
First Ceiling	8
Max Ridge Height	25'
Roof Framing	Stick
Exterior Walls	2x4

* Alternate foundation options available at an additional charge.
Please call 1-800-235-5700 for more information.

Mbr.
14⁰ x 13⁰
8'-0" CLG.
WHIRL-POOL

Bfst.
11⁴ x 10⁰
10'-0" CLG.
SNACK BAR

Grt. rm.
14⁰ x 18⁶
10'-8" CEILING

TRANSOMS

Kit.
11⁴ x 9⁰

Din.
11⁰ x 14⁰

Gar.
19⁴ x 22⁰

COVERED STOOP

53'-0"

40'-8"

© Design Basics, Inc.

FIRST FLOOR

Br.4
10⁰ x 10⁷

OPEN TO BELOW

Br.3
10⁰ x 10⁷

DN

Br.2
11⁰ x 10⁸

SECOND FLOOR

To order your Blueprints, call 1-800-235-5700

Units	Single
Price Code	E
Total Finished	2,257 sq. ft.
First Finished	1,540 sq. ft.
Second Finished	717 sq. ft.
Basement Unfinished	1,545 sq. ft.
Garage Unfinished	503 sq. ft.
Porch Unfinished	144 sq. ft.
Dimensions	57'x56'8''
Foundation	Basement
	Crawlspace
	Slab
Bedrooms	4
Full Baths	2
Half Baths	1
First Ceiling	9'
Second Ceiling	8'
Max Ridge Height	33'6''
Roof Framing	Truss

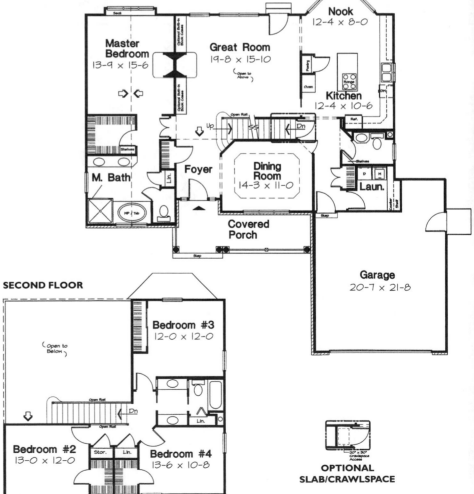

FIRST FLOOR

Nook 12-4 x 8-0

Master Bedroom 13-9 x 15-6

Great Room 19-8 x 15-10 (Open to Above)

Kitchen 12-4 x 10-6

M. Bath

Foyer

Dining Room 14-3 x 11-0

Laun.

Covered Porch

Garage 20-7 x 21-8

SECOND FLOOR

Bedroom #3 12-0 x 12-0

(Open to Below)

Bedroom #2 13-0 x 12-0

Bedroom #4 13-6 x 10-8

OPTIONAL SLAB/CRAWLSPACE

To order your Blueprints, call 1-800-235-5700

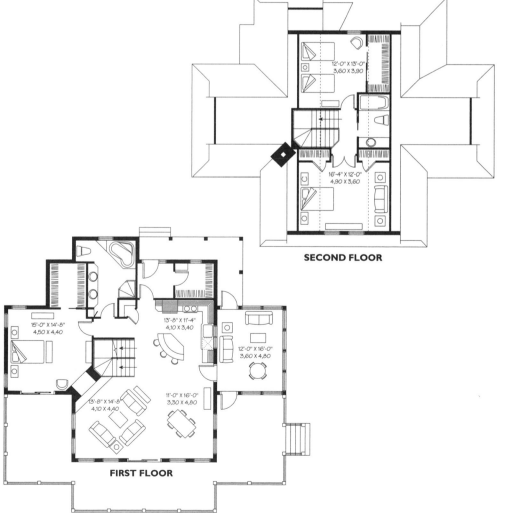

SECOND FLOOR

12'-0" X 13'-0"
3,60 X 3,90

16'-4" X 12'-0"
4,90 X 3,60

Units	Single
Price Code	C
Total Finished	1,832 sq. ft.
First Finished	1,212 sq. ft.
Second Finished	620 sq. ft.
Basement Unfinished	1,212 sq. ft.
Dimensions	38'x40'
Foundation	Basement
Bedrooms	3
Full Baths	2
First Ceiling	8'
Max Ridge Height	26'4''

15'-0" X 14'-8"
4,50 X 4,40

13'-8" X 11'-4"
4,10 X 3,40

12'-0" X 16'-0"
3,60 X 4,80

13'-8" X 14'-8"
4,10 X 4,40

11'-0" X 16'-0"
3,30 X 4,80

FIRST FLOOR

To order your Blueprints, call 1-800-235-5700

Units	Single
Price Code	I
Total Finished	2,889 sq. ft.
First Finished	2,151 sq. ft.
Second Finished	738 sq. ft.
Bonus Unfinished	534 sq. ft.
Garage Unfinished	612 sq. ft.
Porch Unfinished	617 sq. ft.
Dimensions	99'x56'
Foundation	Crawlspace
Bedrooms	3
Full Baths	2
Half Baths	I
Max Ridge Height	32'
Exterior Walls	2x6

* Alternate foundation options available at an additional charge.
Please call 1-800-235-5700 for more information.

FIRST FLOOR

SECOND FLOOR

Units	Single
Price Code	E
Total Finished	2,342 sq. ft.
First Finished	1,234 sq. ft.
Second Finished	1,108 sq. ft.
Dimensions	56'x74'6''
Foundation	Crawlspace
Bedrooms	3
Full Baths	2
Half Baths	I
First Ceiling	9'
Second Ceiling	8'
Max Ridge Height	34'6''
Roof Framing	Truss
Exterior Walls	2x6

SECOND FLOOR

FIRST FLOOR

SECOND FLOOR

FUTURE BONUS ROOM
12-0 x 11-0

SLOPE CLG.

10-0 x 21-0

DOWN

WALK-IN CLOSET

BEDROOM 2
14-8 x 13-6

HALL

CHASE

DOWN

FUTURE BEDROOM 4
11-0 x 12-0

CLOS.

BEDROOM 3
14-6 x 11-6

SLOPE CLG.

WALK-IN CLOSET

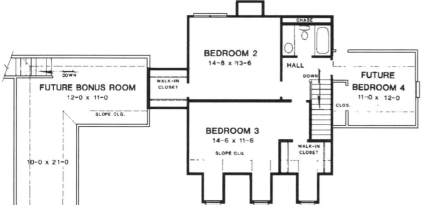

FIRST FLOOR

LAUNDRY

BREAKFAST
10-6 x 11-6

KITCHEN
12-0 x 11-6

WOOD DECK
24-0 x 12-0

FAMILY ROOM
19-8 x 13-6

BATH

BATH

M

M. BEDROOM
13-8 x 16-8

GARAGE
22-0 x 22-0

DINING
12-0 x 11-6

LIBANY LIVING
13-6 x 11-6

ENTRY

PORCH
24-0 x 6-0

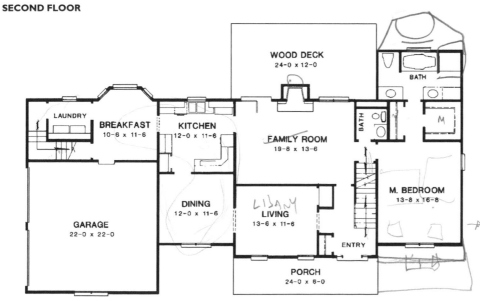

Units	Single
Price Code	E
Total Finished	2,297 sq. ft.
First Finished	1,580 sq. ft.
Second Finished	717 sq. ft.
Bonus Unfinished	410 sq. ft.
Basement Unfinished	1,342 sq. ft.
Garage Unfinished	484 sq. ft.
Porch Unfinished	144 sq. ft.
Dimensions	72'x40'
Foundation	Basement Crawlspace
Bedrooms	3
Full Baths	2
Half Baths	1
First Ceiling	8'
Second Ceiling	8'
Vaulted Ceiling	11'4"
Max Ridge Height	25'6"
Roof Framing	Stick
Exterior Walls	2x4

Units	Single
Price Code	K
Total Finished	3,136 sq. ft.
First Finished	1,673 sq. ft.
Second Finished	1,463 sq. ft.
Dimensions	60'10"x62'
Foundation	Crawlspace
Bedrooms	3
Full Baths	2
Half Baths	1
Max Ridge Height	34'4"
Exterior Walls	2x6

* Alternate foundation options available at an additional charge.
Please call 1-800-235-5700 for more information.

FIRST FLOOR

SECOND FLOOR

FIRST FLOOR

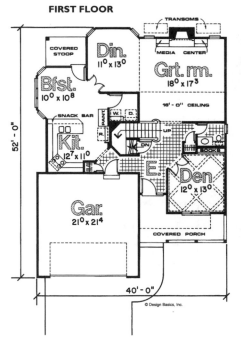

Units	Single
Price Code	D
Total Finished	2,229 sq. ft.
First Finished	1,195 sq. ft.
Second Finished	1,034 sq. ft.
Basement Unfinished	1,195 sq. ft.
Garage Unfinished	469 sq. ft.
Dimensions	40'x52'
Foundation	Basement
	Crawlspace
	Slab
Bedrooms	4
Full Baths	2
Half Baths	1
First Ceiling	8'
Max Ridge Height	27'
Roof Framing	Stick
Exterior Walls	2x4

* Alternate foundation options available at an additional charge.
Please call 1-800-235-5700 for more information.

SECOND FLOOR

© Design Basics, Inc.

To order your Blueprints, call 1-800-235-5700

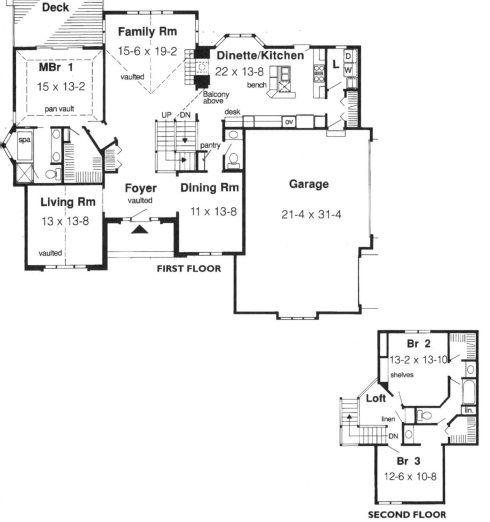

Deck

Family Rm
15-6 x 19-2
vaulted

Dinette/Kitchen
22 x 13-8
bench

D
W

L

MBr 1
15 x 13-2
pan vault

Balcony above

UP DN

desk

ov

spa

pantry

Foyer
vaulted

Dining Rm
11 x 13-8

Garage
21-4 x 31-4

Living Rm
13 x 13-8
vaulted

vaulted

FIRST FLOOR

Br 2
13-2 x 13-10
shelves

Loft
linen

lin.

DN

Br 3
12-6 x 10-8

SECOND FLOOR

Units	Single
Price Code	E
Total Finished	2,372 sq. ft.
First Finished	1,752 sq. ft.
Second Finished	620 sq. ft.
Basement Unfinished	1,726 sq. ft.
Garage Unfinished	714 sq. ft.
Dimensions	64'x52'
Foundation	Basement
	Crawlspace
	Slab
Bedrooms	3
Full Baths	2
Half Baths	1
First Ceiling	8'
Second Ceiling	8'
Max Ridge Height	29'6''
Roof Framing	Stick
Exterior Walls	2x4,2x6

Units	Single
Price Code	A
Total Finished	1,360 sq. ft.
First Finished	864 sq. ft.
Second Finished	496 sq. ft.
Basement Unfinished	864 sq. ft.
Dimensions	27'x32'
Foundation	Basement
Bedrooms	2
Full Baths	2
Exterior Walls	2x6

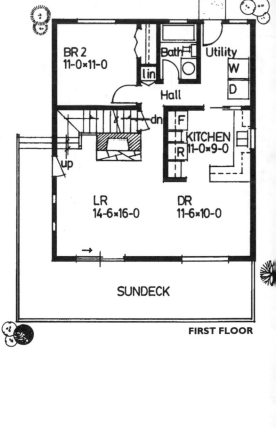

FIRST FLOOR

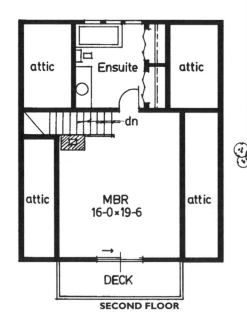

SECOND FLOOR

To order your Blueprints, call 1-800-235-5700

Units	Single
Price Code	C
Total Finished	1,763 sq. ft.
First Finished	909 sq. ft.
Second Finished	854 sq. ft.
Basement Unfinished	899 sq. ft.
Garage Unfinished	491 sq. ft.
Dimensions	48'x44'
Foundation	Basement
	Crawlspace
	Slab
Bedrooms	3
Full Baths	2
Half Baths	1
First Ceiling	8'
Second Ceiling	8'
Tray Ceiling	9'
Max Ridge Height	29'
Roof Framing	Stick
Exterior Walls	2x4,2x6

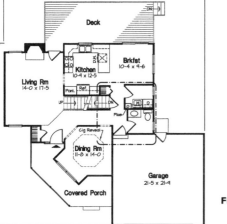

FIRST FLOOR

SECOND FLOOR

Units	Single
Price Code	H
Total Finished	2,755 sq. ft.
First Finished	2,073 sq. ft.
Second Finished	682 sq. ft.
Garage Unfinished	528 sq. ft.
Porch Unfinished	120 sq. ft.
Dimensions	64'x76'2''
Foundation	Crawlspace
Bedrooms	3
Full Baths	2
Half Baths	1
Max Ridge Height	28'
Exterior Walls	2x6

** Alternate foundation options available at an additional charge.
Please call 1-800-235-5700 for more information.*

FIRST FLOOR

SECOND FLOOR

To order your Blueprints, call 1-800-235-5700

Units	Single
Price Code	A
Total Finished	1,470 sq. ft.
First Finished	1,035 sq. ft.
Second Finished	435 sq. ft.
Basement Unfinished	1,018 sq. ft.
Porch Unfinished	192 sq. ft.
Dimensions	35'x42'
Foundation	Basement
	Crawlspace
	Slab
Bedrooms	3
Full Baths	2
First Ceiling	8'
Second Ceiling	8'
Max Ridge Height	27'
Roof Framing	Stick
Exterior Walls	2x4,2x6

**OPTIONAL
CRAWLSPACE/SLAB**

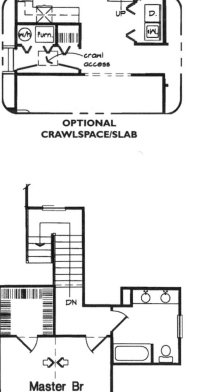

SECOND FLOOR

Master Br
14-3 x 12-11

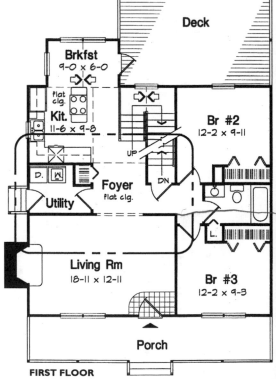

FIRST FLOOR

Deck

Brkfst
9-0 x 6-0

Br #2
12-2 x 9-11

Kit.
11-6 x 9-8

Foyer
flat clg.

Utility

Living Rm
18-11 x 12-11

Br #3
12-2 x 9-3

Porch

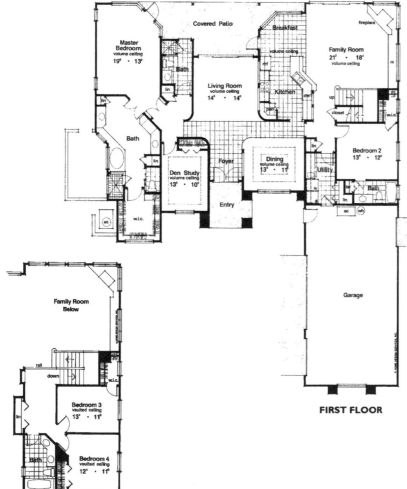

Covered Patio

Master Bedroom
volume ceiling
19⁶ · 13⁸

Bath

Breakfast

fireplace

Family Room
21² · 18⁴
volume ceiling

Living Room
volume ceiling
14⁶ · 14⁰

Kitchen

Bath

Den Study
volume ceiling
13⁰ · 10⁰

Foyer

Dining
volume ceiling
13⁴ · 11⁰

Entry

Bedroom 2
13⁴ · 12⁰

Utility

Bath

ac   w.i.c.

ac   wf

Garage

FIRST FLOOR

Family Room Below

down

rail

w.i.c.

Bedroom 3
vaulted ceiling
13⁴ · 11⁸

Bath

Bedroom 4
vaulted ceiling
12⁴ · 11⁸

SECOND FLOOR

Units	Single
Price Code	H
Total Finished	3,164 sq. ft.
First Finished	2,624 sq. ft.
Second Finished	540 sq. ft.
Garage Unfinished	802 sq. ft.
Dimensions	66'×83'
Foundation	Slab
Bedrooms	5
Full Baths	3
3/4 Baths	1
Max Ridge Height	27'
Roof Framing	Truss
Exterior Walls	2×4

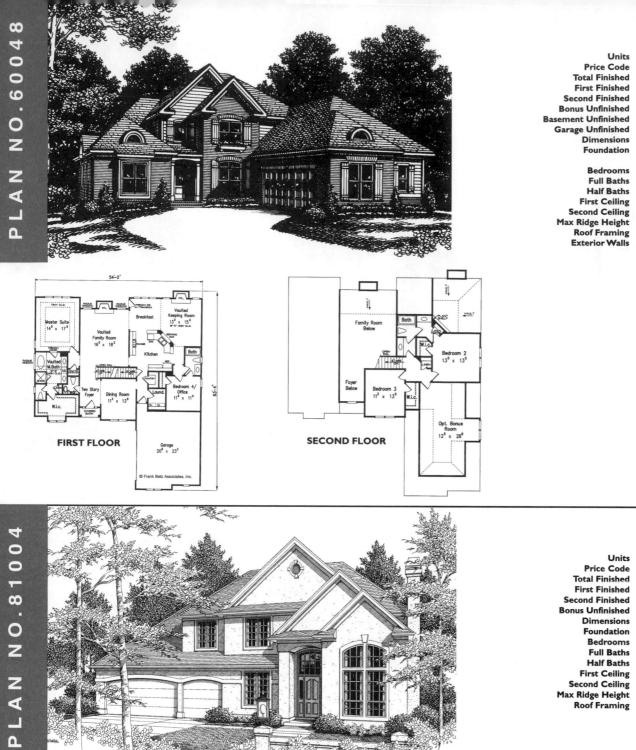

Units	Single
Price Code	F
Total Finished	2,508 sq. ft.
First Finished	1,946 sq. ft.
Second Finished	562 sq. ft.
Bonus Unfinished	366 sq. ft.
Basement Unfinished	1,946 sq. ft.
Garage Unfinished	520 sq. ft.
Dimensions	54'x63'4"
Foundation	Basement
	Crawlspace
Bedrooms	4
Full Baths	3
Half Baths	1
First Ceiling	9'
Second Ceiling	8'
Max Ridge Height	30'4"
Roof Framing	Stick
Exterior Walls	2x4

FIRST FLOOR

SECOND FLOOR

© Frank Betz Associates, Inc.

Units	Single
Price Code	F
Total Finished	2,707 sq. ft.
First Finished	1,547 sq. ft.
Second Finished	1,160 sq. ft.
Bonus Unfinished	288 sq. ft.
Dimensions	60'x50'
Foundation	Crawlspace
Bedrooms	3
Full Baths	2
Half Baths	1
First Ceiling	9'
Second Ceiling	8'
Max Ridge Height	34'
Roof Framing	Stick

FIRST FLOOR

SECOND FLOOR

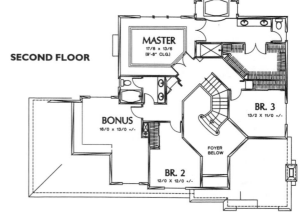

To order your Blueprints, call 1-800-235-5700

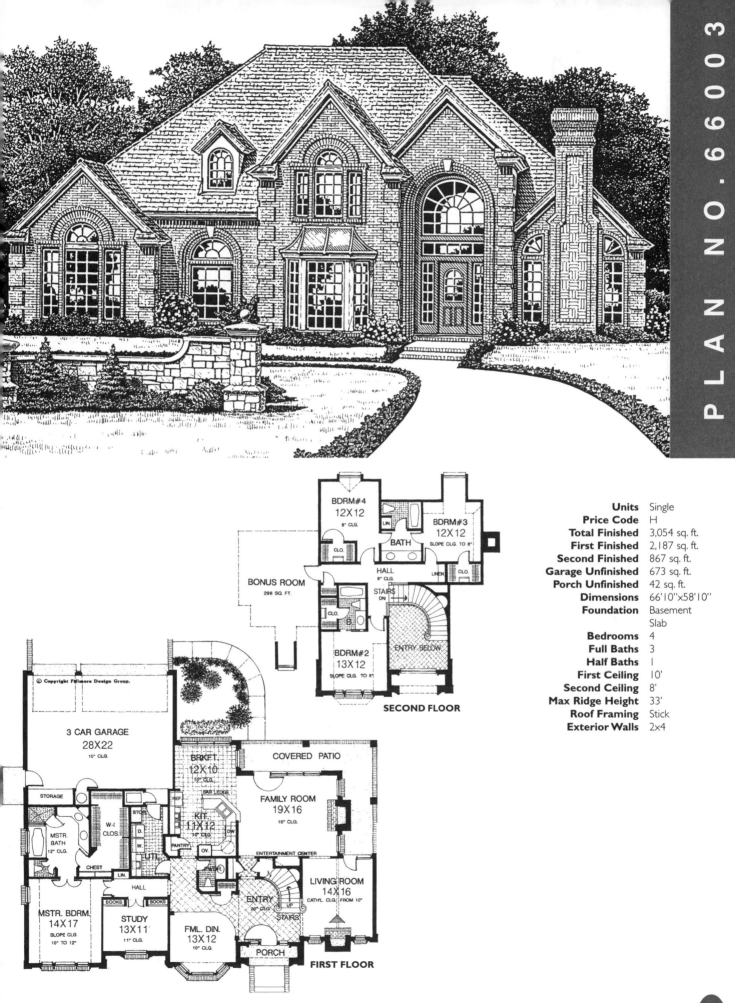

SECOND FLOOR

BDRM#4
12X12
8' CLG.

BDRM#3
12X12
SLOPE CLG. TO 8'

BATH

BONUS ROOM
296 SQ. FT.

HALL
9' CLG.

STAIRS
DN

BDRM#2
13X12
SLOPE CLG. TO 9'

ENTRY BELOW

FIRST FLOOR

© Copyright Fillmore Design Group.

3 CAR GARAGE
28X22
10' CLG.

STORAGE

BRKFT.
12X10
10' CLG.

COVERED PATIO

W-I
CLOS.

STO.

KIT.
11X12
10' CLG.

BAR LEDGE

REF.

FAMILY ROOM
19X16
10' CLG.

MSTR.
BATH
12' CLG.

D.

W.

PANTRY

UTIL.

OV.

ENTERTAINMENT CENTER

CHEST

LIN.

LIVING ROOM
14X16
CATH'L. CLG. FROM 10'

MSTR. BDRM.
14X17
SLOPE CLG.
10' TO 12'

HALL

BOOKS

BOOKS

STUDY
13X11
11' CLG.

ENTRY
20' CLG.

FML. DIN.
13X12
10' CLG.

UP

STAIRS

PORCH

Units	Single
Price Code	H
Total Finished	3,054 sq. ft.
First Finished	2,187 sq. ft.
Second Finished	867 sq. ft.
Garage Unfinished	673 sq. ft.
Porch Unfinished	42 sq. ft.
Dimensions	66'10''x58'10''
Foundation	Basement
	Slab
Bedrooms	4
Full Baths	3
Half Baths	1
First Ceiling	10'
Second Ceiling	8'
Max Ridge Height	33'
Roof Framing	Stick
Exterior Walls	2x4

Units	Single
Price Code	F
Total Finished	2,667 sq. ft.
First Finished	1,385 sq. ft.
Second Finished	1,282 sq. ft.
Basement Unfinished	1,320 sq. ft.
Garage Unfinished	627 sq. ft.
Porch Unfinished	80 sq. ft.
Dimensions	64'6"x36'
Foundation	Basement
Bedrooms	4
Full Baths	3
Max Ridge Height	24'
Roof Framing	Truss
Exterior Walls	2x6

SECOND FLOOR

BR 2
10-0 x 15-0

BR 4
9-0 x 11-0

whirl-pool

WIC

ENS

BATH

Dressing

railing

lin

dn

MBR
13-6 x 20-0

Gas FP

BR 3
13-6 x 13-6

foyer below

FIRST FLOOR

workbench

D W

Utility

NOOK
11-0 x 14-0

dw

R

PATIO

Gas FP

FAMILY RM
15-0 x 13-6

KITCHEN
14-6 x 10-0

desk

DOUBLE GARAGE
22-0 x 24-0 / 30-0

brm

lin

pantry

F

Powder Rm

french doors

dn

DINING
13-6 x 16-0

dn

railing

LIVINGROOM
13-6 x 17-6

Gas FP

FOYER
(open to above)

up

dn

Covered Porch

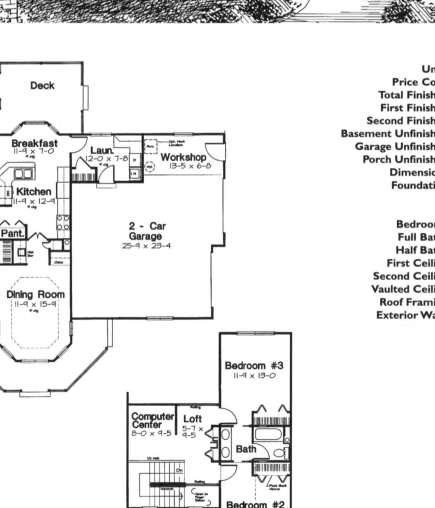

FIRST FLOOR

Sun Terrace

Deck

M.Bath
13-9 x 11-9

Great Room
15-5 x 17-9
Open to Above

Breakfast
11-9 x 7-0
9' clg

Laun.
12-0 x 7-8
9' clg

Workshop
13-5 x 6-8

Kitchen
11-9 x 12-9
9' clg

Master Bedroom
13-9 x 13-5
9' clg

Pdr.
9' clg

Pant.

2 - Car Garage
25-9 x 23-4

Foyer

Dining Room
11-9 x 15-9
9' clg

Covered Porch

SECOND FLOOR

Computer Center
8-0 x 9-5

Loft
5-7 x 9-5

Bedroom #3
11-9 x 13-0

Bath

Bedroom #2
11-9 x 13-4

Units	Single
Price Code	D
Total Finished	2,044 sq. ft.
First Finished	1,403 sq. ft.
Second Finished	641 sq. ft.
Basement Unfinished	1,394 sq. ft.
Garage Unfinished	680 sq. ft.
Porch Unfinished	231 sq. ft.
Dimensions	68'x47'
Foundation	Basement Crawlspace Slab
Bedrooms	3
Full Baths	2
Half Baths	1
First Ceiling	9'
Second Ceiling	8'
Vaulted Ceiling	12'9''
Roof Framing	Truss
Exterior Walls	2x4

Units	Single
Price Code	A
Total Finished	1,471 sq. ft.
First Finished	895 sq. ft.
Second Finished	576 sq. ft.
Basement Unfinished	895 sq. ft.
Garage Unfinished	37 sq. ft.
Porch Unfinished	44 sq. ft.
Dimensions	26'×36'
Foundation	Basement
Bedrooms	3
Full Baths	2
First Ceiling	8'2''
Second Ceiling	8'2''
Max Ridge Height	23'8''
Roof Framing	Truss
Exterior Walls	2x6

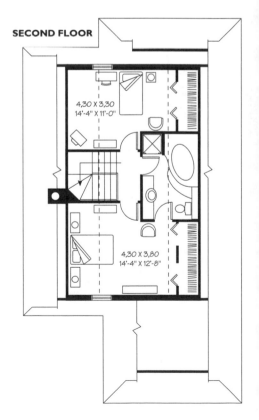

FIRST FLOOR

3,00 X 3,30
10'-0" X 11'-0"

4,30 X 3,00
14'-4" X 10'-0"

3,60 X 3,80
12'-0" X 12'-8"

3,80 X 3,50
12'-8" X 11'-8"

4,20 X 3,50
14'-0" X 11'-8"

SECOND FLOOR

4,30 X 3,30
14'-4" X 11'-0"

4,30 X 3,80
14'-4" X 12'-8"

To order your Blueprints, call 1-800-235-5700

Units	Single
Price Code	G
Total Finished	2,887 sq. ft.
First Finished	1,375 sq. ft.
Second Finished	1,512 sq. ft.
Bonus Unfinished	243 sq. ft.
Basement Unfinished	1,375 sq. ft.
Garage Unfinished	736 sq. ft.
Dimensions	58'4"x48'8"
Foundation	Basement
	Crawlspace
Bedrooms	4
Full Baths	3
First Ceiling	9'
Second Ceiling	8'
Roof Framing	Stick
Exterior Walls	2x4

FIRST FLOOR

58'-4"

French Dr. w/Transom

Breakfast

Arched Opng.

Decorative Cols.

Two Story Family Room 17⁰ x 19²

Three Car Garage 20⁰ x 33⁵

Island

Ovens

Kitchen

Pass Thru

Plant Shelf Above

DW

Ref.

Serv. Unit

Pantry

Stairs

Coats

Arched Opng.

Open Rail

Pwdr.

Dining Room 12⁰ x 14⁸

Two Story Foyer

Living Room 12⁴ x 12²

Covered Porch

© Frank Betz Associates, Inc.

49'-0"

SECOND FLOOR

Radius Window

Tray Clg.

W.i.c.

Vaulted M.Bath 12'-6" High Clg.

Master Suite 14⁰ x 18⁸

Plant Shelf Above

Family Room Below

Bedroom 4 12⁶ x 12⁰

Laund.

Overlook

W.i.c.

Bath

Bath

Linen

Bedroom 3 12⁰ x 12²

Overlook

Open Rail

Foyer Below

Bedroom 2 12⁴ x 12⁸

Tray Clg.

Units	Single
Price Code	C
Total Finished	1,951 sq. ft.
First Finished	1,082 sq. ft.
Second Finished	869 sq. ft.
Basement Unfinished	1,082 sq. ft.
Garage Unfinished	478 sq. ft.
Dimensions	50'x40'
Foundation	Basement
	Crawlspace
	Slab
Bedrooms	3
Full Baths	2
Half Baths	1
First Ceiling	8
Max Ridge Height	25'
Roof Framing	Stick
Exterior Walls	2x4

* Alternate foundation options available at an additional charge. Please call 1-800-235-5700 for more information.

FIRST FLOOR

Fam. rm. 18⁰x14⁰

Bfst. 10⁰x14⁰

Kit. 9⁰x11⁰

Desk

Par. 11⁰x12⁰

10'-0" Clg.

Din. 11⁰x12²

Gar. 20⁰x24⁰

Covered Stoop

Trans.

50'-0"

40'-0"

© Design Basics, Inc.

SECOND FLOOR

Br. 2 11⁰x10⁸

Br. 3 10³x10⁸

Mbr. 13⁰x15⁰

Seat

8'-0" Ceiling

Plant Shelf

Open to Below

Whirlpool

Trans.

Lin.

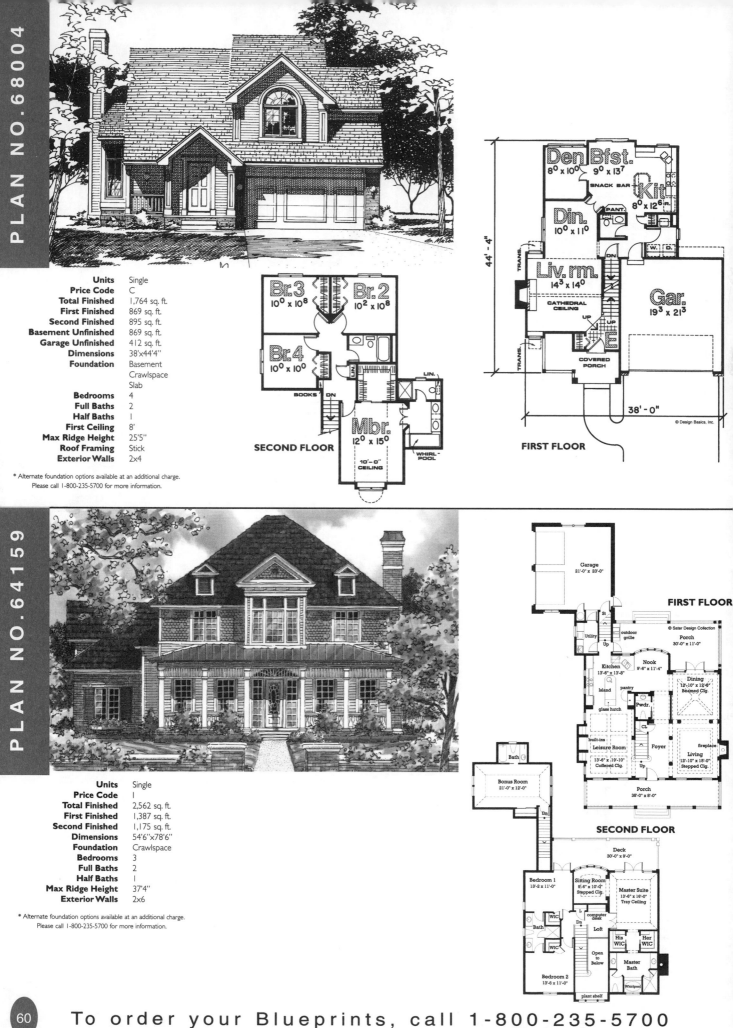

Units	Single
Price Code	C
Total Finished	1,764 sq. ft.
First Finished	869 sq. ft.
Second Finished	895 sq. ft.
Basement Unfinished	869 sq. ft.
Garage Unfinished	412 sq. ft.
Dimensions	38'x44'4''
Foundation	Basement
	Crawlspace
	Slab
Bedrooms	4
Full Baths	2
Half Baths	1
First Ceiling	8'
Max Ridge Height	25'5''
Roof Framing	Stick
Exterior Walls	2x4

* Alternate foundation options available at an additional charge.
Please call 1-800-235-5700 for more information.

SECOND FLOOR

FIRST FLOOR

© Design Basics, Inc.

FIRST FLOOR

© Sater Design Collection

SECOND FLOOR

Units	Single
Price Code	I
Total Finished	2,562 sq. ft.
First Finished	1,387 sq. ft.
Second Finished	1,175 sq. ft.
Dimensions	54'6''x78'6''
Foundation	Crawlspace
Bedrooms	3
Full Baths	2
Half Baths	1
Max Ridge Height	37'4''
Exterior Walls	2x6

* Alternate foundation options available at an additional charge.
Please call 1-800-235-5700 for more information.

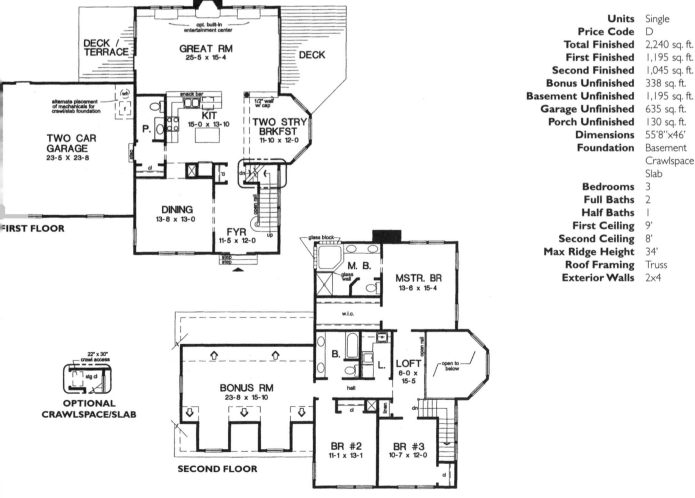

FIRST FLOOR

DECK / TERRACE

GREAT RM
25-5 x 15-4

DECK

opt. built-in entertainment center

alternate placement of mechanicals for crawl/slab foundation

snack bar

KIT
15-0 x 13-10

P.

TWO CAR GARAGE
23-5 x 23-8

TWO STRY BRKFST
11-10 x 12-0

1/2" wall w/ cap

DINING
13-8 x 13-0

FYR
11-5 x 12-0

dn

open rail

up

step
step

22" x 30" crawl access

stg cl

OPTIONAL CRAWLSPACE/SLAB

glass block

M. B.

MSTR. BR
13-6 x 15-4

glass wall

w.i.c.

BONUS RM
23-8 x 15-10

B.

L.

LOFT
6-0 x 15-5

open rail

open to below

hall

linen

dn

SECOND FLOOR

BR #2
11-1 x 13-1

BR #3
10-7 x 12-0

Units	Single
Price Code	D
Total Finished	2,240 sq. ft.
First Finished	1,195 sq. ft.
Second Finished	1,045 sq. ft.
Bonus Unfinished	338 sq. ft.
Basement Unfinished	1,195 sq. ft.
Garage Unfinished	635 sq. ft.
Porch Unfinished	130 sq. ft.
Dimensions	55'8''x46'
Foundation	Basement
	Crawlspace
	Slab
Bedrooms	3
Full Baths	2
Half Baths	1
First Ceiling	9'
Second Ceiling	8'
Max Ridge Height	34'
Roof Framing	Truss
Exterior Walls	2x4

Units	Single
Price Code	B
Total Finished	1,575 sq. ft.
First Finished	802 sq. ft.
Second Finished	773 sq. ft.
Dimensions	38'x47'
Foundation	Basement
Bedrooms	3
Full Baths	2
Half Baths	1
First Ceiling	8'
Second Ceiling	8'
Max Ridge Height	26'6'
Roof Framing	Truss
Exterior Walls	2x4

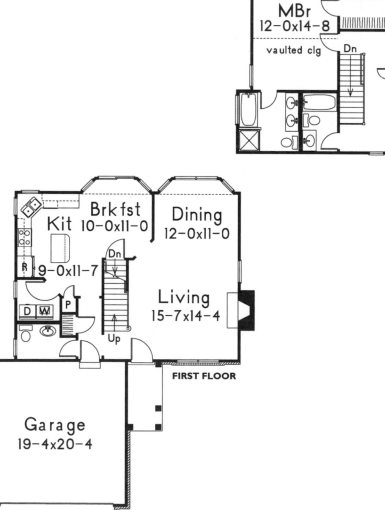

MBr
12-0x14-8
vaulted clg

Br 2
12-0x11-0

Br 3
12-0x11-3
vaulted clg

plant shel

SECOND FLOOR

Brk fst
10-0x11-0

Kit

Dining
12-0x11-0

9-0x11-7

Living
15-7x14-4

FIRST FLOOR

Garage
19-4x20-4

To order your Blueprints, call 1-800-235-5700

SECOND FLOOR

BEDROOM 3
12'-0" x 11'-6"

BEDROOM 2
12'-8" x 11'-6"

MR. BATH
& DRSG

WIC

WIC

BATH 2

BEDROOM 4
13'-8" x 10'-5"

MR BEDROOM
13'-8" x 19'-2"
(VAULTED CEILING)

FIRST FLOOR

DINING RM.
13'-8" x 13'-10"

KITCHEN
14'-10" x 13'-0"

COUNTER

NOOK
12'-0" x 15'-0"
(+ BAY)

FLAGSTONE TERRACE

FAMILY ROOM
20'-10" x 15'-0"
(VAULTED CEILING)

PANTRY

UTILITY

W D

LIVING ROOM
13'-8" x 18'-0"

PR

ENTRY
12'-3" x 13'-0"

STUDY
13'-8" x 11'-0"
(+ BAY)

GARAGE
23'-4" x 31'-8"

PORCH

Units	Single
Price Code	H
Total Finished	3,219 sq. ft.
First Finished	1,884 sq. ft.
Second Finished	1,335 sq. ft.
Basement Unfinished	1,872 sq. ft.
Garage Unfinished	753 sq. ft.
Porch Unfinished	43 sq. ft.
Dimensions	68'3"x50'8"
Foundation	Basement
Bedrooms	4
Full Baths	2
Half Baths	1
First Ceiling	9'
Second Ceiling	8'
Max Ridge Height	35'
Roof Framing	Stick
Exterior Walls	2x6

SECOND FLOOR

BEDROOM
12-4 x 16-8

GREAT ROOM
(BELOW)

CLOSET

BATH

BALCONY

DOWN

FOYER
(BELOW)

BEDROOM
11-4 x 22-0

CLOSET

FIRST FLOOR

WOOD DECK
26-0 x 12-0

BREAKFAST
9-0 x 11-0

HEARTH

BATH
16-0 x 10-4

SPA TUB

LINEN

KITCHEN
12-8 x 14-0

ISLAND

PANTRY

GREAT ROOM
14-4 x 22-6
(TWO STORY)

WALK-IN
CLOSET

WALK-IN
CLOSET

DINING
11-0 x 13-0

BALCONY ABOVE

LAUNDRY

PORCH

FOYER
(TWO STORY)

MASTER
BEDROOM
16-0 x 16-4
12' CLG.

GARAGE
21-4 x 22-0

PORCH

50'-5"

53'-10"

Units	Single
Price Code	G
Total Finished	2,754 sq. ft.
First Finished	1,822 sq. ft.
Second Finished	932 sq. ft.
Basement Unfinished	1,822 sq. ft.
Garage Unfinished	484 sq. ft.
Dimensions	53'10"x50'5"
Foundation	Basement Crawlspace
Bedrooms	3
Full Baths	2
Half Baths	1
Max Ridge Height	27'8"
Roof Framing	Stick
Exterior Walls	2x4

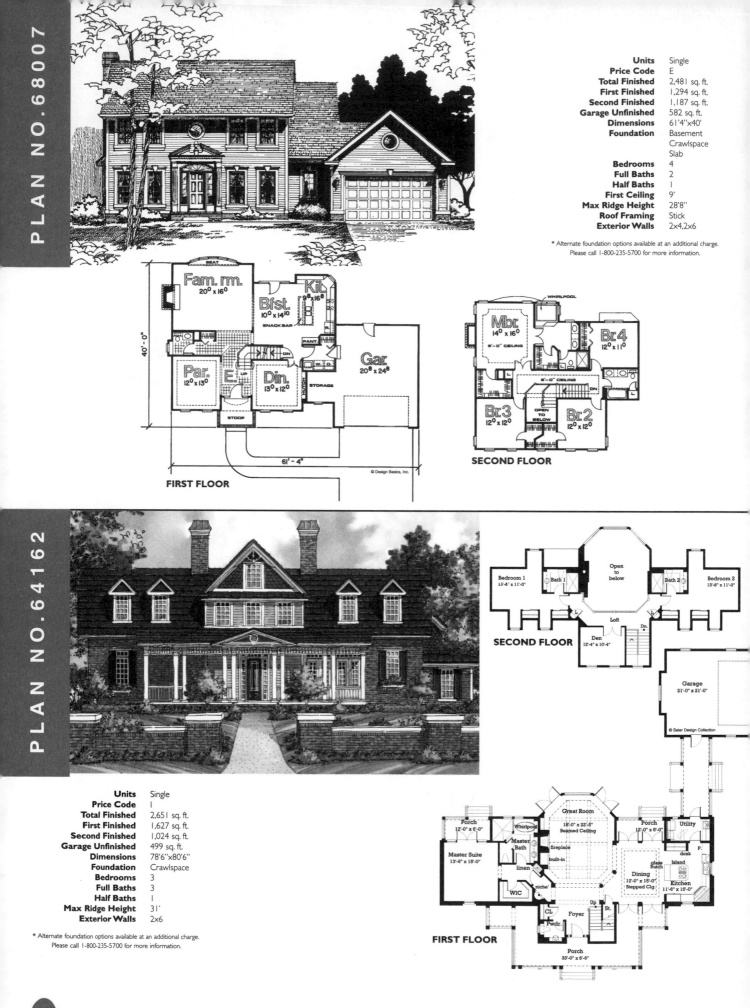

Units	Single
Price Code	E
Total Finished	2,481 sq. ft.
First Finished	1,294 sq. ft.
Second Finished	1,187 sq. ft.
Garage Unfinished	582 sq. ft.
Dimensions	61'4"x40'
Foundation	Basement
	Crawlspace
	Slab
Bedrooms	4
Full Baths	2
Half Baths	1
First Ceiling	9'
Max Ridge Height	28'8"
Roof Framing	Stick
Exterior Walls	2x4,2x6

* Alternate foundation options available at an additional charge.
Please call 1-800-235-5700 for more information.

FIRST FLOOR

© Design Basics, Inc.

SECOND FLOOR

SECOND FLOOR

FIRST FLOOR

© Sater Design Collection

Units	Single
Price Code	I
Total Finished	2,651 sq. ft.
First Finished	1,627 sq. ft.
Second Finished	1,024 sq. ft.
Garage Unfinished	499 sq. ft.
Dimensions	78'6"x80'6"
Foundation	Crawlspace
Bedrooms	3
Full Baths	3
Half Baths	1
Max Ridge Height	31'
Exterior Walls	2x6

* Alternate foundation options available at an additional charge.
Please call 1-800-235-5700 for more information.

To order your Blueprints, call 1-800-235-5700

FIRST FLOOR

6,60 X 4,20
22'-0" X 14'-0"

6,00 X 6,00
20'-0" X 20'-0"

6,00 X 6,00
20'-0" X 20'-0"

3,90 X 5,10
13'-0" X 17'-0"

3,00 X 3,60
10'-0" X 12'-0"

3,00 X 1,80
10'-0" X 6'-0"

Units	Single
Price Code	E
Total Finished	2,300 sq. ft.
First Finished	1,067 sq. ft.
Second Finished	1,233 sq. ft.
Basement Unfinished	1,067 sq. ft.
Dimensions	58'x33'
Foundation	Basement
Bedrooms	4
Full Baths	2
Half Baths	1
First Ceiling	9'2"
Second Ceiling	8'2"
Max Ridge Height	24'6"
Roof Framing	Truss
Exterior Walls	2x6

SECOND FLOOR

5,40 X 4,30
18'-0" X 14'-4"

4,50 X 4,50
15'-0" X 15'-0"

3,80 X 4,80
12'-8" X 16'-0"

3,00 X 4,20
10'-0" X 14'-0"

3,00 X 3,60
10'-0" X 12'-0"

To order your Blueprints, call 1-800-235-5700

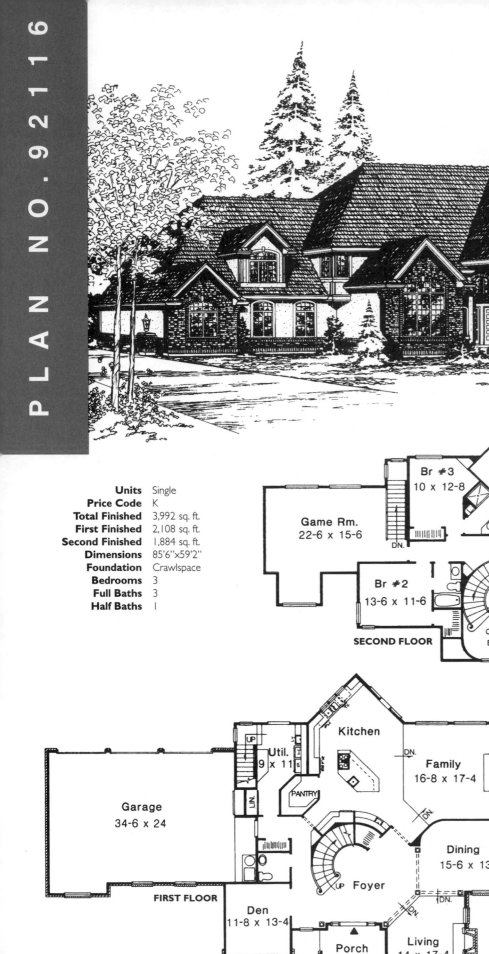

Units	Single
Price Code	K
Total Finished	3,992 sq. ft.
First Finished	2,108 sq. ft.
Second Finished	1,884 sq. ft.
Dimensions	85'6''x59'2''
Foundation	Crawlspace
Bedrooms	3
Full Baths	3
Half Baths	I

Br #3
10 x 12-8

Master Bedroom

Game Rm.
22-6 x 15-6

DN.

Br #2
13-6 x 11-6

M.Bath

OPEN TO
BELOW

DN.

SECOND FLOOR

Kitchen

UP

Util.
9 x 11

Family
16-8 x 17-4

DN.

PANTRY

LIN.

DN.

Garage
34-6 x 24

Dining
15-6 x 13

UP   Foyer

FIRST FLOOR

Den
11-8 x 13-4

Porch

Living
14 x 17-4

DN.

To order your Blueprints, call 1-800-235-5700

Units	Single
Price Code	B
Total Finished	1,668 sq. ft.
First Finished	1,057 sq. ft.
Second Finished	611 sq. ft.
Basement Unfinished	511 sq. ft.
Garage Unfinished	546 sq. ft.
Dimensions	40'4''x38'
Foundation	Basement
Bedrooms	3
Full Baths	2
Half Baths	1
First Ceiling	8'
Second Ceiling	8'
Max Ridge Height	23'
Roof Framing	Stick
Exterior Walls	2x4

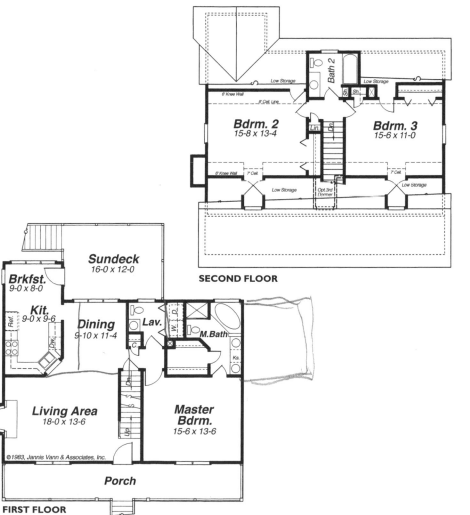

SECOND FLOOR

Bdrm. 2
15-8 x 13-4

Bdrm. 3
15-6 x 11-0

Bath 2

6' Knee Wall
8' Ceil. Line
7' Ceil.
7' Ceil.
Low Storage
Opt.3rd Dormer

Sundeck
16-0 x 12-0

Brkfst.
9-0 x 8-0

Kit.
9-0 x 9-6

Dining
9-10 x 11-4

Lav.

M.Bath

Living Area
18-0 x 13-6

Master Bdrm.
15-6 x 13-6

©1983, Jannis Vann & Associates, Inc.

Porch

FIRST FLOOR

Units	Single
Price Code	J
Total Finished	3,559 sq. ft.
First Finished	1,865 sq. ft.
Second Finished	1,694 sq. ft.
Basement Unfinished	1,865 sq. ft.
Garage Unfinished	481 sq. ft.
Dimensions	59'x50'
Foundation	Basement
	Crawlspace
Bedrooms	5
Full Baths	3
First Ceiling	9'
Second Ceiling	8'
Max Ridge Height	34'
Roof Framing	Stick
Exterior Walls	2x4

SECOND FLOOR

Vaulted Sitting Room

RADIUS WINDOWS

TRAY CLG.

Master Suite 20' x 15⁰

Family Room Below

Bedroom 4 13' x 11⁰

BOOKSHELVES

ARCHED OPNG.

Bath

Master Bath

W.i.c.

STAIRS DN.

W.i.c.

ARCHED OPNG.

LINEN

Bedroom 2 13⁰ x 11⁵

OVERLOOK STAIRS DN.

Bedroom 3 13' x 13²

Foyer Below

W.i.c.

Bath

TRAY CLG.

FIRST FLOOR

Breakfast

FRENCH DOOR

WET BAR

SURFACE UNIT

SERVING BAR

PLANT/LEDGE ABOVE

Two Story Family Room 20' x 15⁹

FRENCH DOORS

BOOKSHELVES

Study/ Bedroom 5 13' x 11⁸

Kitchen

FPL

DBL OVEN

REF

DESK

STAIRS UP

BOOKSHELVES

WALK-IN PANTRY

Laundry

SINK

Bath

STORAGE

COATS

STAIRS DN.

Garage 20⁵ x 21⁵

Dining Room 13⁰ x 14⁰

ARCHED OPENINGS

Living Room 13' x 15⁵

Two Story Foyer

STAIRS UP

FRENCH DOORS

Covered Porch

© Frank Betz Associates, Inc.

To order your Blueprints, call 1-800-235-5700

Units	Single
Price Code	F
Total Finished	2,539 sq. ft.
First Finished	1,200 sq. ft.
Second Finished	1,339 sq. ft.
Dimensions	56'x40'
Foundation	Crawlspace
Bedrooms	5
Full Baths	3
Half Baths	1
Max Ridge Height	31'
Roof Framing	Stick
Exterior Walls	2x6

FIRST FLOOR

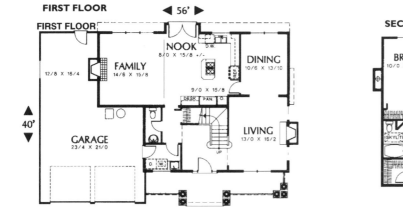

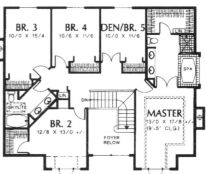

SECOND FLOOR

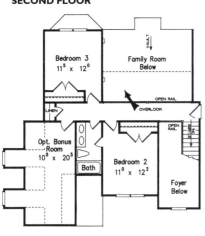

FIRST FLOOR

© Frank Betz Associates, Inc.

Units	Single
Price Code	D
Total Finished	2,115 sq. ft.
First Finished	1,581 sq. ft.
Second Finished	534 sq. ft.
Bonus Unfinished	250 sq. ft.
Basement Unfinished	1,581 sq. ft.
Garage Unfinished	423 sq. ft.
Dimensions	53'x43'4''
Foundation	Basement Crawlspace
Bedrooms	3
Full Baths	2
First Ceiling	9'
Second Ceiling	8'
Max Ridge Height	29'6''
Roof Framing	Stick
Exterior Walls	2x4

To order your Blueprints, call 1-800-235-5700

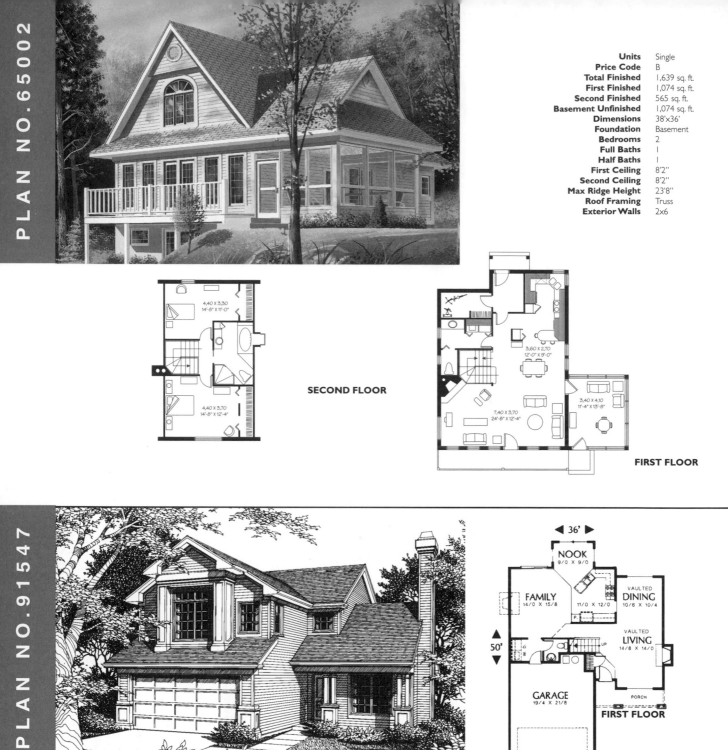

Units	Single
Price Code	B
Total Finished	1,639 sq. ft.
First Finished	1,074 sq. ft.
Second Finished	565 sq. ft.
Basement Unfinished	1,074 sq. ft.
Dimensions	38'x36'
Foundation	Basement
Bedrooms	2
Full Baths	1
Half Baths	1
First Ceiling	8'2''
Second Ceiling	8'2''
Max Ridge Height	23'8''
Roof Framing	Truss
Exterior Walls	2x6

SECOND FLOOR

FIRST FLOOR

Units	Single
Price Code	B
Total Finished	1,726 sq. ft.
First Finished	913 sq. ft.
Second Finished	813 sq. ft.
Dimensions	36'x50'
Foundation	Crawlspace
Bedrooms	3
Full Baths	2
Half Baths	1
Max Ridge Height	26'
Roof Framing	Truss
Exterior Walls	2x6

FIRST FLOOR

SECOND FLOOR

To order your Blueprints, call 1-800-235-5700

MAIN FLOOR

Covered Porch

FRENCH DOOR

FPL.

ARCHED OPENING

Vaulted Breakfast

FRENCH DOOR

Master Suite
12³ x 15⁵

TRAY CLG.

Vaulted Great Room
14³ x 20³
12'-10" HIGH CLG.

SERVING BAR

PASS THRU

Kitchen
12'-10" HIGH CLG.

R NGE

D.W.

Bedroom 2
11³ x 10⁰

Bath

PANTRY

PLANT SHELF ABOVE

ARCHED OPENING

FRENCH DOOR

Vltd. M.Bath

LINEN

LINEN

SHWR

PLANT SHELF ABOVE

OPEN RAIL

TRAY CLG.

Dining Room
10⁰ x 11³

Bedroom 3
11³ x 10³

W.i.c.

STAIRS UP

Foyer

STAIRS DN.

Units Single
Price Code B
Total Finished 1,609 sq. ft.
First Finished 1,509 sq. ft.
Lower Finished 100 sq. ft.
Basement Unfinished 954 sq. ft.
Garage Unfinished 484 sq. ft.
Dimensions 49'x34'4''
Foundation Basement
Bedrooms 3
Full Baths 2
Max Ridge Height 28'
Roof Framing Stick
Exterior Walls 2x4

Unfinished Basement

Garage
21² x 21⁵

STAIRS UP

D.

W.

COATS

© Frank Betz Associates, Inc.

LOWER FLOOR

Units	Single
Price Code	H
Total Finished	3,072 sq. ft.
First Finished	1,437 sq. ft.
Second Finished	1,635 sq. ft.
Garage Unfinished	474 sq. ft.
Dimensions	36'x62'
Foundation	Slab
Bedrooms	4
Full Baths	3
Half Baths	1
Roof Framing	Truss
Exterior Walls	2x6

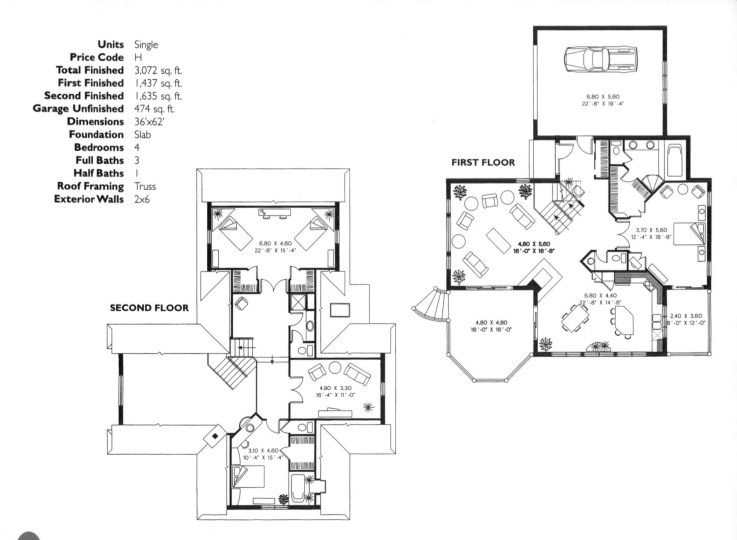

SECOND FLOOR

FIRST FLOOR

72

To order your Blueprints, call 1-800-235-5700

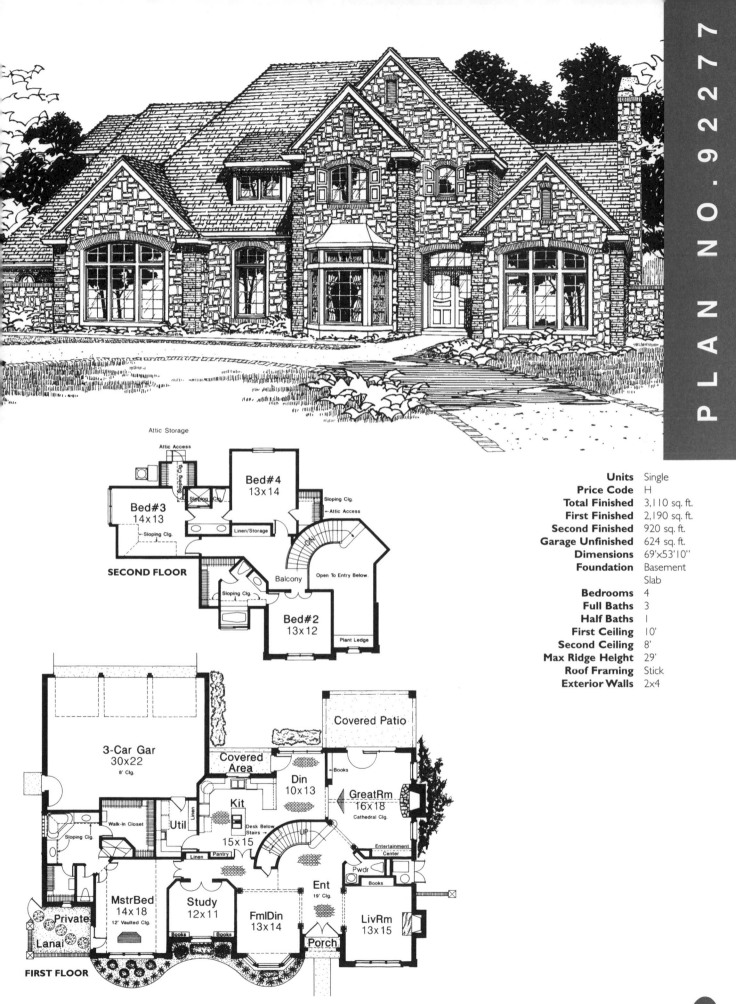

SECOND FLOOR

Attic Storage

Attic Access

Sloping Clg.

Bed#3
14x13

Sloping Clg.

Sloping Clg.

Bed#4
13x14

Sloping Clg.

Attic Access

Linen/Storage

Balcony

Open To Entry Below.

Sloping Clg.

Bed#2
13x12

Plant Ledge

Units	Single
Price Code	H
Total Finished	3,110 sq. ft.
First Finished	2,190 sq. ft.
Second Finished	920 sq. ft.
Garage Unfinished	624 sq. ft.
Dimensions	69'x53'10"
Foundation	Basement
	Slab
Bedrooms	4
Full Baths	3
Half Baths	1
First Ceiling	10'
Second Ceiling	8'
Max Ridge Height	29'
Roof Framing	Stick
Exterior Walls	2x4

FIRST FLOOR

3-Car Gar
30x22
8' Clg.

Walk-In Closet

Sloping Clg.

Linen

Util

Kit
15x15

Desk Below Stairs

Linen

Pantry

UP

Covered Area

Covered Patio

Din
10x13

books

GreatRm
16x18
Cathedral Clg.

Entertainment Center

Pwdr

books

MstrBed
14x18
12' Vaulted Clg.

Private

Lanai

Study
12x11

Books   Books

FmlDin
13x14

Ent
19' Clg.

Porch

LivRm
13x15

Units	Single
Price Code	F
Total Finished	2,574 sq. ft.
First Finished	1,135 sq. ft.
Second Finished	1,439 sq. ft.
Bonus Unfinished	193 sq. ft.
Basement Unfinished	1,112 sq. ft.
Dimensions	49'x38'
Foundation	Basement
	Crawlspace
	Slab
Bedrooms	4
Full Baths	2
Half Baths	1
Max Ridge Height	30'4''
Roof Framing	Truss
Exterior Walls	2x4

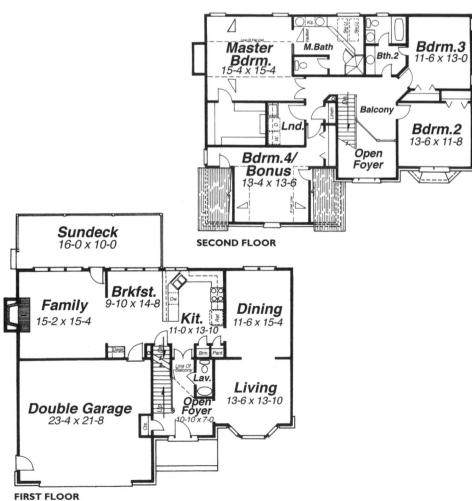

SECOND FLOOR

FIRST FLOOR

Units	Single
Price Code	A
Total Finished	972 sq. ft.
Main Finished	972 sq. ft.
Basement Unfinished	972 sq. ft.
Dimensions	30'x35'
Foundation	Basement
Bedrooms	2
Full Baths	1
Main Ceiling	8'2''
Max Ridge Height	17'6''
Exterior Walls	2x6

MAIN FLOOR

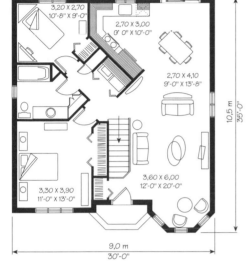

FIRST FLOOR

© Design Basics, Inc.

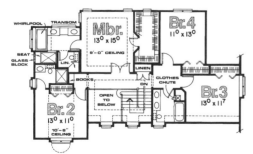

SECOND FLOOR

Units	Single
Price Code	E
Total Finished	2,498 sq. ft.
First Finished	1,298 sq. ft.
Second Finished	1,200 sq. ft.
Garage Unfinished	528 sq. ft.
Dimensions	51'4''x46'
Foundation	Basement
	Crawlspace
	Slab
Bedrooms	4
Full Baths	2
Half Baths	1
3/4 Baths	1
First Ceiling	8'
Max Ridge Height	29'
Roof Framing	Stick
Exterior Walls	2x4

* Alternate foundation options available at an additional charge.
Please call 1-800-235-5700 for more information.

To order your Blueprints, call 1-800-235-5700

75

Units	Single
Price Code	K
Total Finished	3,813 sq. ft.
First Finished	2,553 sq. ft.
Second Finished	1,260 sq. ft.
Garage Unfinished	714 sq. ft.
Dimensions	82'×52'
Foundation	Crawlspace
	Slab
Bedrooms	4
Full Baths	3
Half Baths	1
First Ceiling	9'
Second Ceiling	9'
Max Ridge Height	36'
Roof Framing	Stick
Exterior Walls	2x4

SECOND FLOOR

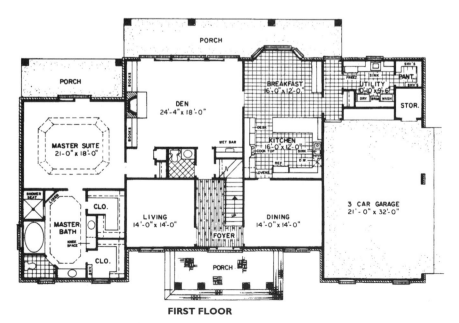

FIRST FLOOR

To order your Blueprints, call 1-800-235-5700

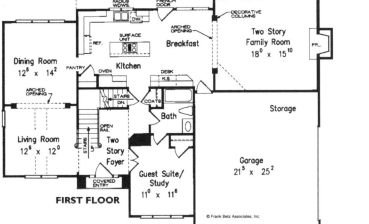

FIRST FLOOR

- Dining Room 12⁸ x 14²
- Living Room 12⁸ x 12⁰
- Kitchen
- Breakfast
- Two Story Family Room 18⁰ x 15¹⁰
- Storage
- Garage 21⁵ x 25²
- Two Story Foyer
- Bath
- Guest Suite/Study 11⁰ x 11⁶
- Pantry
- Coats
- Covered Entry

© Frank Betz Associates, Inc.

SECOND FLOOR

- Bath
- Bedroom 2 12⁰ x 11¹⁰
- Bedroom 3 12⁶ x 11¹⁰
- W.i.c.
- Laund.
- Family Room Below
- Foyer Below
- W.i.c.
- Master Suite 18⁰ x 15²
- Vaulted M.Bath
- Sitting Room 10¹⁰ x 10⁰
- Linen
- Overlook

Units	Single
Price Code	F
Total Finished	2,685 sq. ft.
First Finished	1,374 sq. ft.
Second Finished	1,311 sq. ft.
Basement Unfinished	1,374 sq. ft.
Garage Unfinished	560 sq. ft.
Dimensions	57'4"x42'
Foundation	Basement Crawlspace
Bedrooms	4
Full Baths	3
Max Ridge Height	33'
Roof Framing	Stick
Exterior Walls	2x4

To order your Blueprints, call 1-800-235-5700

Units	Single
Price Code	A
Total Finished	920 sq. ft.
Main Finished	920 sq. ft.
Porch Unfinished	152 sq. ft.
Dimensions	38'x28'
Foundation	Basement
Bedrooms	2
Full Baths	1
Main Ceiling	8'
Max Ridge Height	20'6''
Roof Framing	Truss
Exterior Walls	2x6

MAIN FLOOR

5.70 X 3.50
19'-0" X 11'-8"

3.65 X 3.50
12'-2" X 11'-8"

4.60 X 3.60
15'-4" X 12'-0"

2.70 X 3.00
9'-0" X 10'-0"

8.4 m
28'-0"

3.6 m
12'-0"

7.8 m
26'-0"

VAULTED
MASTER
12/8 X 16/4

GREAT RM
BELOW

BR. 2
11/8 X 11/0

BR. 3
11/8 X 11/4

SECOND FLOOR

TWO STORY
GREAT RM.
14/0 X 17/4

DEN/PARLOR
11/8 X 10/8
(9' CLG.)

NOOK
12/8 X 11/0
(9' CLG.)

14/8 X 11/0

DINING
12/0 X 11/0
(9' CLG.)

FIRST FLOOR

GARAGE
20/4 X 20/2

Units	Single
Price Code	D
Total Finished	2,170 sq. ft.
First Finished	1,176 sq. ft.
Second Finished	994 sq. ft.
Porch Unfinished	90 sq. ft.
Dimensions	40'x64'
Foundation	Crawlspace
Bedrooms	2
Full Baths	2
Half Baths	1
Max Ridge Height	32'
Roof Framing	Truss
Exterior Walls	2x6

To order your Blueprints, call 1-800-235-5700

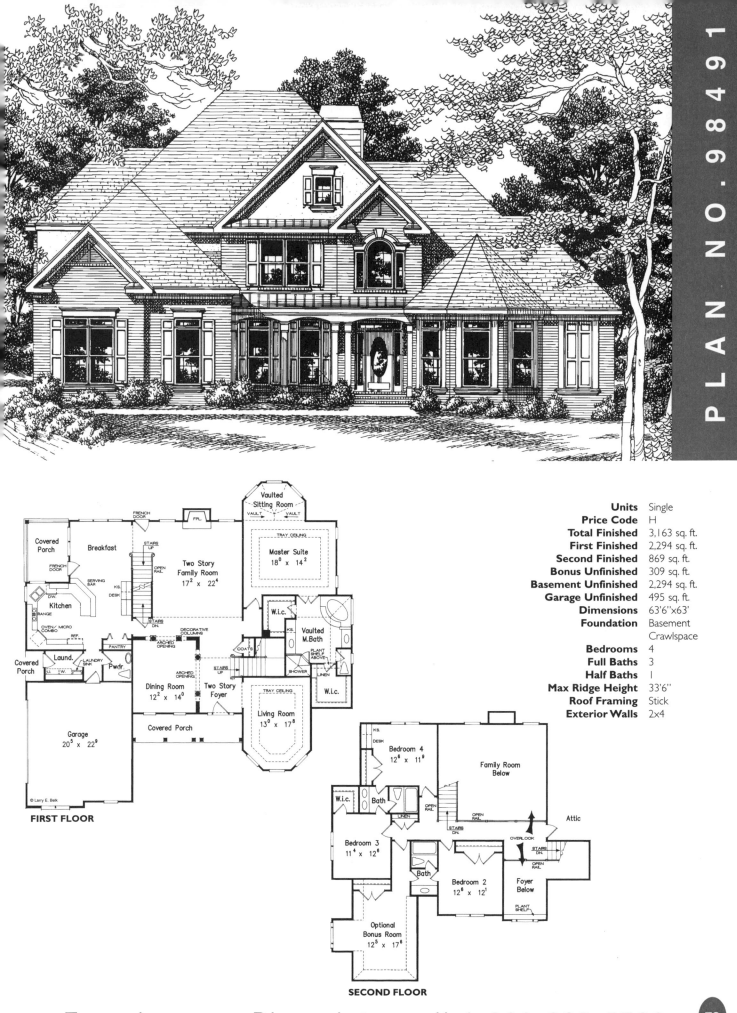

FIRST FLOOR

Covered Porch

Breakfast

FRENCH DOOR

FPL

Vaulted Sitting Room

VAULT   VAULT

TRAY CEILING

STAIRS UP

OPEN RAIL

Master Suite
18⁰ x 14²

Two Story Family Room
17² x 22⁴

KB. DESK

STAIRS DN.

Kitchen

DW.

SERVING BAR

RANGE

OVEN/ MICRO COMBO

REF.

PANTRY

ARCHED OPENING

DECORATIVE COLUMNS

W.i.c.

KB.

Vaulted M.Bath

COATS

PLANT SHELF ABOVE

Covered Porch

Laund.

LAUNDRY SINK

Pwdr.

D. W.

Dining Room
12² x 14⁰

ARCHED OPENING

Two Story Foyer

STAIRS UP

SHOWER

LINEN

W.i.c.

Garage
20⁵ x 22⁸

Covered Porch

Living Room
13⁰ x 17⁸

TRAY CEILING

© Larry E. Belk

SECOND FLOOR

KB. DESK

Bedroom 4
12⁶ x 11⁹

Family Room Below

W.i.c.

Bath

LINEN

OPEN RAIL

OPEN RAIL

Attic

STAIRS DN.

OVERLOOK

Bedroom 3
11⁴ x 12⁶

Bath

Bedroom 2
12⁶ x 12¹

STAIRS DN.

OPEN RAIL

Foyer Below

PLANT SHELF

Optional Bonus Room
12⁵ x 17⁶

PLANT SHELF

Units	Single
Price Code	H
Total Finished	3,163 sq. ft.
First Finished	2,294 sq. ft.
Second Finished	869 sq. ft.
Bonus Unfinished	309 sq. ft.
Basement Unfinished	2,294 sq. ft.
Garage Unfinished	495 sq. ft.
Dimensions	63'6''x63'
Foundation	Basement Crawlspace
Bedrooms	4
Full Baths	3
Half Baths	I
Max Ridge Height	33'6''
Roof Framing	Stick
Exterior Walls	2x4

To order your Blueprints, call 1-800-235-5700

Units	Single
Price Code	D
Total Finished	2,083 sq. ft.
First Finished	1,113 sq. ft.
Second Finished	970 sq. ft.
Basement Unfinished	1,113 sq. ft.
Garage Unfinished	480 sq. ft.
Porch Unfinished	581 sq. ft.
Dimensions	74'x41'6"
Foundation	Basement
	Crawlspace
	Slab
Bedrooms	3
Full Baths	2
Half Baths	1
First Ceiling	8'
Second Ceiling	8'
Max Ridge Height	28'6"
Roof Framing	Stick
Exterior Walls	2x4,2x6

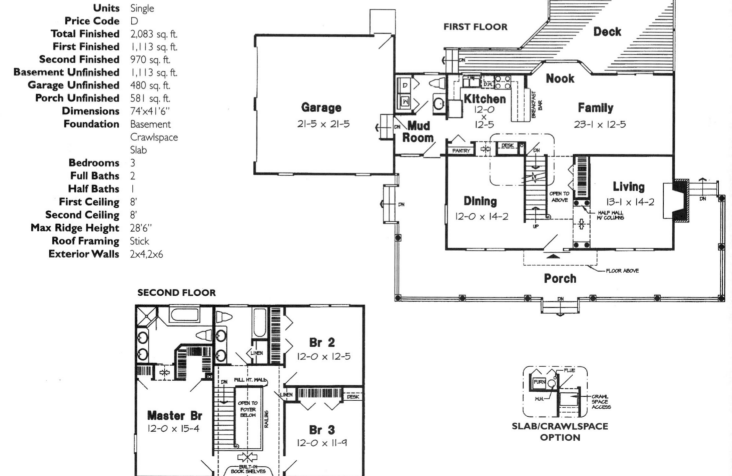

FIRST FLOOR

Deck

Nook

Kitchen
12-0 x 12-5

Family
23-1 x 12-5

Garage
21-5 x 21-5

Mud Room

PANTRY DESK

Dining
12-0 x 14-2

OPEN TO ABOVE

Living
13-1 x 14-2

HALF WALL W/ COLUMNS

UP

FLOOR ABOVE

Porch

SECOND FLOOR

Master Br
12-0 x 15-4

FULL HT. WALL

LINEN

Br 2
12-0 x 12-5

OPEN TO FOYER BELOW

RAILING

LINEN

DESK

Br 3
12-0 x 11-9

BUILT-IN BOOK SHELVES

WINDOW SEAT

FURN

FLUE

W.H.

CRAWL SPACE ACCESS

SLAB/CRAWLSPACE OPTION

To order your Blueprints, call 1-800-235-5700

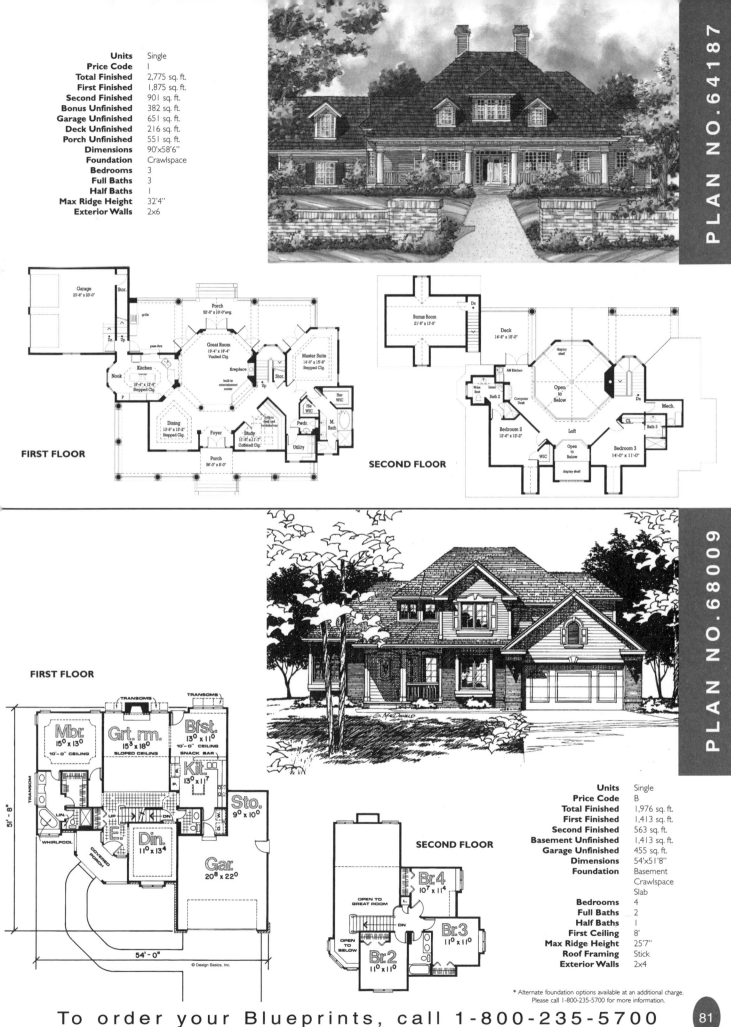

Units	Single
Price Code	I
Total Finished	2,775 sq. ft.
First Finished	1,875 sq. ft.
Second Finished	901 sq. ft.
Bonus Unfinished	382 sq. ft.
Garage Unfinished	651 sq. ft.
Deck Unfinished	216 sq. ft.
Porch Unfinished	551 sq. ft.
Dimensions	90'x58'6"
Foundation	Crawlspace
Bedrooms	3
Full Baths	3
Half Baths	1
Max Ridge Height	32'4"
Exterior Walls	2x6

FIRST FLOOR

SECOND FLOOR

PLAN NO. 68009

FIRST FLOOR

SECOND FLOOR

Units	Single
Price Code	B
Total Finished	1,976 sq. ft.
First Finished	1,413 sq. ft.
Second Finished	563 sq. ft.
Basement Unfinished	1,413 sq. ft.
Garage Unfinished	455 sq. ft.
Dimensions	54'x51'8"
Foundation	Basement
	Crawlspace
	Slab
Bedrooms	4
Full Baths	2
Half Baths	1
First Ceiling	8'
Max Ridge Height	25'7"
Roof Framing	Stick
Exterior Walls	2x4

* Alternate foundation options available at an additional charge.
Please call 1-800-235-5700 for more information.

To order your Blueprints, call 1-800-235-5700

Units	Single
Price Code	D
Total Finished	2,101 sq. ft.
First Finished	1,626 sq. ft.
Second Finished	475 sq. ft.
Basement Unfinished	1,512 sq. ft.
Garage Unfinished	438 sq. ft.
Dimensions	59'x60'8''
Foundation	Basement
Bedrooms	3
Full Baths	2
Half Baths	1
First Ceiling	8'
Second Ceiling	8'
Max Ridge Height	31'
Roof Framing	Truss
Exterior Walls	2x4

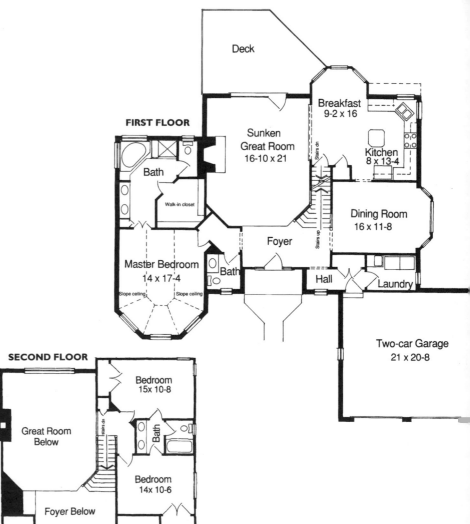

FIRST FLOOR

Deck

Breakfast
9-2 x 16

Sunken
Great Room
16-10 x 21

Kitchen
8 x 13-4

Bath

Walk-in closet

Dining Room
16 x 11-8

Foyer

Master Bedroom
14 x 17-4

Bath

Slope ceiling   Slope ceiling

Hall

Laundry

Two-car Garage
21 x 20-8

SECOND FLOOR

Bedroom
15x 10-8

Great Room
Below

Bath

Bedroom
14x 10-6

Foyer Below

SECOND FLOOR

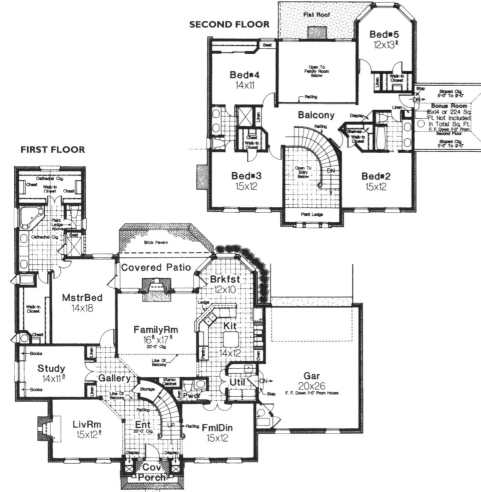

Flat Roof

Bed#5
12x13²

Bed#4
14x11

Open To
Family Room
Below

Railing

Balcony

Bonus Room
16x14 or 224 Sq.
Ft. Not Included
In Total Sq. Ft.
F.F. Down 1'-0" From
Second Floor

Sloped Clg.
5'-0" To 9'-0"

Sloped Clg.
5'-0" To 9'-0"

Bed#3
15x12

Open To
Entry
Below

Bed#2
15x12

Plant Ledge

FIRST FLOOR

Cathedral Clg.

Plant
Ledge
Above

Cathedral Clg.

MstrBed
14x18

Covered Patio

Brick Pavers

Brkfst
12x10

Kit
14x12

FamilyRm
16⁶x17²
20'-0" Clg.

Line Of
Balcony

Gar
20x26
F.F. Down 1'-0" From House

Study
14x11³

Gallery

Line Of
Balcony

Storage

Stereo
Cabinet

Util

Pwdr

Step

LivRm
15x12⁹

Ent
20'-0" Clg.

Railing

FmlDin
15x12

Display

Display

Cov
Porch

Units	Single
Price Code	I
Total Finished	3,381 sq. ft.
First Finished	2,208 sq. ft.
Second Finished	1,173 sq. ft.
Bonus Unfinished	224 sq. ft.
Garage Unfinished	520 sq. ft.
Porch Unfinished	104 sq. ft.
Dimensions	72'x63'10"
Foundation	Crawlspace
	Slab
Bedrooms	5
Full Baths	2
Half Baths	1
3/4 Baths	1
First Ceiling	10'
Second Ceiling	9'
Max Ridge Height	33'6"
Roof Framing	Stick
Exterior Walls	2x4

Units	Single
Price Code	K
Total Finished	3,342 sq. ft.
First Finished	1,865 sq. ft.
Second Finished	1,477 sq. ft.
Bonus Unfinished	282 sq. ft.
Garage Unfinished	584 sq. ft.
Dimensions	78'x78'8"
Foundation	Crawlspace
Bedrooms	4
Full Baths	2
Half Baths	1
Max Ridge Height	34'4"
Exterior Walls	2x6

* Alternate foundation options available at an additional charge.
Please call 1-800-235-5700 for more information.

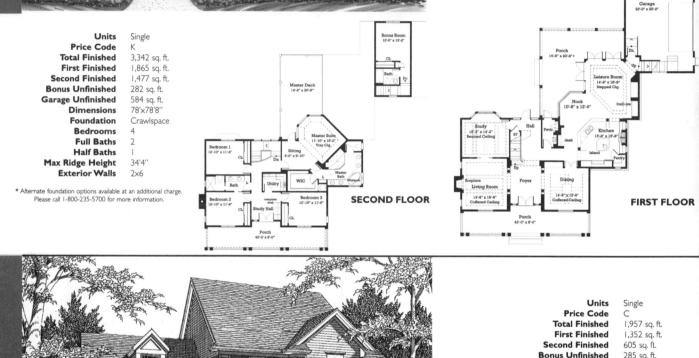

SECOND FLOOR

FIRST FLOOR

Units	Single
Price Code	C
Total Finished	1,957 sq. ft.
First Finished	1,352 sq. ft.
Second Finished	605 sq. ft.
Bonus Unfinished	285 sq. ft.
Dimensions	60'x43'
Foundation	Crawlspace
Bedrooms	3
Full Baths	2
Half Baths	1
Primary Roof Pitch	10:12
Max Ridge Height	35'6"
Roof Framing	Truss
Exterior Walls	2x6

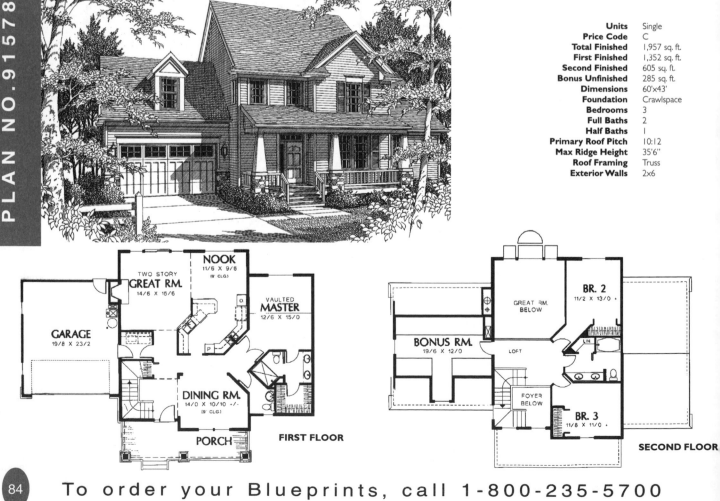

FIRST FLOOR

SECOND FLOOR

To order your Blueprints, call 1-800-235-5700

FIRST FLOOR

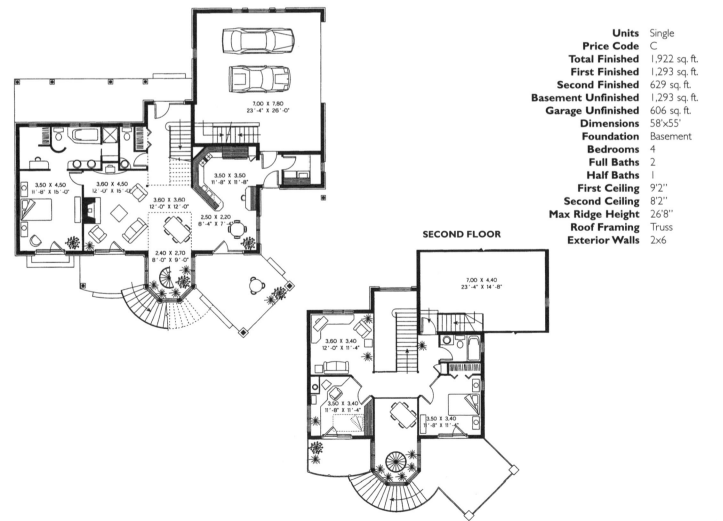

7,00 X 7,80
23'-4" X 26'-0"

3,50 X 3,50
11'-8" X 11'-8"

3,50 X 4,50
11'-8" X 15'-0"

3,60 X 4,50
12'-0" X 15'-0"

3,60 X 3,60
12'-0" X 12'-0"

2,50 X 2,20
8'-4" X 7'-1"

2,40 X 2,70
8'-0" X 9'-0"

Units	Single
Price Code	C
Total Finished	1,922 sq. ft.
First Finished	1,293 sq. ft.
Second Finished	629 sq. ft.
Basement Unfinished	1,293 sq. ft.
Garage Unfinished	606 sq. ft.
Dimensions	58'x55'
Foundation	Basement
Bedrooms	4
Full Baths	2
Half Baths	1
First Ceiling	9'2"
Second Ceiling	8'2"
Max Ridge Height	26'8"
Roof Framing	Truss
Exterior Walls	2x6

SECOND FLOOR

7,00 X 4,40
23'-4" X 14'-8"

3,60 X 3,40
12'-0" X 11'-4"

3,50 X 3,40
11'-8" X 11'-4"

3,50 X 3,40
11'-8" X 11'-4"

Units	Single
Price Code	H
Total Finished	3,220 sq. ft.
First Finished	2,125 sq. ft.
Second Finished	1,095 sq. ft.
Basement Unfinished	2,125 sq. ft.
Dimensions	89'9''x57'
Foundation	Basement
	Crawlspace
	Slab
Bedrooms	4
Full Baths	2
3/4 Baths	1
Max Ridge Height	30'
Roof Framing	Truss
Exterior Walls	2x6

SECOND FLOOR

M.B.

M.B.R.
13/6 X 18/10

B

B.R.
12 X 12/9

VAULTED
FOYER

BALC

WALK-IN CLOSET

VIEW DECK

VAULTED
FAMILY
14/0 X 19/0+

KIT

DINE
12/4 X 16/9

VAULTED
LIVING
17/5 X 14/7

B.R. 4/
DEN
15/4 X 13/7

PANTRY

UTIL

GALLERY

BUFFET

VAULTED
FOYER

ENT

B.R. 3
12/0 X 13/6

3 CAR GARAGE

FIRST FLOOR

Units	Single
Price Code	K
Total Finished	3,082 sq. ft.
First Finished	2,138 sq. ft.
Second Finished	944 sq. ft.
Bonus Unfinished	427 sq. ft.
Dimensions	77'2''x64'
Foundation	Crawlspace
Bedrooms	3
Full Baths	3
Half Baths	1
Max Ridge Height	34'2''
Exterior Walls	2x6

* Alternate foundation options available at an additional charge.
Please call 1-800-235-5700 for more information.

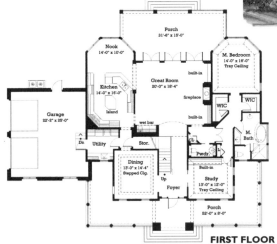

FIRST FLOOR

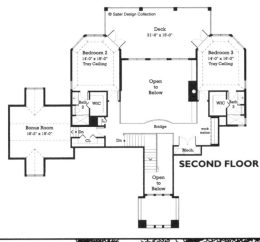

© Sater Design Collection

SECOND FLOOR

Units	Single
Price Code	A
Total Finished	1,491 sq. ft.
First Finished	1,061 sq. ft.
Second Finished	430 sq. ft.
Basement Unfinished	540 sq. ft.
Garage Unfinished	409 sq. ft.
Dimensions	40'4''x36'2''
Foundation	Basement
	Crawlspace
Bedrooms	3
Full Baths	2
First Ceiling	8'
Second Ceiling	8'
Max Ridge Height	22'6''
Roof Framing	Stick
Exterior Walls	2x4

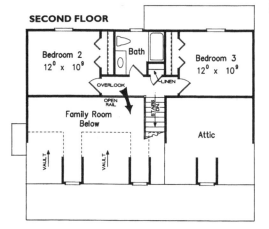

SECOND FLOOR

FIRST FLOOR

copyright © 1998 frank betz associates, inc.

Units	Single
Price Code	C
Total Finished	1,850 sq. ft.
First Finished	961 sq. ft.
Second Finished	889 sq. ft.
Bonus Unfinished	386 sq. ft.
Basement Unfinished	961 sq. ft.
Garage Unfinished	501 sq. ft.
Dimensions	53'10"x34'6"
Foundation	Basement Crawlspace
Bedrooms	4
Full Baths	2
Half Baths	1
Max Ridge Height	31'
Roof Framing	Stick
Exterior Walls	2x4

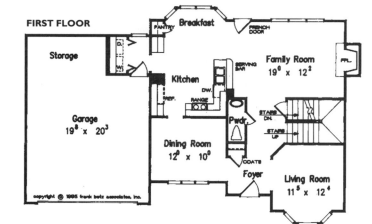

FIRST FLOOR

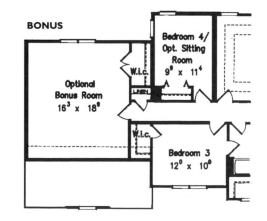

BONUS

SECOND FLOOR

To order your Blueprints, call 1-800-235-5700

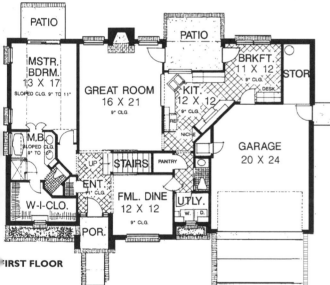

FIRST FLOOR

PATIO

MSTR.
BDRM.
13 X 17
SLOPED CLG. 9" TO 11"

GREAT ROOM
16 X 21
9" CLG.

PATIO

BRKFT.
11 X 12
9" CLG.

STOR

KIT.
12 X 12
9" CLG.

DESK

REF.

NICHE

M.B.
SLOPED CLG.
9" TO

STAIRS

UP

PANTRY

GARAGE
20 X 24

ENT.
11" CLG.

FML. DINE
12 X 12
9" CLG.

UTLY.
W. D.

W-I-CLO.

POR.

Units	Single
Price Code	D
Total Finished	2,175 sq. ft.
First Finished	1,472 sq. ft.
Second Finished	703 sq. ft.
Garage Unfinished	540 sq. ft.
Porch Unfinished	36 sq. ft.
Dimensions	58'x39'10''
Foundation	Slab
Bedrooms	4
Full Baths	2
Half Baths	1
First Ceiling	9'
Second Ceiling	8'
Max Ridge Height	25'
Roof Framing	Stick
Exterior Walls	2x4

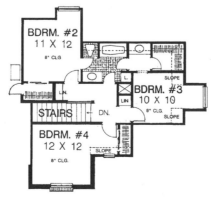

BDRM. #2
11 X 12
8" CLG

BDRM. #3
10 X 10
8" CLG.

SLOPE

SLOPE

L

LIN.

LIN

STAIRS

DN.

BDRM. #4
12 X 12
8" CLG.

SLOPE

SECOND FLOOR

To order your Blueprints, call 1-800-235-5700

Units	Single
Price Code	K
Total Finished	3,096 sq. ft.
First Finished	2,083 sq. ft.
Second Finished	1,013 sq. ft.
Garage Unfinished	497 sq. ft.
Porch Unfinished	369 sq. ft.
Dimensions	74'x88'
Foundation	Crawlspace
Bedrooms	3
Full Baths	3
Half Baths	1
Max Ridge Height	33'
Exterior Walls	2x6

* Alternate foundation options available at an additional charge. Please call 1-800-235-5700 for more information.

FIRST FLOOR

SECOND FLOOR

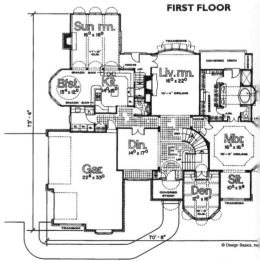

FIRST FLOOR

Units	Single
Price Code	K
Total Finished	3,765 sq. ft.
First Finished	2,804 sq. ft.
Second Finished	961 sq. ft.
Garage Unfinished	773 sq. ft.
Dimensions	70'8''x73'4''
Foundation	Basement
	Crawlspace
	Slab
Bedrooms	4
Full Baths	2
Half Baths	1
3/4 Baths	1
First Ceiling	8'
Max Ridge Height	32'4''
Roof Framing	Stick
Exterior Walls	2x4

SECOND FLOOR

* Alternate foundation options available at an additional charge. Please call 1-800-235-5700 for more information.

To order your Blueprints, call 1-800-235-5700

Units	Single
Price Code	H
Total Finished	3,029 sq. ft.
First Finished	2,115 sq. ft.
Second Finished	914 sq. ft.
Basement Unfinished	2,115 sq. ft.
Garage Unfinished	448 sq. ft.
Dimensions	60'×52'
Foundation	Basement
	Slab
Bedrooms	4
Full Baths	3
Half Baths	1
Max Ridge Height	34'
Roof Framing	Stick/Truss
Exterior Walls	2×4

SECOND FLOOR

upper grand room

upper foyer

breakfast below

shed vault

up

open rail

open rail

knee wall

open rail

br
12'-2" x 13'-8"

br
11'-6" x 14'-8"

br
15'-0" x 12'-2"

br

linen

w.i.c.

glass blocks

offset per elev.

FIRST FLOOR

2 story grand room
17'-0" x 20'-0"

brk
23'-9" x 16'-0"

k
island

mbr
17'-7.5" x 15'-0"

2 story foyer

din
12'-6" x 14'-9"

liv
14'-4" x 11'-5"

gar

laundry

pantry

powder rm.

w.i.c.

tub

plant shelf

up

shed vault

open rail

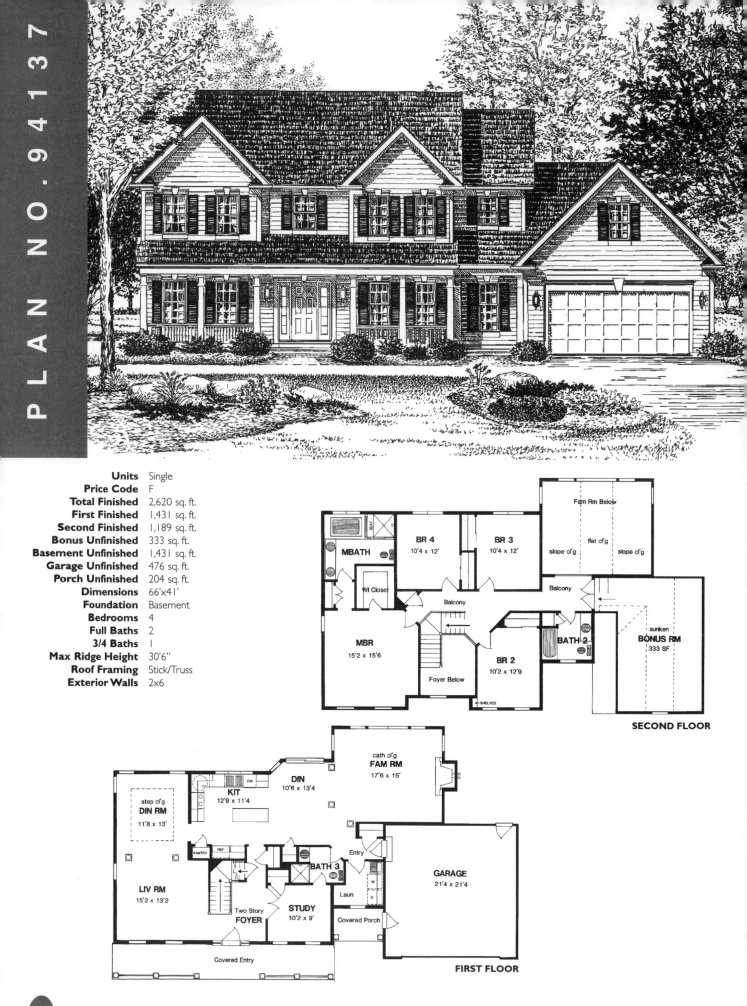

Units	Single
Price Code	F
Total Finished	2,620 sq. ft.
First Finished	1,431 sq. ft.
Second Finished	1,189 sq. ft.
Bonus Unfinished	333 sq. ft.
Basement Unfinished	1,431 sq. ft.
Garage Unfinished	476 sq. ft.
Porch Unfinished	204 sq. ft.
Dimensions	66'x41'
Foundation	Basement
Bedrooms	4
Full Baths	2
3/4 Baths	1
Max Ridge Height	30'6''
Roof Framing	Stick/Truss
Exterior Walls	2x6

SECOND FLOOR

Fam Rm Below

flat cl'g

slope cl'g   slope cl'g

MBATH

WI Closet

Balcony   Balcony

BR 4
10'4 x 12'

BR 3
10'4 x 12'

sunken
BONUS RM
333 SF

MBR
15'2 x 15'6

BATH 2

BR 2
10'2 x 12'9

Foyer Below

SHELVES

FIRST FLOOR

step cl'g
DIN RM
11'8 x 13'

KIT
12'9 x 11'4

DW

DIN
10'6 x 13'4

cath cl'g
FAM RM
17'6 x 15'

PANTRY   REF

Entry

LIV RM
15'2 x 13'2

BATH 3

Laun

GARAGE
21'4 x 21'4

Two Story
FOYER

STUDY
10'2 x 9'

Covered Porch

Covered Entry

To order your Blueprints, call 1-800-235-5700

FIRST FLOOR

Patio

Kit
13x14

Din
12x11

FamRm
17x17

3 Car Garage
21x36

To Opt.
Basement

Stairs

Gallery
TILE FLOOR

LivRm
13x16
CATH. CLNG.

Util

FrmlDin
14x14

Ent
TILE FLOOR

Porch

SECOND FLOOR

Future Room
22x16
(Not Included In Sq. Ftg.)

Bed#2
12x12

Bed#3
12x12

STAIRS

Sitting
Area
9x12

MstrBd
14x16

Units	Single
Price Code	E
Total Finished	2,455 sq. ft.
First Finished	1,447 sq. ft.
Second Finished	1,008 sq. ft.
Bonus Unfinished	352 sq. ft.
Garage Unfinished	756 sq. ft.
Porch Unfinished	210 sq. ft.
Dimensions	65'x37'11''
Foundation	Basement Slab
Bedrooms	3
Full Baths	2
Half Baths	1
First Ceiling	9'
Second Ceiling	8'
Max Ridge Height	30'
Roof Framing	Stick
Exterior Walls	2x4

Units	Single
Price Code	F
Total Finished	2,537 sq. ft.
First Finished	1,794 sq. ft.
Second Finished	743 sq. ft.
Dimensions	66'x55'11.5''
Foundation	Slab
Bedrooms	4
Full Baths	2
Half Baths	1
Max Ridge Height	33'
Roof Framing	Stick
Exterior Walls	2x4

* Alternate foundation options available at an additional charge.
Please call 1-800-235-5700 for more information.

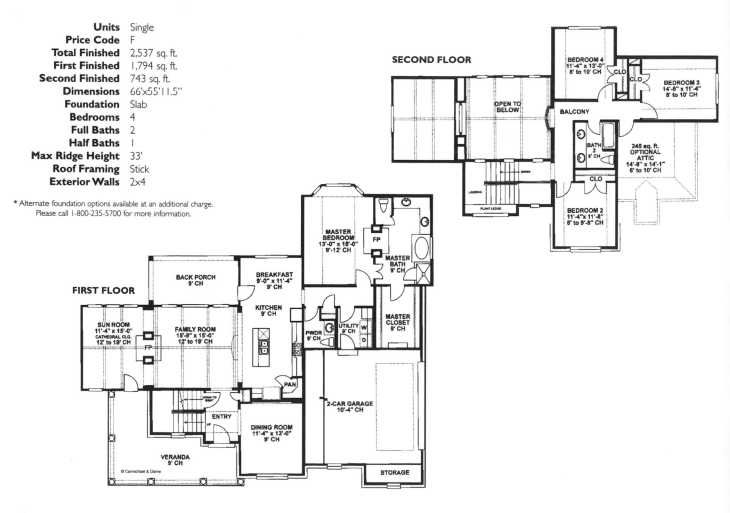

To order your Blueprints, call 1-800-235-5700

Units	Single
Price Code	G
Total Finished	2,778 sq. ft.
First Finished	1,279 sq. ft.
Second Finished	1,499 sq. ft.
Bonus Unfinished	240 sq. ft.
Basement Unfinished	1,279 sq. ft.
Garage Unfinished	660 sq. ft.
Dimensions	53'x46'6''
Foundation	Basement
	Crawlspace
Bedrooms	4
Full Baths	2
Half Baths	1
First Ceiling	9'
Second Ceiling	8'

53'-0"
46'-6"

Two Story
Family Room
15⁹ x 18⁰

Breakfast

PANTRY

FRENCH DOOR

FPL.

SERVING BAR

Kitchen

DW.

REF.

SURFACE UNIT

OVEN

Three Car
Garage
19⁸ x 32⁵

Pwdr.

COATS

ST. RM.

STAIRS DN.

Living Room
12⁸ x 12²

Two Story
Foyer

Dining Room
12⁸ x 13⁰

© Frank Betz Associates, Inc.

COVERED ENTRY

FIRST FLOOR

Family Room
Below

Bedroom 2
12⁸ x 13⁴

Bath

TRAY CEILING

Master Suite
18⁰ x 14⁰

W.i.c.

LINEN

PLANT SHELF ABOVE

Vaulted
M.Bath

RADIUS WINDOW

LINEN

OVERLOOK

STAIRS DN.

Laund.

SHWR.

Bedroom 3
12⁶ x 14⁸

Foyer
Below

Bedroom 4
12⁸ x 13⁰

W.i.c.

W.i.c.

LINEN

WINDOW SEAT

SECOND FLOOR

Units	Single
Price Code	B
Total Finished	1,647 sq. ft.
First Finished	1,288 sq. ft.
Second Finished	359 sq. ft.
Foundation	Slab
Bedrooms	3
Full Baths	1
First Ceiling	8'
Second Ceiling	11'
Vaulted Ceiling	20'
Max Ridge Height	25'3''
Roof Framing	Stick
Exterior Walls	2x4

BEDROOM 1
11'-10" x 10'-0"

COATS

BEDROOM 2
11'-4" x 10'-0"

46'-0"
+ PORCH

LINEN

W/D

PANTRY

GREAT ROOM
27'-4" x 29'-5"
20' HIGH CEILING

DECK/PATIO
11'-6" x 18'-8"

VAULT

VAULT

DECK
7'-6" x 36'-0"

PORCH
24'-4" x 7'-6"

28'-0"

FIRST FLOOR

LOFT
23'-1" x 15'-6"

40" KNEE WALL

DN.

VAULT

VAULT

OPEN BELOW
20' HIGH CEILING

VAULT

VAULT

SECOND FLOOR

To order your Blueprints, call 1-800-235-5700

Units	Single
Price Code	L
Total Finished	4,759 sq. ft.
First Finished	3,546 sq. ft.
Second Finished	1,213 sq. ft.
Garage Unfinished	822 sq. ft.
Porch Unfinished	719 sq. ft.
Dimensions	95'4"x83'
Foundation	Slab
Bedrooms	4
Full Baths	2
Half Baths	1
3/4 Baths	1
First Ceiling	10'
Second Ceiling	9'
Max Ridge Height	37'8"
Roof Framing	Truss
Exterior Walls	2x6

* Alternate foundation options available at an additional charge.
  Please call 1-800-235-5700 for more information.

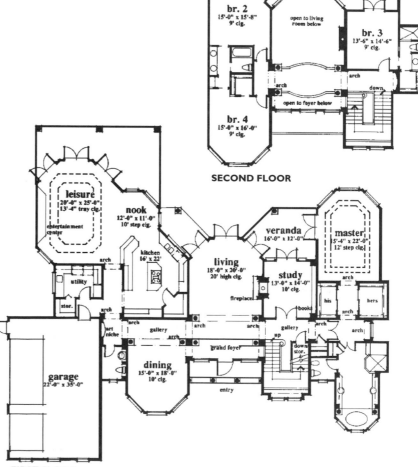

SECOND FLOOR

FIRST FLOOR

To order your Blueprints, call 1-800-235-5700

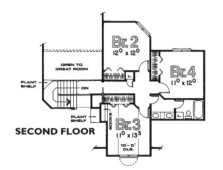

SECOND FLOOR

Br. 2
12⁰ x 12⁰

Br. 4
11⁰ x 12⁰

OPEN TO GREAT ROOM

PLANT SHELF

DN

PLANT SHELF

Br. 3
11⁰ x 13³
10'-0" CLG.

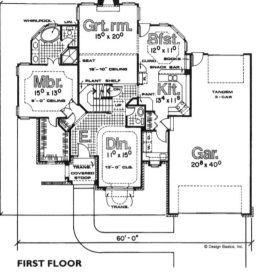

Whirlpool

LIN.

Grt. rm.
15⁰ x 20⁰

Bfst.
12⁰ x 11⁰

SEAT

18'-10" CEILING

CURIO

BOOKS

SNACK BAR

Mbr.
15⁰ x 13⁰
9'-0" CEILING

PLANT SHELF

DN

UP

Kit.
13⁴ x 11⁸

PANT.

TANDEM 3-CAR

Din.
11⁰ x 15⁰
13'-0" CLG.

Gar.
20⁸ x 40⁰

TRANS.

COVERED STOOP

TRANS.

60'-0"

© Design Basics, Inc.

FIRST FLOOR

Units	Single
Price Code	D
Total Finished	2,215 sq. ft.
First Finished	1,518 sq. ft.
Second Finished	697 sq. ft.
Basement Unfinished	1,518 sq. ft.
Garage Unfinished	769 sq. ft.
Dimensions	60'x53'4"
Foundation	Basement
	Crawlspace
	Slab
Bedrooms	4
Full Baths	2
Half Baths	I
First Ceiling	8'
Max Ridge Height	26'
Roof Framing	Stick
Exterior Walls	2x4

* Alternate foundation options available at an additional charge.
Please call 1-800-235-5700 for more information.

Units	Single
Price Code	B
Total Finished	1,574 sq. ft.
First Finished	787 sq. ft.
Second Finished	787 sq. ft.
Basement Unfinished	787 sq. ft.
Dimensions	32'4"x24'4"
Foundation	Basement
Bedrooms	3
Full Baths	2
First Ceiling	8'2"
Max Ridge Height	32'4"
Roof Framing	Truss
Exterior Walls	2x6

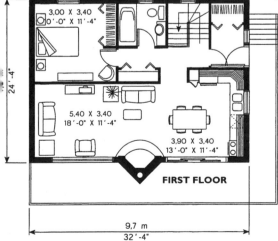

3,00 X 3,40
0'-0" X 11'-4"

5,40 X 3,40
18'-0" X 11'-4"

3,90 X 3,40
13'-0" X 11'-4"

24'-4"

9,7 m
32'-4"

FIRST FLOOR

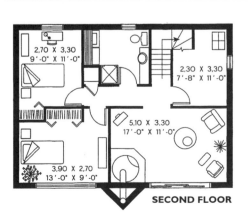

2,70 X 3,30
9'-0" X 11'-0"

2,30 X 3,30
7'-8" X 11'-0"

5,10 X 3,30
17'-0" X 11'-0"

3,90 X 2,70
13'-0" X 9'-0"

SECOND FLOOR

Units	Single
Price Code	E
Total Finished	2,332 sq. ft.
First Finished	1,214 sq. ft.
Second Finished	1,118 sq. ft.
Garage Unfinished	511 sq. ft.
Dimensions	54'x43'4''
Foundation	Basement
Bedrooms	4
Full Baths	2
Half Baths	1
Max Ridge Height	26'3''
Roof Framing	Stick
Exterior Walls	2×4

* Alternate foundation options available at an additional charge.
Please call 1-800-235-5700 for more information.

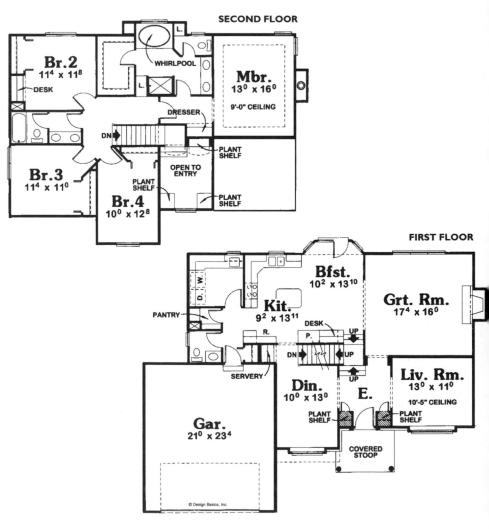

Units	Single
Price Code	I
Total Finished	3,423 sq. ft.
First Finished	2,787 sq. ft.
Second Finished	636 sq. ft.
Garage Unfinished	832 sq. ft.
Porch Unfinished	212 sq. ft.
Dimensions	101'x58'8''
Foundation	Crawlspace
	Slab
Bedrooms	4
Full Baths	2
Half Baths	I
First Ceiling	9'
Second Ceiling	7'-9'
Max Ridge Height	28'6''
Roof Framing	Stick
Exterior Walls	2x4

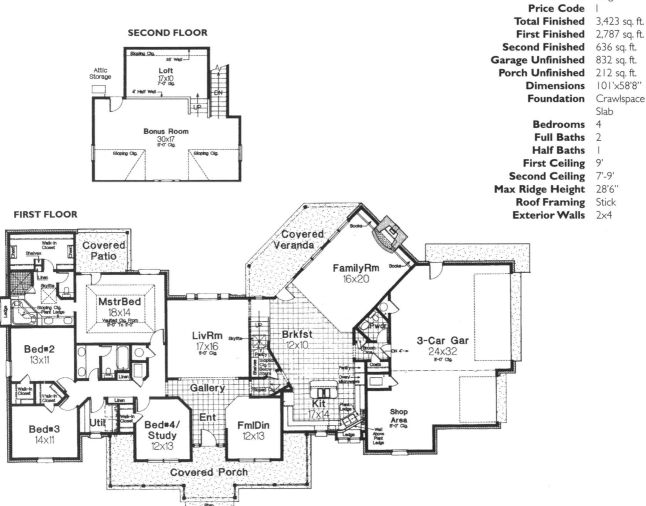

SECOND FLOOR

FIRST FLOOR

Units	Single
Price Code	B
Total Finished	834 sq. ft.
Main Finished	834 sq. ft.
Garage Unfinished	208 sq. ft.
Dimensions	48'x44'
Foundation	Basement
Bedrooms	2
Full Baths	1

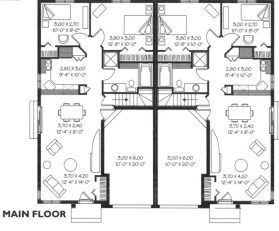

MAIN FLOOR

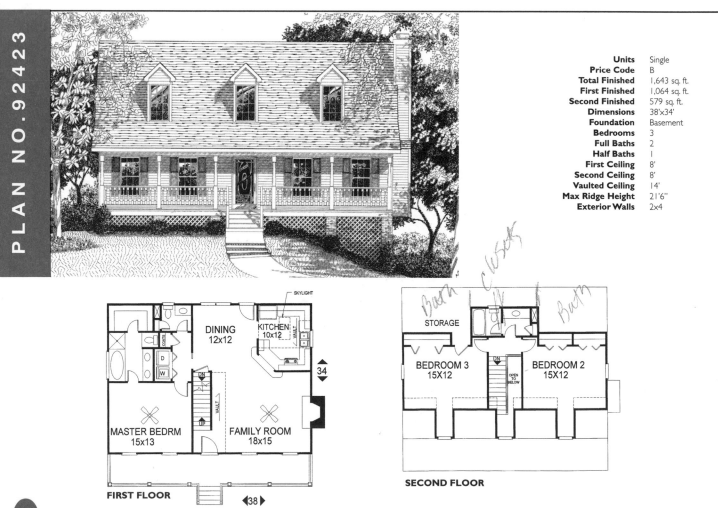

Units	Single
Price Code	B
Total Finished	1,643 sq. ft.
First Finished	1,064 sq. ft.
Second Finished	579 sq. ft.
Dimensions	38'x34'
Foundation	Basement
Bedrooms	3
Full Baths	2
Half Baths	1
First Ceiling	8'
Second Ceiling	8'
Vaulted Ceiling	14'
Max Ridge Height	21'6"
Exterior Walls	2x4

FIRST FLOOR

SECOND FLOOR

To order your Blueprints, call 1-800-235-5700

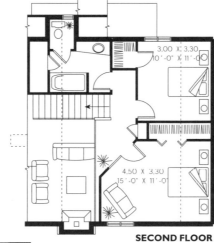

SECOND FLOOR

Units	Single
Price Code	A
Total Finished	1,360 sq. ft.
First Finished	858 sq. ft.
Second Finished	502 sq. ft.
Basement Unfinished	858 sq. ft.
Dimensions	35'x29'8''
Foundation	Basement
Bedrooms	3
Full Baths	2
Max Ridge Height	26'6''
Roof Framing	Truss
Exterior Walls	2x6

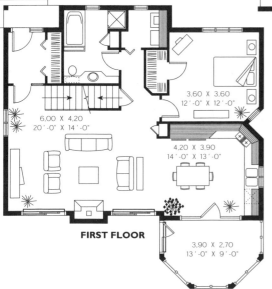

FIRST FLOOR

To order your Blueprints, call 1-800-235-5700

Units	Single
Price Code	K
Total Finished	3,936 sq. ft.
First Finished	2,751 sq. ft.
Second Finished	1,185 sq. ft.
Bonus Unfinished	343 sq. ft.
Garage Unfinished	790 sq. ft.
Porch Unfinished	36 sq. ft.
Dimensions	79'x66'4"
Foundation	Basement
	Slab
Bedrooms	4
Full Baths	3
Half Baths	1
First Ceiling	10'
Max Ridge Height	35'
Roof Framing	Stick
Exterior Walls	2x4

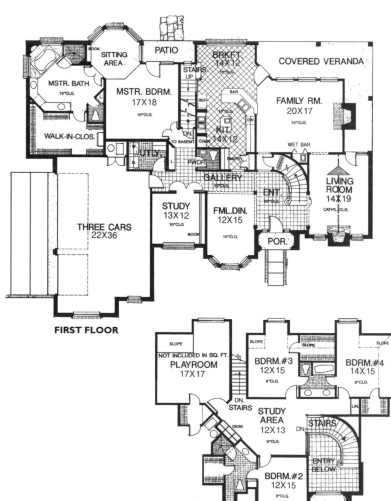

FIRST FLOOR

SECOND FLOOR

To order your Blueprints, call 1-800-235-5700

FIRST FLOOR

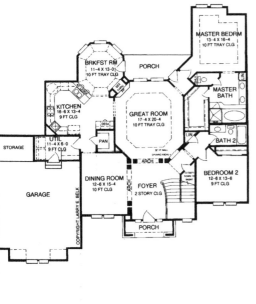

MASTER BEDRM
13-4 X 16-4
10 FT TRAY CLG

BRKFST RM
11-4 X 13-0
10 FT TRAY CLG

PORCH

MASTER BATH

KITCHEN
16-6 X 13-4
9 FT CLG

GREAT ROOM
17-4 X 20-4
10 FT TRAY CLG

DESK

BATH 2

STORAGE

UTIL
11-4 X 6-0
9 FT CLG

PAN

LIN

ARCH

GARAGE

DINING ROOM
12-6 X 15-4
10 FT CLG

FOYER
2 STORY CLG

BEDROOM 2
12-6 X 13-6
9 FT CLG

PORCH

COPYRIGHT LARRY E. BELK

SECOND FLOOR

BEDROOM 4
13-4 X 10-4

EXPANDABLE
17-4 X 18-0

LIN

BATH 3

UP

OPEN TO
FOYER
BELOW

BEDROOM 3
13-0 X 11-6

PLANT
LEDGE

Units	Single
Price Code	F
Total Finished	2,611 sq. ft.
First Finished	2,050 sq. ft.
Second Finished	561 sq. ft.
Bonus Unfinished	272 sq. ft.
Garage Unfinished	599 sq. ft.
Porch Unfinished	145 sq. ft.
Dimensions	64'10''x64'
Foundation	Basement
	Crawlspace
	Slab
Bedrooms	4
Full Baths	3
Max Ridge Height	29'
Roof Framing	Stick
Exterior Walls	2x4

FIRST FLOOR

Living

Covered Porch

Breakfast

Master Bath

Kitchen

Ba.

Master Bedroom

Dining

Foyer

Porch

Garage

SECOND FLOOR

Open to Below

Bath #2

Bedroom #4

Bedroom #2

Bedroom #3

Utility

Units	Single
Price Code	E
Total Finished	2,473 sq. ft.
First Finished	1,504 sq. ft.
Second Finished	969 sq. ft.
Porch Unfinished	212 sq. ft.
Dimensions	36'x53'
Foundation	Crawlspace
	Slab
Bedrooms	4
Full Baths	2
Half Baths	1
First Ceiling	10'
Second Ceiling	9'
Max Ridge Height	32'6''
Roof Framing	Stick
Exterior Walls	2x4

Units	Single
Price Code	B
Total Finished	1,595 sq. ft.
First Finished	931 sq. ft.
Second Finished	664 sq. ft.
Dimensions	32'4''x40'
Foundation	Basement
	Crawlspace
	Slab
Bedrooms	4
Full Baths	2
Half Baths	1
Max Ridge Height	28'
Roof Framing	Stick
Exterior Walls	2x4

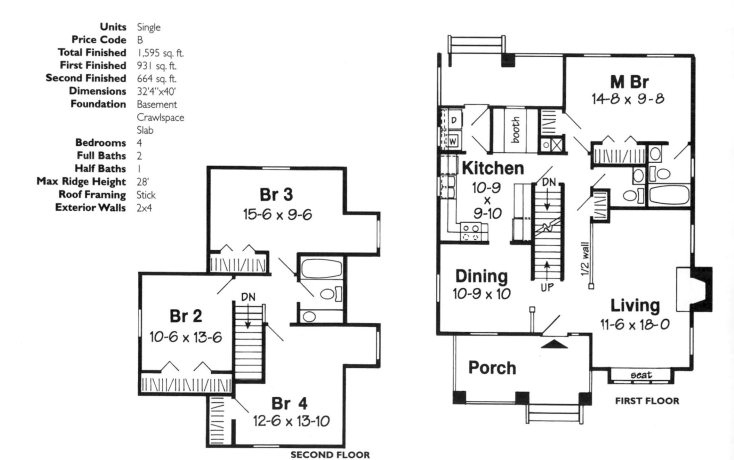

Br 3
15-6 x 9-6

DN

Br 2
10-6 x 13-6

Br 4
12-6 x 13-10

SECOND FLOOR

M Br
14-8 x 9-8

D

W

booth

Kitchen
10-9 x 9-10

DN

UP

1/2 wall

Dining
10-9 x 10

Living
11-6 x 18-0

Porch

seat

FIRST FLOOR

To order your Blueprints, call 1-800-235-5700

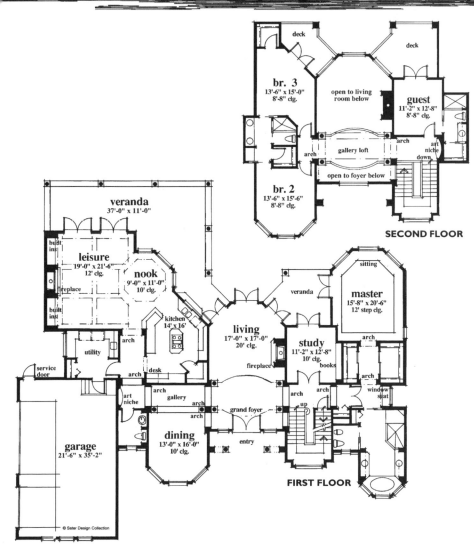

br. 3
13'-6" x 15'-0"
8'-8" clg.

open to living room below

guest
11'-2" x 12'-8"
8'-8" clg.

arch

gallery loft

arch

art niche

down

open to foyer below

br. 2
13'-6" x 15'-6"
8'-8" clg.

SECOND FLOOR

veranda
37'-0" x 11'-0"

built ins

leisure
19'-0" x 21'-6"
12' clg.

fireplace

nook
9'-0" x 11'-0"
10' clg.

built ins

kitchen
14' x 16'

arch

utility

sitting

veranda

master
15'-8" x 20'-6"
12' step clg.

arch

desk

living
17'-0" x 17'-0"
20' clg.

study
11'-2" x 12'-8"
10' clg.

books

service door

art niche

arch

gallery

arch

arch

fireplace

arch

arch

arch

arch

window seat

garage
21'-6" x 35'-2"

dining
13'-0" x 16'-0"
10' clg.

grand foyer

entry

up

© Sater Design Collection

FIRST FLOOR

Units	Single
Price Code	L
Total Finished	4,106 sq. ft.
First Finished	3,027 sq. ft.
Second Finished	1,079 sq.ft.
Basement Unfinished	3,027 sq. ft.
Garage Unfinished	802 sq. ft.
Porch Unfinished	884 sq. ft.
Dimensions	87'4''x80'4''
Foundation	Basement
	Slab
	Combo
	Basement/Slab
Bedrooms	4
Full Baths	1
Half Baths	1
3/4 Baths	2
Max Ridge Height	38'
Roof Framing	Truss
Exterior Walls	2x6

* Alternate foundation options available at an additional charge.
Please call 1-800-235-5700 for more information.

Units	Single
Price Code	B
Total Finished	1,598 sq. ft.
First Finished	812 sq. ft.
Second Finished	786 sq. ft.
Garage Unfinished	560 sq. ft.
Dimensions	52'x28'
Foundation	Crawlspace
	Slab
Bedrooms	3
Full Baths	2
Half Baths	1
First Ceiling	8'
Second Ceiling	8'
Vaulted Ceiling	15'
Max Ridge Height	25'10''
Roof Framing	Truss
Exterior Walls	2x4

FIRST FLOOR

SECOND FLOOR

Units	Single
Price Code	C
Total Finished	2,113 sq. ft.
First Finished	1,612 sq. ft.
Second Finished	501 sq. ft.
Bonus Unfinished	291 sq. ft.
Basement Unfinished	1,612 sq. ft.
Garage Unfinished	452 sq. ft.
Dimensions	52'x50'10''
Foundation	Basement
	Crawlspace
Bedrooms	4
Full Baths	3
First Ceiling	9'
Second Ceiling	8'
Max Ridge Height	29'
Roof Framing	Stick
Exterior Walls	2x4

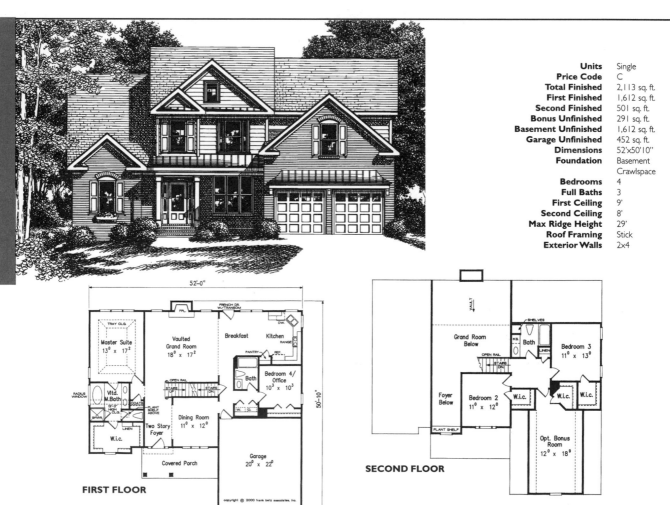

FIRST FLOOR

SECOND FLOOR

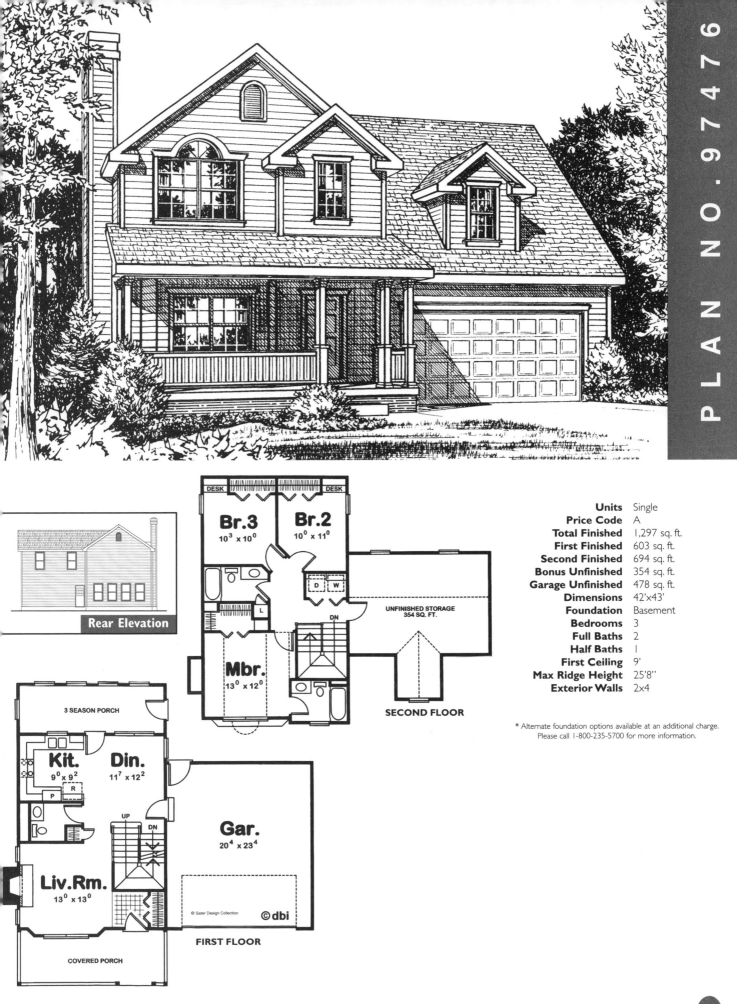

Rear Elevation

Br.3
10³ x 10⁰

Br.2
10⁰ x 11⁰

DESK   DESK

D   W

L

DN

UNFINISHED STORAGE
354 SQ. FT.

Mbr.
13⁰ x 12⁰

SECOND FLOOR

3 SEASON PORCH

Kit.
9⁰ x 9²

Din.
11⁷ x 12²

P   R

UP   DN

Gar.
20⁴ x 23⁴

Liv.Rm.
13⁰ x 13⁰

© Sater Design Collection   © dbi

FIRST FLOOR

COVERED PORCH

Units	Single
Price Code	A
Total Finished	1,297 sq. ft.
First Finished	603 sq. ft.
Second Finished	694 sq. ft.
Bonus Unfinished	354 sq. ft.
Garage Unfinished	478 sq. ft.
Dimensions	42'x43'
Foundation	Basement
Bedrooms	3
Full Baths	2
Half Baths	1
First Ceiling	9'
Max Ridge Height	25'8''
Exterior Walls	2x4

* Alternate foundation options available at an additional charge.
Please call 1-800-235-5700 for more information.

Units	Single
Price Code	A
Total Finished	1,240 sq. ft.
First Finished	620 sq. ft.
Second Finished	620 sq. ft.
Dimensions	22'x32'
Foundation	Basement
Bedrooms	3
Full Baths	1
Half Baths	1

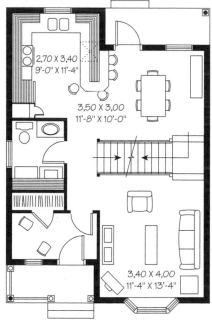

SECOND FLOOR

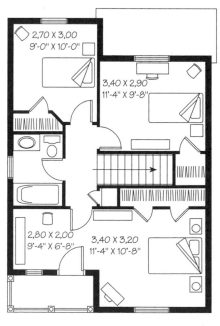

FIRST FLOOR

To order your Blueprints, call 1-800-235-5700

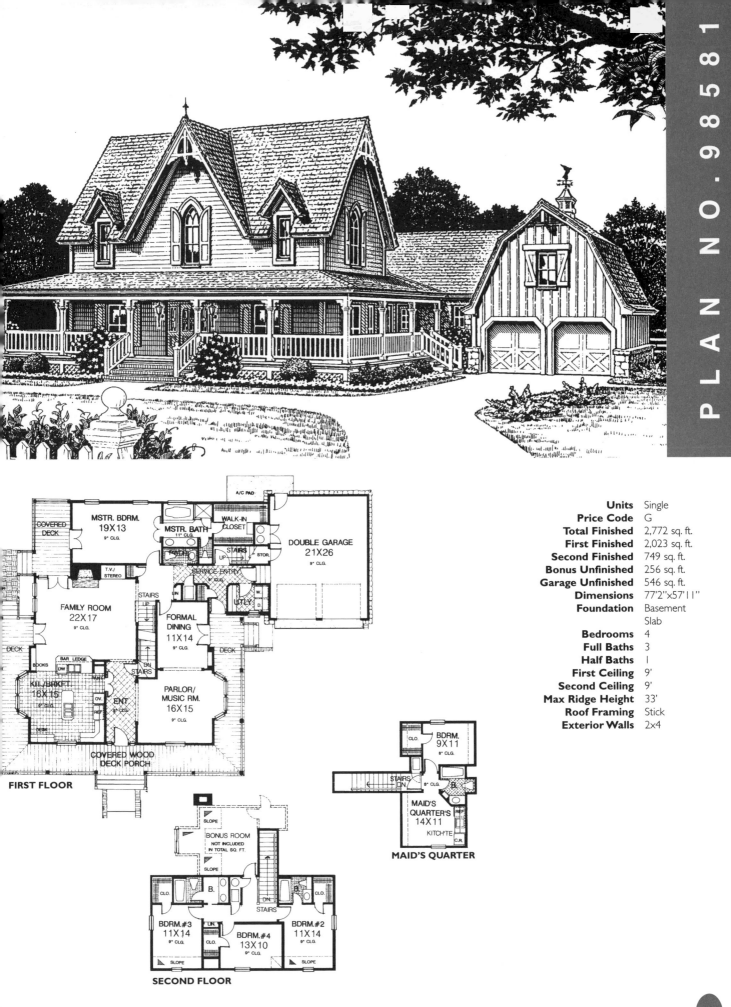

FIRST FLOOR

- COVERED DECK
- MSTR. BDRM. 19X13 — 9' CLG.
- MSTR. BATH 11' CLG.
- WALK-IN CLOSET
- DOUBLE GARAGE 21X26 — 9' CLG.
- STAIRS UP
- STOR.
- T.V./ STEREO
- SERVICE ENTRY
- FAMILY ROOM 22X17 — 9' CLG.
- STAIRS UP
- FORMAL DINING 11X14 — 9' CLG.
- UTLY.
- DECK
- BAR LEDGE
- BOOKS
- DW
- DN STAIRS
- KIT/BRKFT 16X15 — 9' CLG.
- OV.
- REF.
- ENT 9' CLG.
- PARLOR/ MUSIC RM. 16X15 — 9' CLG.
- DECK
- A/C PAD
- COVERED WOOD DECK PORCH

SECOND FLOOR

- BONUS ROOM NOT INCLUDED IN TOTAL SQ. FT.
- SLOPE
- CLO.
- B.
- CLO.
- BDRM.#3 11X14 — 9' CLG.
- LN.
- CLO.
- BDRM.#4 13X10 — 9' CLG.
- STAIRS DN.
- BDRM.#2 11X14 — 9' CLG.
- SLOPE

MAID'S QUARTER

- CLO.
- BDRM. 9X11 — 8' CLG.
- STAIRS DN.
- B.
- MAID'S QUARTER'S 14X11 — 8' CLG.
- REF.
- KITCH'TE
- C.R.

Units	Single
Price Code	G
Total Finished	2,772 sq. ft.
First Finished	2,023 sq. ft.
Second Finished	749 sq. ft.
Bonus Unfinished	256 sq. ft.
Garage Unfinished	546 sq. ft.
Dimensions	77'2"×57'11"
Foundation	Basement Slab
Bedrooms	4
Full Baths	3
Half Baths	1
First Ceiling	9'
Second Ceiling	9'
Max Ridge Height	33'
Roof Framing	Stick
Exterior Walls	2x4

Units	Single
Price Code	F
Total Finished	2,647 sq. ft.
First Finished	1,378 sq. ft.
Second Finished	1,269 sq. ft.
Basement Unfinished	1,378 sq. ft.
Garage Unfinished	717 sq. ft.
Dimensions	71'x45'
Foundation	Basement
	Crawlspace
	Slab
Bedrooms	3
Full Baths	2
3/4 Baths	1
First Ceiling	9'
Second Ceiling	8'
Max Ridge Height	29'
Roof Framing	Stick
Exterior Walls	2x4

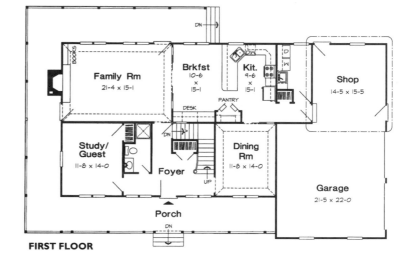

FIRST FLOOR

Family Rm 21-4 x 15-1
Brkfst 10-6 x 15-1
Kit. 9-6 x 15-1
Shop 14-5 x 15-5
BOOKS
PANTRY
DESK
Study/ Guest 11-8 x 14-0
DN
Foyer
UP
Dining Rm 11-8 x 14-0
Garage 21-5 x 22-0
Porch
DN

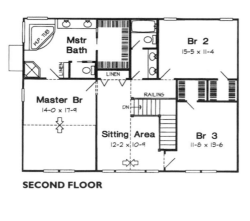

SECOND FLOOR

Mstr Bath
WLP TUB
LINEN
LINEN
Br 2 15-5 x 11-4
Master Br 14-0 x 17-9
RAILING
DN
Sitting Area 12-2 x 10-9
Br 3 11-8 x 13-6

OPTIONAL SECOND FLOOR

RAILING
DN
Br 4 12-2 x 10-9
Br 3 11-8 x 13-6

OPTIONAL CRAWLSPACE/SLAB

HW
FURN
Shop 14-5 x 15-5

To order your Blueprints, call 1-800-235-5700

Units	Single
Price Code	D
Total Finished	2,257 sq. ft.
First Finished	1,274 sq. ft.
Second Finished	983 sq. ft.
Garage Unfinished	437 sq. ft.
Porch Unfinished	183 sq. ft.
Dimensions	50'x46'
Foundation	Basement
Bedrooms	3
Full Baths	2
Half Baths	1
First Ceiling	9'
Second Ceiling	8'
Max Ridge Height	30'11'
Roof Framing	Truss
Exterior Walls	2x6

FIRST FLOOR

SECOND FLOOR

SECOND FLOOR

FIRST FLOOR

© Design Basics, Inc.

Units	Single
Price Code	E
Total Finished	2,497 sq. ft.
First Finished	1,535 sq. ft.
Second Finished	962 sq. ft.
Garage Unfinished	533 sq. ft.
Dimensions	60'x44'
Foundation	Basement
	Crawlspace
	Slab
Bedrooms	4
Full Baths	2
Half Baths	1
3/4 Baths	1
First Ceiling	8'
Max Ridge Height	26'6''
Roof Framing	Stick
Exterior Walls	2x4

* Alternate foundation options available at an additional charge.
Please call 1-800-235-5700 for more information.

To order your Blueprints, call 1-800-235-5700

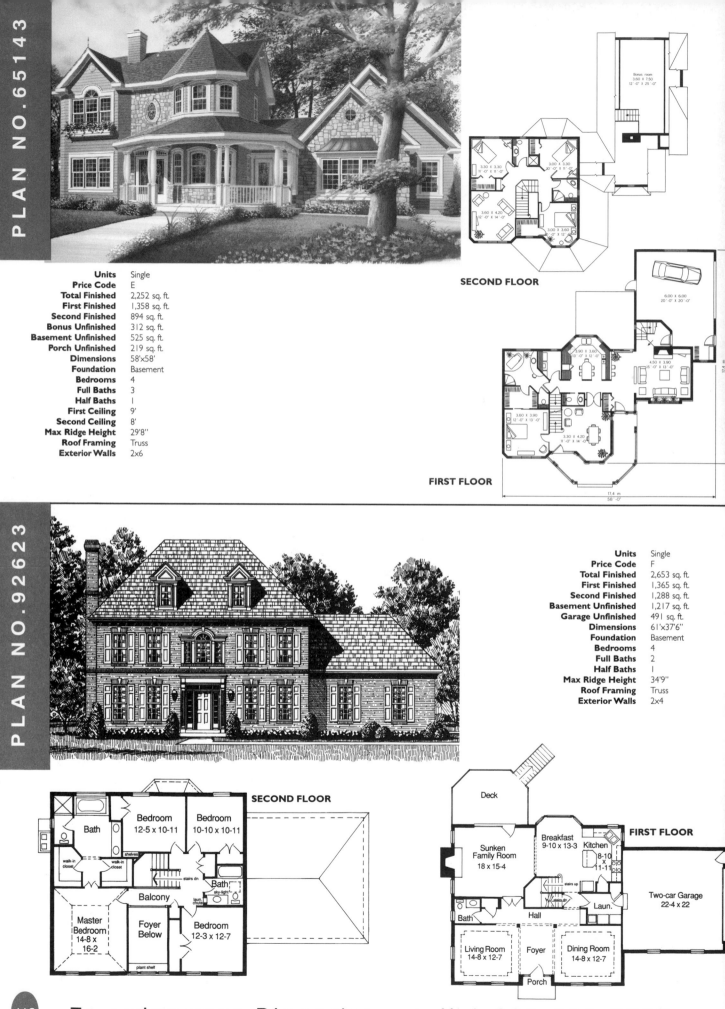

Units	Single
Price Code	E
Total Finished	2,252 sq. ft.
First Finished	1,358 sq. ft.
Second Finished	894 sq. ft.
Bonus Unfinished	312 sq. ft.
Basement Unfinished	525 sq. ft.
Porch Unfinished	219 sq. ft.
Dimensions	58'x58'
Foundation	Basement
Bedrooms	4
Full Baths	3
Half Baths	1
First Ceiling	9'
Second Ceiling	8'
Max Ridge Height	29'8"
Roof Framing	Truss
Exterior Walls	2x6

SECOND FLOOR

FIRST FLOOR

Units	Single
Price Code	F
Total Finished	2,653 sq. ft.
First Finished	1,365 sq. ft.
Second Finished	1,288 sq. ft.
Basement Unfinished	1,217 sq. ft.
Garage Unfinished	491 sq. ft.
Dimensions	61'x37'6"
Foundation	Basement
Bedrooms	4
Full Baths	2
Half Baths	1
Max Ridge Height	34'9"
Roof Framing	Truss
Exterior Walls	2x4

SECOND FLOOR

Bath

Bedroom 12-5 x 10-11

Bedroom 10-10 x 10-11

walk-in closet

walk-in closet

shelves

stairs dn

Bath

sky-light

laun. chute

Balcony

Master Bedroom 14-8 x 16-2

Foyer Below

Bedroom 12-3 x 12-7

plant shelf

Deck

Sunken Family Room 18 x 15-4

Breakfast 9-10 x 13-3

Kitchen 8-10 x 11-11

FIRST FLOOR

Hall

stairs up

Laun.

Two-car Garage 22-4 x 22

Bath

Living Room 14-8 x 12-7

Foyer

Dining Room 14-8 x 12-7

Porch

Units	Single
Price Code	D
Total Finished	2,012 sq. ft.
First Finished	1,324 sq. ft.
Second Finished	688 sq. ft.
Garage Unfinished	425 sq. ft.
Dimensions	56'x41'
Foundation	Basement
Bedrooms	4
Full Baths	2

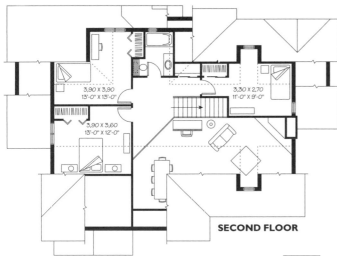

3,90 X 3,90
13'-0" X 13'-0"

3,30 X 2,70
11'-0" X 9'-0"

3,90 X 3,60
13'-0" X 12'-0"

SECOND FLOOR

5,70 X 6,00
19'-0" X 20'-0"

3,60 X 4,40
12'-0" X 14'-8"

3,90 X 5,70
13'-0" X 19'-0"

4,80 X 4,50
16'-0" X 15'-0"

3,60 X 3,80
12'-0" X 12'-8"

FIRST FLOOR

12,3 m
41'-0"

16,5 m
55'-0"

To order your Blueprints, call 1-800-235-5700

PLAN NO. 97610

Units	Single
Price Code	C
Total Finished	1,800 sq. ft.
First Finished	1,378 sq. ft.
Second Finished	422 sq. ft.
Bonus Unfinished	244 sq. ft.
Basement Unfinished	1,378 sq. ft.
Dimensions	48'x45'10''
Foundation	Basement
	Crawlspace
Bedrooms	3
Full Baths	2
Half Baths	1
Primary Roof Pitch	10:12
Max Ridge Height	27'
Roof Framing	Stick
Exterior Walls	2x4

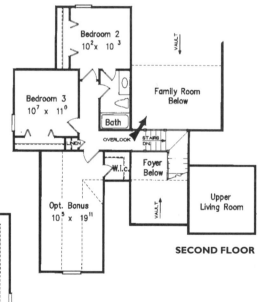

SECOND FLOOR

FIRST FLOOR

© Frank Betz Associates, Inc.

114

To order your Blueprints, call 1-800-235-5700

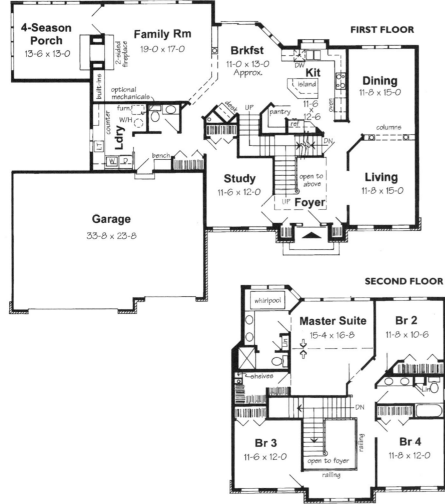

FIRST FLOOR

4-Season Porch
13-6 x 13-0

Family Rm
19-0 x 17-0

2-sided fireplace

built-ins

Brkfst
11-0 x 13-0
Approx.

DW

Kit
island
11-6 x 12-6
oven
ref

Dining
11-8 x 15-0

optional mechanicals

furn.
W/H

counter

Ldry

LT

W. D.

bench

desk

UP

pantry

DN

Study
11-6 x 12-0

open to above

columns

Living
11-8 x 15-0

UP **Foyer**

Garage
33-8 x 23-8

SECOND FLOOR

whirlpool

Master Suite
15-4 x 16-8

Br 2
11-8 x 10-6

Lin

shelves

Lin

DN

Br 3
11-6 x 12-0

open to foyer

railing

railing

Br 4
11-8 x 12-0

Units	Single
Price Code	I
Total Finished	3,339 sq. ft.
First Finished	2,076 sq. ft.
Second Finished	1,263 sq. ft.
Basement Unfinished	2,076 sq. ft.
Garage Unfinished	801 sq. ft.
Dimensions	72'x54'4''
Foundation	Basement
	Crawlspace
	Slab
Bedrooms	4
Full Baths	2
Half Baths	I
First Ceiling	9'
Second Ceiling	8'
Max Ridge Height	32'
Roof Framing	Stick
Exterior Walls	2x6

Units Single
Price Code H
Total Finished 3,219 sq. ft.
First Finished 2,337 sq. ft.
Second Finished 882 sq. ft.
Bonus Unfinished 357 sq. ft.
Garage Unfinished 640 sq. ft.
Porch Unfinished 120 sq. ft.
Dimensions 70'x63'2''
Foundation Basement
Slab
Bedrooms 4
Full Baths 3
Half Baths 1
Max Ridge Height 32'6''
Roof Framing Stick
Exterior Walls 2x4

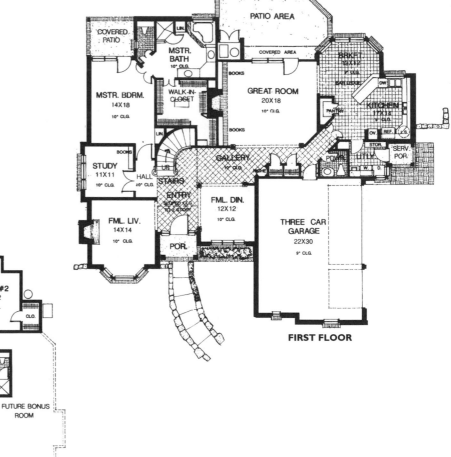

FIRST FLOOR

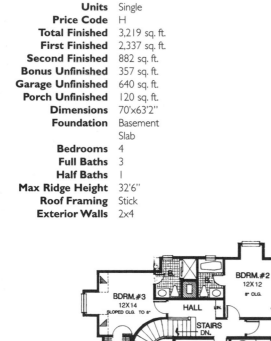

SECOND FLOOR

To order your Blueprints, call 1-800-235-5700

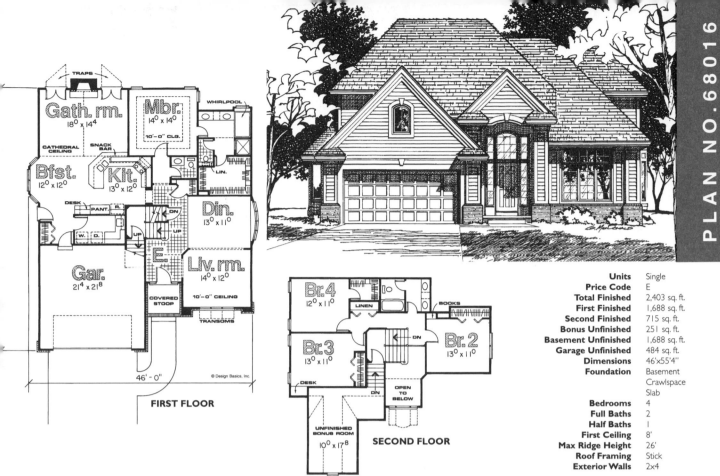

FIRST FLOOR

Gath. rm. 18⁰ x 14⁴
Mbr. 14⁰ x 14⁰
10'-0" CLG.
WHIRLPOOL
CATHEDRAL CEILING
SNACK BAR
Bfst. 12⁰ x 12⁰
Kit. 13⁰ x 12⁰
LIN.
DESK
PANT.
R.
Din. 13⁰ x 11⁰
W. D.
UP
E.
Liv. rm. 14⁰ x 12⁰
Gar. 21⁴ x 21⁸
COVERED STOOP
10'-0" CEILING
TRANSOMS
46'-0"
© Design Basics, Inc.
TRAPS

SECOND FLOOR

Br. 4 12⁰ x 11⁰
LINEN
BOOKS
Br. 3 13⁰ x 11⁰
DN
Br. 2 13⁰ x 11⁰
DESK
OPEN TO BELOW
DN
UNFINISHED BONUS ROOM 10⁰ x 17⁸

Units	Single
Price Code	E
Total Finished	2,403 sq. ft.
First Finished	1,688 sq. ft.
Second Finished	715 sq. ft.
Bonus Unfinished	251 sq. ft.
Basement Unfinished	1,688 sq. ft.
Garage Unfinished	484 sq. ft.
Dimensions	46'x55'4"
Foundation	Basement Crawlspace Slab
Bedrooms	4
Full Baths	2
Half Baths	1
First Ceiling	8'
Max Ridge Height	26'
Roof Framing	Stick
Exterior Walls	2x4

* Alternate foundation options available at an additional charge. Please call 1-800-235-5700 for more information.

Units	Single
Price Code	A
Total Finished	1,176 sq. ft.
Main Finished	1,176 sq. ft.
Garage Unfinished	401 sq. ft.
Dimensions	58'x28'
Foundation	Basement
Bedrooms	3
Full Baths	1

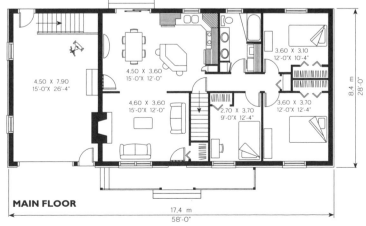

4.50 X 7.90 15'-0"X 26'-4"
4.50 X 3.60 15'-0"X 12'-0"
4.60 X 3.60 15'-0"X 12'-0"
2.70 X 3.70 9'-0"X 12'-4"
3.60 X 3.10 12'-0"X 10'-4"
3.60 X 3.70 12'-0"X 12'-4"
8.4 m 28'-0"
17.4 m 58'-0"

MAIN FLOOR

Units	Single
Price Code	C
Total Finished	2,179 sq. ft.
First Finished	1,668 sq. ft.
Second Finished	511 sq. ft.
Bonus Unfinished	302 sq. ft.
Basement Unfinished	1,668 sq. ft.
Garage Unfinished	410 sq. ft.
Dimensions	50'x56'
Foundation	Basement
	Crawlspace
Bedrooms	4
Full Baths	3
First Ceiling	9'
Second Ceiling	8'
Max Ridge Height	29'6''
Roof Framing	Stick
Exterior Walls	2x4

FIRST FLOOR

SECOND FLOOR

Units	Single
Price Code	E
Total Finished	2,403 sq. ft.
First Finished	1,710 sq. ft.
Second Finished	693 sq. ft.
Basement Unfinished	1,620 sq. ft.
Garage Unfinished	467 sq. ft.
Porch Unfinished	43 sq. ft.
Dimensions	63'4''x48'
Foundation	Basement
	Slab
Bedrooms	4
Full Baths	3
Half Baths	1
First Ceiling	8'
Second Ceiling	8'
Vaulted Ceiling	11'
Tray Ceiling	17'
Max Ridge Height	20'
Roof Framing	Truss
Exterior Walls	2x4

FIRST FLOOR

SECOND FLOOR

To order your Blueprints, call 1-800-235-5700

SECOND FLOOR

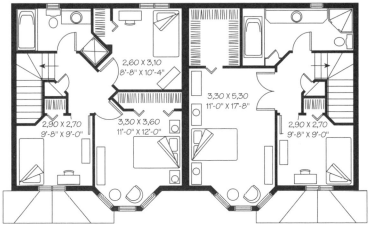

2,60 X 3,10
8'-8" X 10'-4"

3,30 X 5,30
11'-0" X 17'-8"

2,90 X 2,70
9'-8" X 9'-0"

3,30 X 3,60
11'-0" X 12'-0"

2,90 X 2,70
9'-8" X 9'-0"

Units	Single
Price Code	D
Total Finished	2,172 sq. ft.
First Finished	1,086 sq. ft.
Second Finished	1,086 sq. ft.
Dimensions	44'x28'8''
Bedrooms	3
Full Baths	I
Half Baths	I

FIRST FLOOR

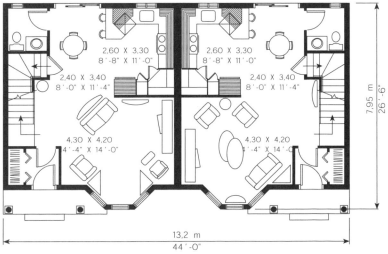

2,60 X 3,30
8'-8" X 11'-0"

2,60 X 3,30
8'-8" X 11'-0"

2,40 X 3,40
8'-0" X 11'-4"

2,40 X 3,40
8'-0" X 11'-4"

4,30 X 4,20
4'-4" X 14'-0"

4,30 X 4,20
4'-4" X 14'-0"

7,95 m
26'-6"

13,2 m
44'-0"

To order your Blueprints, call 1-800-235-5700

119

Units	Single
Price Code	G
Total Finished	2,898 sq. ft.
First Finished	2,135 sq. ft.
Second Finished	763 sq. ft.
Bonus Unfinished	538 sq. ft.
Garage Unfinished	436 sq. ft.
Porch Unfinished	540 sq. ft.
Dimensions	62'6''x70'
Foundation	Crawlspace
Bedrooms	5
Full Baths	3
First Ceiling	9'
Second Ceiling	8'
Roof Framing	Stick

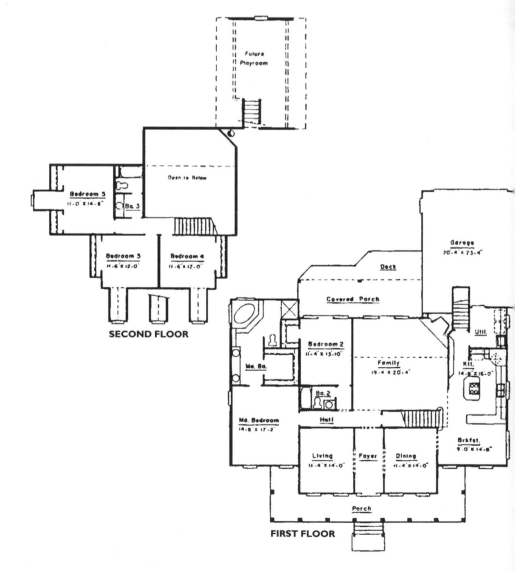

SECOND FLOOR

FIRST FLOOR

SECOND FLOOR

RADIUS WINDOW

Family Room Below

Laund.
BUILT-IN SHELVES
Sitting Area
10⁰ x 11³

TRAY CLG.
Master Suite
18⁰ x 14⁰

SINK
FPL.
LINEN
BUILT-IN SHELVES

OPEN RAIL
OVERLOOK

Bath

FRENCH DOORS
Vaulted M.Bath

Bedroom 3
12⁰ x 12³

OVERLOOK
OPEN RAIL

Bath

Bedroom 2
13² x 13⁹

Foyer Below

SHWR

LINEN

PLANT SHELF ABOVE

W.i.c.

Vaulted Bedroom 4
14⁵ x 14³
10'-0" HIGH CLG.

PLANT SHELF

LINEN

VLT.   VLT.

Units	Single
Price Code	I
Total Finished	3,266 sq. ft.
First Finished	1,577 sq. ft.
Second Finished	1,689 sq. ft.
Basement Unfinished	1,577 sq. ft.
Garage Unfinished	694 sq. ft.
Dimensions	59'4"x49'
Foundation	Basement Crawlspace
Bedrooms	5
Full Baths	4
Half Baths	I
First Ceiling	9'
Second Ceiling	8'
Max Ridge Height	32'6"
Roof Framing	Stick
Exterior Walls	2x4

FIRST FLOOR

FRENCH DOOR

Breakfast

Kitchen
DW.
SURF. UNIT
REF.
ISLAND
SERVING BAR

Study/ Bedroom 5
12⁰ x 12⁰

Two Story Family Room
20² x 14¹⁰

FPL.

DECORATIVE COLUMN

COATS
PANTRY
Pwdr.
ARCHED OPENING

OVENS

Bath

Three Car Garage
20⁵ x 32²

Dining Room
13² x 13⁴

Two Story Foyer

Living Room
13⁰ x 13⁶

Covered Porch

copyright © 1997 frank betz associates, inc.

Units	Single
Price Code	A
Total Finished	1,304 sq. ft.
First Finished	681 sq. ft.
Second Finished	623 sq. ft.
Garage Unfinished	260 sq. ft.
Dimensions	28'x40'
Foundation	Basement
Bedrooms	3
Full Baths	1
Half Baths	1

SECOND FLOOR

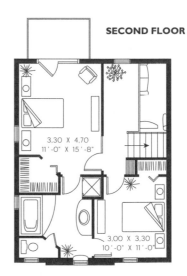

FIRST FLOOR

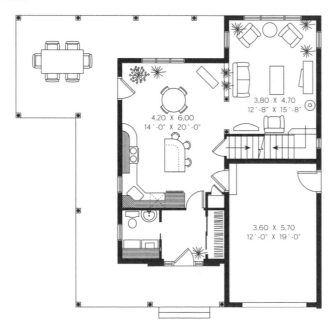

To order your Blueprints, call 1-800-235-5700

FIRST FLOOR

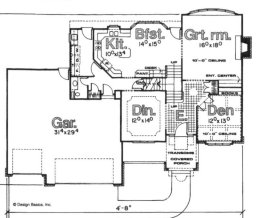

SECOND FLOOR

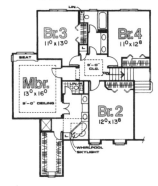

Units	Single
Price Code	F
Total Finished	2,601 sq. ft.
First Finished	1,421 sq. ft.
Second Finished	1,180 sq. ft.
Garage Unfinished	887 sq. ft.
Dimensions	64'8''x48'
Foundation	Basement
	Crawlspace
	Slab
Bedrooms	4
Full Baths	2
Half Baths	1
First Ceiling	8'
Max Ridge Height	29'9''
Roof Framing	Stick
Exterior Walls	2x4

* Alternate foundation options available at an additional charge.
Please call 1-800-235-5700 for more information.

Units	Single
Price Code	H
Total Finished	2,896 sq. ft.
First Finished	1,264 sq. ft.
Second Finished	1,632 sq. ft.
Garage Unfinished	532 sq. ft.
Porch Unfinished	21 sq. ft.
Dimensions	62'x48'4''
Foundation	Basement
Bedrooms	5
Full Baths	2
Half Baths	1
First Ceiling	8'
Second Ceiling	8'
Max Ridge Height	35'10''
Roof Framing	Truss
Exterior Walls	2x6

Photography supplied by Drummond Designs, Inc.

FIRST FLOOR

SECOND FLOOR

Units	Single
Price Code	H
Total Finished	3,138 sq. ft.
First Finished	2,341 sq. ft.
Second Finished	797 sq. ft.
Garage Unfinished	635 sq. ft.
Porch Unfinished	418 sq. ft.
Dimensions	65'x79'
Foundation	Slab
Bedrooms	4
Full Baths	4
Roof Framing	Truss

* Alternate foundation options available at an additional charge.
Please call 1-800-235-5700 for more information.

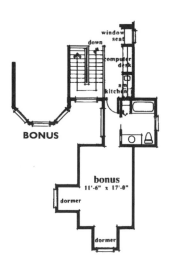

BONUS

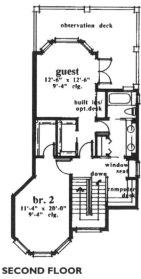

SECOND FLOOR

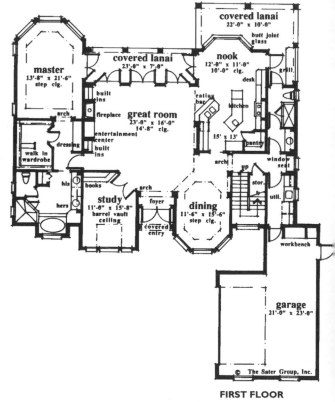

© The Sater Group, Inc.

FIRST FLOOR

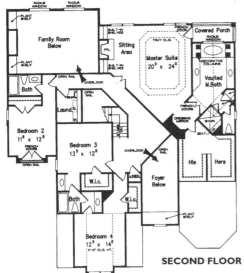

SECOND FLOOR

FIRST FLOOR

© Frank Betz Associates, Inc.

Units	Single
Price Code	L
Total Finished	4,049 sq. ft.
First Finished	2,095 sq. ft.
Second Finished	1,954 sq. ft.
Basement Unfinished	2,095 sq. ft.
Garage Unfinished	681 sq. ft.
Dimensions	56'x63'
Foundation	Basement Crawlspace
Bedrooms	5
Full Baths	4
First Ceiling	9'
Second Ceiling	9'
Primary Roof Pitch	10:12
Max Ridge Height	36'6"
Roof Framing	Stick
Exterior Walls	2x4

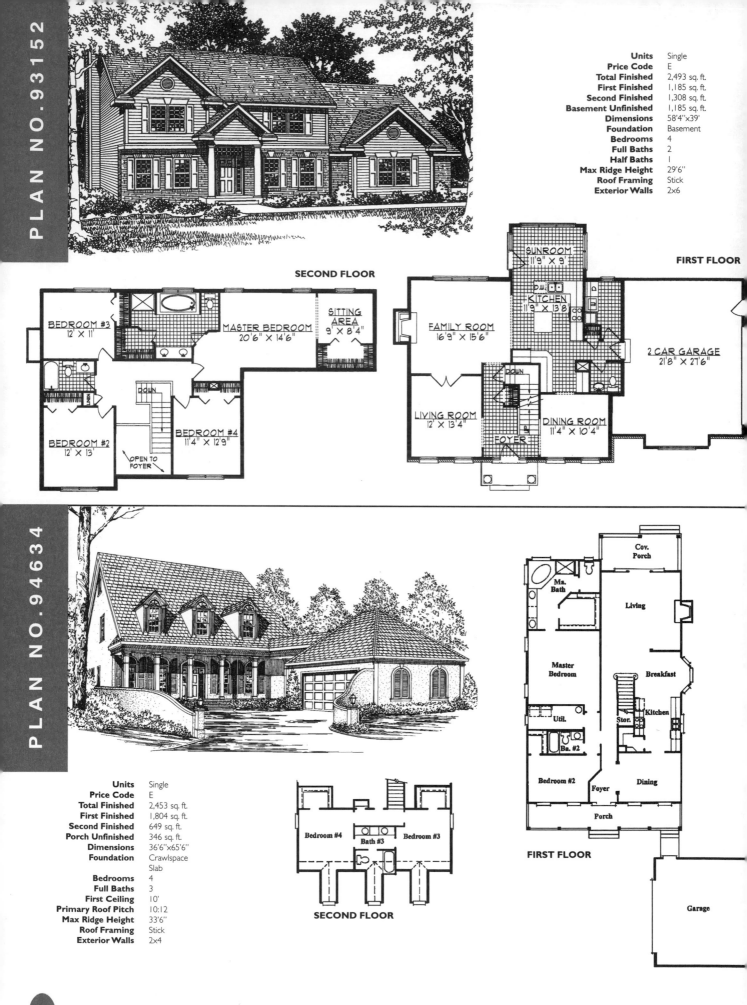

PLAN NO. 93152

Units	Single
Price Code	E
Total Finished	2,493 sq. ft.
First Finished	1,185 sq. ft.
Second Finished	1,308 sq. ft.
Basement Unfinished	1,185 sq. ft.
Dimensions	58'4"x39'
Foundation	Basement
Bedrooms	4
Full Baths	2
Half Baths	1
Max Ridge Height	29'6"
Roof Framing	Stick
Exterior Walls	2x6

SECOND FLOOR

BEDROOM #3
12' X 11'

MASTER BEDROOM
20'6" X 14'6"

SITTING AREA
9' X 8'4"

BEDROOM #2
12' X 13'

DOWN

BEDROOM #4
11'4" X 12'9"

OPEN TO FOYER

FIRST FLOOR

SUNROOM
11'9" X 9'

KITCHEN
11'9" X 13'8"

FAMILY ROOM
16'9" X 15'6"

2 CAR GARAGE
21'8" X 27'6"

DOWN

LIVING ROOM
12' X 13'4"

DINING ROOM
11'4" X 10'4"

FOYER

PLAN NO. 94634

Units	Single
Price Code	E
Total Finished	2,453 sq. ft.
First Finished	1,804 sq. ft.
Second Finished	649 sq. ft.
Porch Unfinished	346 sq. ft.
Dimensions	36'6"x65'6"
Foundation	Crawlspace
	Slab
Bedrooms	4
Full Baths	3
First Ceiling	10'
Primary Roof Pitch	10:12
Max Ridge Height	33'6"
Roof Framing	Stick
Exterior Walls	2x4

SECOND FLOOR

Bedroom #4

Bath #3

Bedroom #3

FIRST FLOOR

Cov. Porch

Ms. Bath

Living

Master Bedroom

Breakfast

Util.

Stor.

Kitchen

Ba. #2

Bedroom #2

Foyer

Dining

Porch

Garage

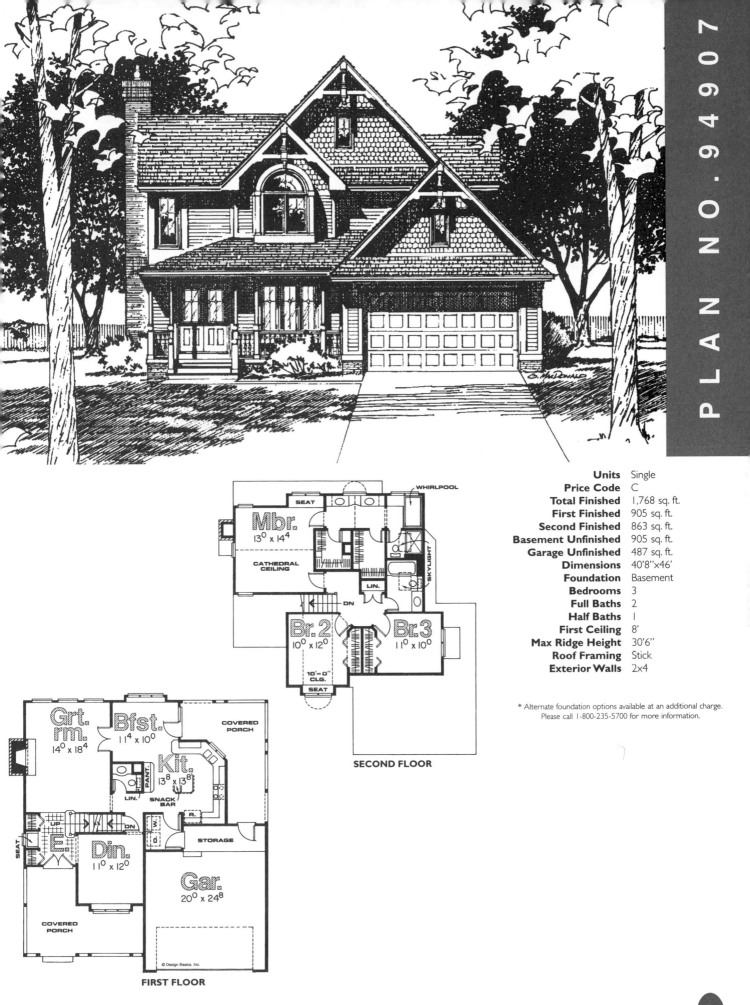

SECOND FLOOR

- SEAT
- WHIRLPOOL
- Mbr. 13⁰ x 14⁴
- CATHEDRAL CEILING
- LIN.
- DN
- SKYLIGHT
- Br. 2 10⁰ x 12⁰
- Br. 3 11⁰ x 10⁰
- 10'-0" CLG.
- SEAT

FIRST FLOOR

- Grt. rm. 14⁰ x 18⁴
- Bfst. 11⁴ x 10⁰
- COVERED PORCH
- Kit. 13⁸ x 13⁸
- PANT.
- LIN.
- SNACK BAR
- UP
- DN
- R.
- D.W.
- STORAGE
- Din. 11⁰ x 12⁰
- SEAT
- Gar. 20⁰ x 24⁸
- COVERED PORCH
- © Design Basics, Inc.

Units	Single
Price Code	C
Total Finished	1,768 sq. ft.
First Finished	905 sq. ft.
Second Finished	863 sq. ft.
Basement Unfinished	905 sq. ft.
Garage Unfinished	487 sq. ft.
Dimensions	40'8''x46'
Foundation	Basement
Bedrooms	3
Full Baths	2
Half Baths	1
First Ceiling	8'
Max Ridge Height	30'6''
Roof Framing	Stick
Exterior Walls	2x4

* Alternate foundation options available at an additional charge.
Please call 1-800-235-5700 for more information.

Units	Single
Price Code	K
Total Finished	3,850 sq. ft.
First Finished	2,306 sq. ft.
Second Finished	1,544 sq. ft.
Dimensions	80'8"x51'8"
Foundation	Basement
Bedrooms	5
Full Baths	3
Half Baths	1

80'-8"

Patio

Brk

Kit. 13-10 18-0

Hearth Rm 12-1x18-3

Sunken Solarium

Up Dn

MBr 16-8x13-0

Dining 12-1x16-0

Great Rm 18-0x21-8

Study 16-8x12-3

Garage 30-4x21-4

Entry

FIRST FLOOR

51'-8"

Br 5 12-1x14-3

Sunken Solarium Below

Dn

Br 2 13-11x15-9

Loft

Br 4 12-1x12-0

Library 15-8x9-8

Br 3 15-5x12-0

open to below

SECOND FLOOR

Units	Single
Price Code	C
Total Finished	2,118 sq. ft.
First Finished	1,638 sq. ft.
Second Finished	480 sq. ft.
Bonus Unfinished	261 sq. ft.
Basement Unfinished	1,638 sq. ft.
Garage Unfinished	410 sq. ft.
Dimensions	53'x51'4"
Foundation	Basement Crawlspace
Bedrooms	4
Full Baths	3
First Ceiling	9'
Second Ceiling	8'
Max Ridge Height	30'
Roof Framing	Stick
Exterior Walls	2x4

53'-0"

TRAY CLG.

FRENCH DOOR

FPL.

Master Suite 13⁰ x 17⁶

Vaulted Family Room 15⁶ x 17³

Vaulted Breakfast

Vaulted Kitchen

RANGE

DW.

PANTRY

REF.

Vaulted M.Bath

Bath

Bedroom 4 11² x 10⁰

Two Story Foyer

Dining Room 11³ x 11¹⁰

Laund.

STORAGE

W.i.c.

LINEN

Garage 19⁵ x 20²

51'-4"

copyright 1998 frank betz associates, inc.

FIRST FLOOR

Family Room Below

Breakfast Below

Kitchen Below

RADIUS WDW.

Bath

Bedroom 3 12⁰ x 12⁶

OPEN RAIL

STAIRS DN.

Foyer Below

Bedroom 2 11³ x 11¹⁰

W.i.c.

LINEN

Opt. Bonus Room 10⁵ x 21⁴

SECOND FLOOR

To order your Blueprints, call 1-800-235-5700

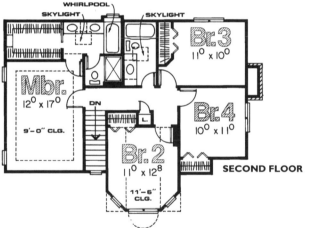

WHIRLPOOL
SKYLIGHT · · · **SKYLIGHT**

Br. 3
11⁰ x 10⁰

Mbr.
12⁰ x 17⁰

9'–0'' CLG.

DN

Br. 4
10⁰ x 11⁰

Br. 2
11⁰ x 12⁸

11'–6''
CLG.

SECOND FLOOR

Units	Single
Price Code	D
Total Finished	2,078 sq. ft.
First Finished	1,113 sq. ft.
Second Finished	965 sq. ft.
Basement Unfinished	1,113 sq. ft.
Garage Unfinished	486 sq. ft.
Dimensions	46'x41'5''
Foundation	Basement
Bedrooms	4
Full Baths	2
Half Baths	1
First Ceiling	8'
Second Ceiling	8'
Max Ridge Height	25'5''
Roof Framing	Stick
Exterior Walls	2x4

* Alternate foundation options available at an additional charge.
Please call 1-800-235-5700 for more information.

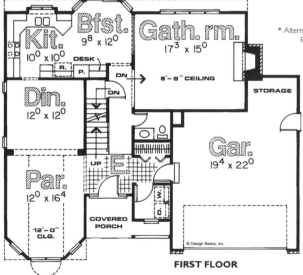

Kit.
10⁰ x 10⁰

Bfst.
9⁸ x 12⁰

Gath. rm.
17³ x 15⁰

DESK

R. · P.

DN

8'– 8'' CEILING

STORAGE

Din.
12⁰ x 12⁰

DN

UP

Gar.
19⁴ x 22⁰

Par.
12⁰ x 16⁴

12'–0''
CLG.

W.

D.

**COVERED
PORCH**

© Design Basics, Inc.

FIRST FLOOR

Units	Single
Price Code	C
Total Finished	1,856 sq. ft.
First Finished	980 sq. ft.
Second Finished	876 sq. ft.
Bonus Unfinished	325 sq. ft.
Basement Unfinished	980 sq. ft.
Garage Unfinished	577 sq. ft.
Porch Unfinished	117 sq. ft.
Dimensions	50'6''x38'
Foundation	Slab
Bedrooms	3
Full Baths	2
Half Baths	1
First Ceiling	8'
Second Ceiling	8'
Tray Ceiling	9'
Max Ridge Height	28'
Roof Framing	Stick
Exterior Walls	2x4

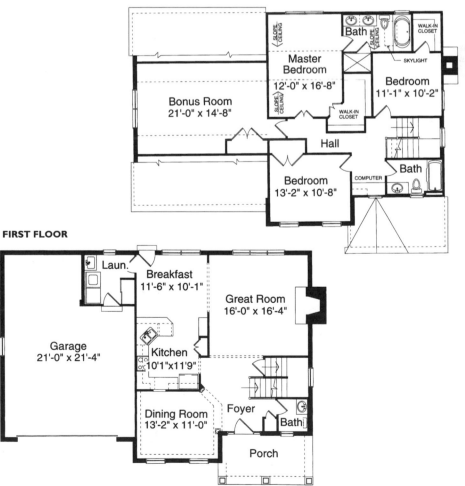

SECOND FLOOR

Bonus Room
21'-0" x 14'-8"

Master
Bedroom
12'-0" x 16'-8"

Bath

WALK-IN
CLOSET

SKYLIGHT

Bedroom
11'-1" x 10'-2"

WALK-IN
CLOSET

Hall

Bedroom
13'-2" x 10'-8"

COMPUTER

Bath

FIRST FLOOR

Laun.

Breakfast
11'-6" x 10'-1"

Great Room
16'-0" x 16'-4"

Garage
21'-0" x 21'-4"

Kitchen
10'1"x11'9"

Dining Room
13'-2" x 11'-0"

Foyer

Bath

Porch

To order your Blueprints, call 1-800-235-5700

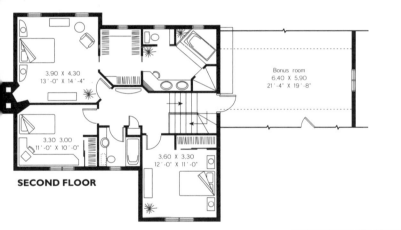

SECOND FLOOR

Bonus room
6.40 X 5.90
21'-4" X 19'-8"

3.90 X 4.30
13'-0" X 14'-4"

3.30 3.00
11'-0" X 10'-0"

3.60 X 3.30
12'-0" X 11'-0"

FIRST FLOOR

5.60 X 3.90
18'-8" X 13'-0"

4.00 X 3.30
13'-4" X 11'-0"

6.40 X 6.80
21'-4" X 22'-8"

4.00 X 4.20
13'-4" X 14'-0"

3.60 X 4.00
12'-0" X 13'-4"

Units	Single
Price Code	D
Total Finished	2,089 sq. ft.
First Finished	1,146 sq. ft.
Second Finished	943 sq. ft.
Bonus Unfinished	313 sq. ft.
Basement Unfinished	483 sq. ft.
Porch Unfinished	168 sq. ft.
Dimensions	56'x38'
Foundation	Basement
Bedrooms	3
Full Baths	2
Half Baths	1
First Ceiling	9'
Second Ceiling	8'
Max Ridge Height	31'3"
Roof Framing	Truss
Exterior Walls	2x6

Units	Single
Price Code	L
Total Finished	4,166 sq. ft.
First Finished	3,168 sq. ft.
Second Finished	998 sq. ft.
Bonus Unfinished	320 sq. ft.
Garage Unfinished	810 sq. ft.
Porch Unfinished	180 sq. ft.
Dimensions	90'x63'5''
Foundation	Basement
	Crawlspace
	Slab
Bedrooms	4
Full Baths	3
Half Baths	1
First Ceiling	10'
Second Ceiling	9'
Max Ridge Height	36'
Roof Framing	Stick
Exterior Walls	2x4

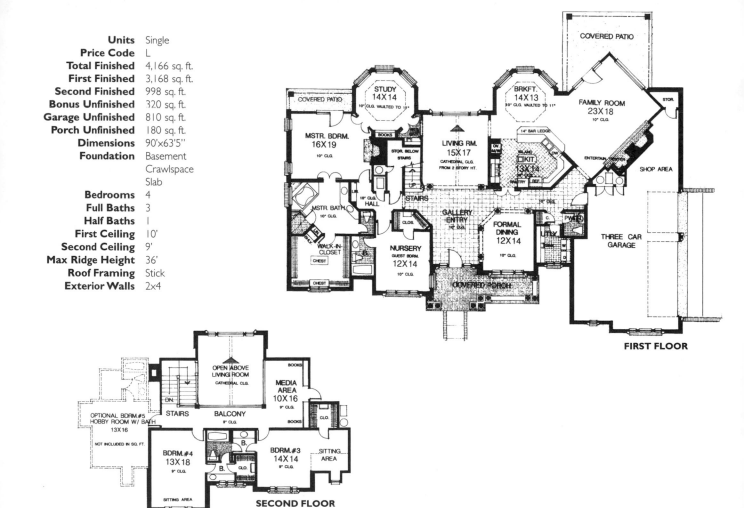

FIRST FLOOR

SECOND FLOOR

To order your Blueprints, call 1-800-235-5700

Units	Single
Price Code	E
Total Finished	2,292 sq. ft.
First Finished	1,246 sq. ft.
Second Finished	1,046 sq. ft.
Basement Unfinished	1,246 sq. ft.
Garage Unfinished	392 sq. ft.
Porch Unfinished	323 sq. ft.
Dimensions	58'x42'2''
Foundation	Basement
Bedrooms	3
Full Baths	2
Half Baths	I
First Ceiling	9'
Second Ceiling	8'
Max Ridge Height	33'1''
Roof Framing	Truss
Exterior Walls	2x6

FIRST FLOOR

SECOND FLOOR

Units	Single
Price Code	E
Total Finished	2,464 sq. ft.
First Finished	1,250 sq. ft.
Second Finished	1,166 sq. ft.
Lower Finished	48 sq. ft.
Basement Unfinished	448 sq. ft.
Garage Unfinished	706 sq. ft.
Dimensions	42'x50'
Foundation	Basement
Bedrooms	4
Full Baths	2
Half Baths	I
Max Ridge Height	30'
Roof Framing	Stick
Exterior Walls	2x4

FIRST FLOOR

SECOND FLOOR

Units	Single
Price Code	B
Total Finished	1,650 sq. ft.
First Finished	891 sq. ft.
Second Finished	759 sq. ft.
Basement Unfinished	891 sq. ft.
Garage Unfinished	484 sq. ft.
Dimensions	44'x40'
Foundation	Basement
Bedrooms	3
Full Baths	2
Half Baths	1
Max Ridge Height	25'6''
Roof Framing	Stick
Exterior Walls	2x4

* Alternate foundation options available at an additional charge.
Please call 1-800-235-5700 for more information.

SECOND FLOOR

Br.2 10⁰ x 11⁶

Mbr. 12⁰ x 16⁰

Br.3 10⁰ x 11⁰

FIRST FLOOR

Grt. rm. 18¹ x 14⁰

Bfst. 10⁰ x 12⁵

Kit. 8¹⁰ x 11³

Din. 10⁰ x 12⁴

Gar. 21³ x 21⁸

COVERED PORCH

© Design Basics, Inc.

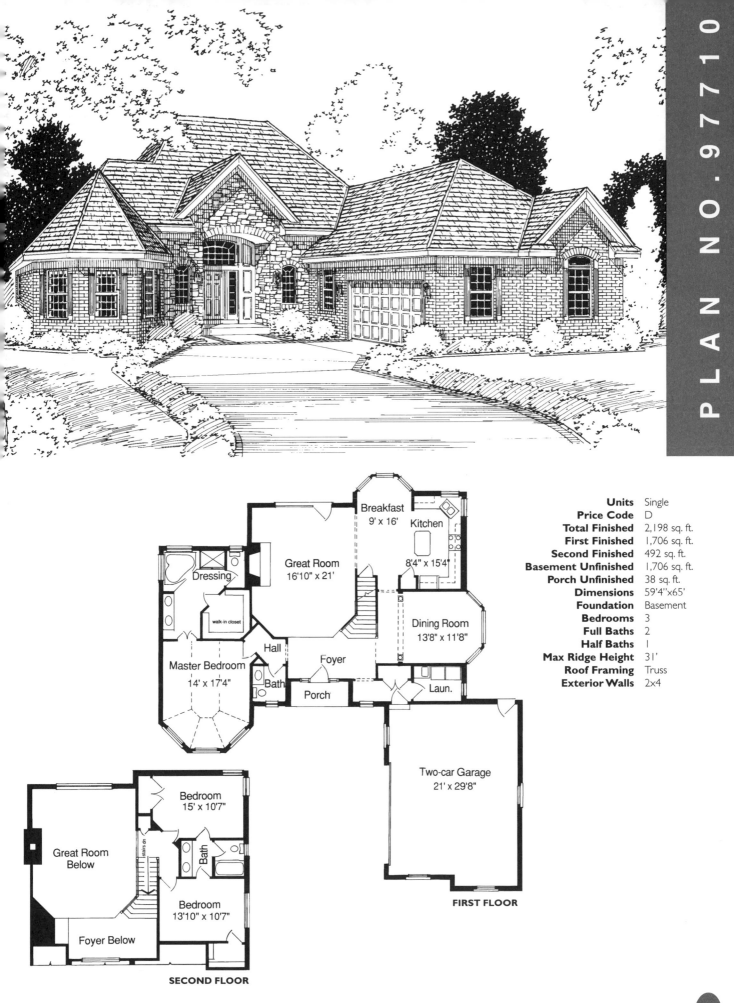

Breakfast 9' x 16'

Kitchen 8'4" x 15'4"

Great Room 16'10" x 21'

Dressing

walk-in closet

Master Bedroom 14' x 17'4"

Hall

Bath

Foyer

Porch

Dining Room 13'8" x 11'8"

Laun.

Two-car Garage 21' x 29'8"

FIRST FLOOR

Bedroom 15' x 10'7"

Bath

Great Room Below

stairs dn

Bedroom 13'10" x 10'7"

Foyer Below

SECOND FLOOR

Units	Single
Price Code	D
Total Finished	2,198 sq. ft.
First Finished	1,706 sq. ft.
Second Finished	492 sq. ft.
Basement Unfinished	1,706 sq. ft.
Porch Unfinished	38 sq. ft.
Dimensions	59'4"x65'
Foundation	Basement
Bedrooms	3
Full Baths	2
Half Baths	1
Max Ridge Height	31'
Roof Framing	Truss
Exterior Walls	2x4

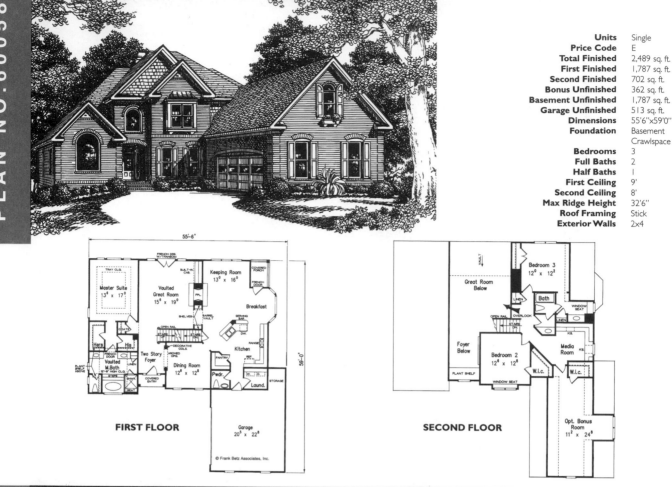

Units	Single
Price Code	E
Total Finished	2,489 sq. ft.
First Finished	1,787 sq. ft.
Second Finished	702 sq. ft.
Bonus Unfinished	362 sq. ft.
Basement Unfinished	1,787 sq. ft.
Garage Unfinished	513 sq. ft.
Dimensions	55'6"x59'0"
Foundation	Basement
	Crawlspace
Bedrooms	3
Full Baths	2
Half Baths	1
First Ceiling	9'
Second Ceiling	8'
Max Ridge Height	32'6"
Roof Framing	Stick
Exterior Walls	2x4

FIRST FLOOR

SECOND FLOOR

© Frank Betz Associates, Inc.

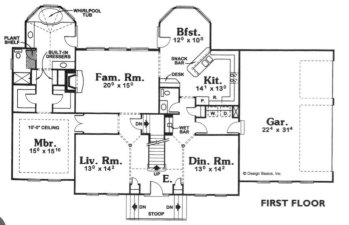

Units	Single
Price Code	H
Total Finished	3,103 sq. ft.
First Finished	2,130 sq. ft.
Second Finished	973 sq. ft.
Garage Unfinished	725 sq. ft.
Dimensions	78'x45'4"
Foundation	Basement
	Crawlspace
	Slab
Bedrooms	4
Full Baths	2
Half Baths	1
3/4 Baths	2
First Ceiling	9'
Max Ridge Height	31'6"
Roof Framing	Stick
Exterior Walls	2x4

* Alternate foundation options available at an additional charge.
Please call 1-800-235-5700 for more information.

FIRST FLOOR

© Design Basics, Inc.

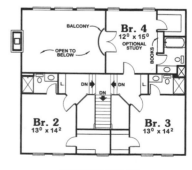

SECOND FLOOR

To order your Blueprints, call 1-800-235-5700

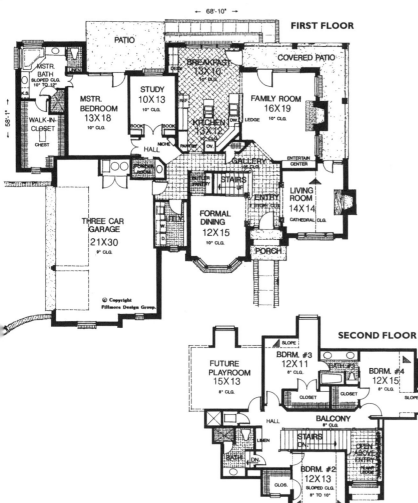

FIRST FLOOR

← 68'-10" →

PATIO

MSTR. BATH
SLOPED CLG. 10' TO 12"

K.S.

WALK-IN CLOSET

CHEST

MSTR. BEDROOM
13X18
10' CLG.

STUDY
10X13
10' CLG.

BOOKS

BOOKS

NICHE

HALL

BREAKFAST
13X10
10' CLG.

REF.

KITCHEN
13X12
10' CLG.

PANTRY

DW.

OV.

LEDGE

COVERED PATIO

FAMILY ROOM
16X19
10' CLG.

ENTERTAIN CENTER

58'-1"

THREE CAR GARAGE
21X30
9' CLG.

UTILITY

W

D

BUTLER PANTRY

GALLERY
10' CLG.

STAIRS
UP

ENTRY
FOYER CLG.

FORMAL DINING
12X15
10' CLG.

PORCH

LIVING ROOM
14X14
CATHEDRAL CLG.

© Copyright
Fillmore Design Group.

SECOND FLOOR

FUTURE PLAYROOM
15X13
8' CLG.

SLOPE

BDRM. #3
12X11
8' CLG.

BATH

CLOSET

CLOSET

BDRM. #4
12X15
8' CLG.

SLOPE

HALL

LINEN

BATH

DN.

STAIRS DN.

BALCONY
8' CLG.

OPEN ABOVE ENTRY

BDRM. #2
12X13
SLOPED CLG.
8' TO 10'

CLOS.

Units	Single
Price Code	H
Total Finished	3,062 sq. ft.
First Finished	2,115 sq. ft.
Second Finished	947 sq. ft.
Bonus Unfinished	195 sq. ft.
Garage Unfinished	635 sq. ft.
Porch Unfinished	32 sq. ft.
Dimensions	68'10"x58'1"
Foundation	Basement
	Crawlspace
	Slab
Bedrooms	4
Full Baths	3
Half Baths	1
First Ceiling	10'
Second Ceiling	8'
Max Ridge Height	32'6"
Roof Framing	Stick
Exterior Walls	2x4

Units	Single
Price Code	D
Total Finished	2,135 sq. ft.
First Finished	1,085 sq. ft.
Second Finished	1,050 sq. ft.
Basement Unfinished	1,050 sq. ft.
Garage Unfinished	440 sq. ft.
Dimensions	50'8''x38'4''
Foundation	Basement
Bedrooms	4
Full Baths	2
Half Baths	1
First Ceiling	9'
Second Ceiling	8'

3.80 X 3.40
12'-8" X 11'-4"

3.30 X 3.00
11'-0" X 10'-0"

3.30 X 3.00
11'-0" X 10'-0"

3.60 X 4.40
12'-0" X 14'-8"

SECOND FLOOR

3.70 X 3.60
12'-4" X 12'-0"

3.30 X 4.00
11'-0" X 13'-4"

3.50 X 4.40
11'-8" X 14'-8"

6.00 X 6.60
20'-0" X 22'-0"

3.60 X 4.40
2'-0" X 14'-8"

11,8 m
39'-4"

FIRST FLOOR

15,2 m
50'-8"

To order your Blueprints, call 1-800-235-5700

Units	Single
Price Code	F
Total Finished	2,707 sq. ft.
First Finished	1,484 sq. ft.
Second Finished	1,223 sq. ft.
Basement Unfinished	1,484 sq. ft.
Dimensions	82'x48'8''
Foundation	Basement
Bedrooms	3
Full Baths	2
Half Baths	1
First Ceiling	9'
Second Ceiling	8'
Max Ridge Height	32'
Roof Framing	Stick
Exterior Walls	2x4

FIRST FLOOR

SECOND FLOOR

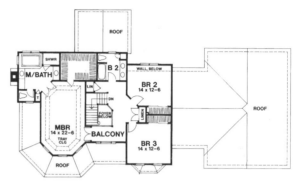

SECOND FLOOR

FIRST FLOOR

© Frank Betz Associates, Inc.

Units	Single
Price Code	A
Total Finished	1,467 sq. ft.
First Finished	1,001 sq. ft.
Second Finished	466 sq. ft.
Bonus Unfinished	292 sq. ft.
Basement Unfinished	1,001 sq. ft.
Garage Unfinished	400 sq. ft.
Dimensions	42x42
Foundation	Basement
	Crawlspace
Bedrooms	3
Full Baths	2
Half Baths	1
Max Ridge Height	29'8''
Roof Framing	Stick
Exterior Walls	2x4

Units	Single
Price Code	E
Total Finished	2,466 sq. ft.
First Finished	1,815 sq. ft.
Second Finished	651 sq. ft.
Bonus Unfinished	185 sq. ft.
Garage Unfinished	440 sq. ft.
Porch Unfinished	64 sq. ft.
Dimensions	55'x55'7''
Foundation	Slab
Bedrooms	4
Full Baths	2
Half Baths	1
First Ceiling	9'
Second Ceiling	8'
Roof Framing	Stick
Exterior Walls	2x4

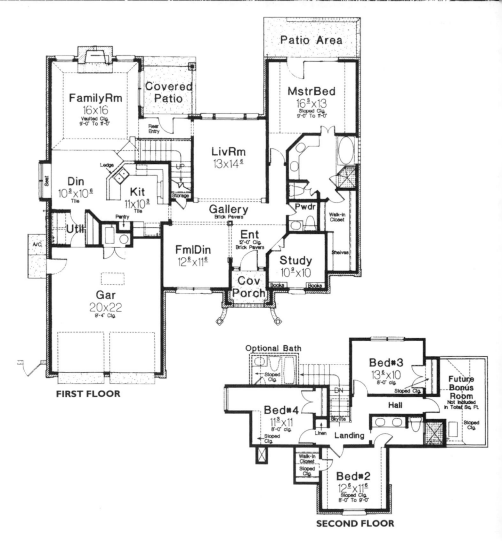

FIRST FLOOR

SECOND FLOOR

To order your Blueprints, call 1-800-235-5700

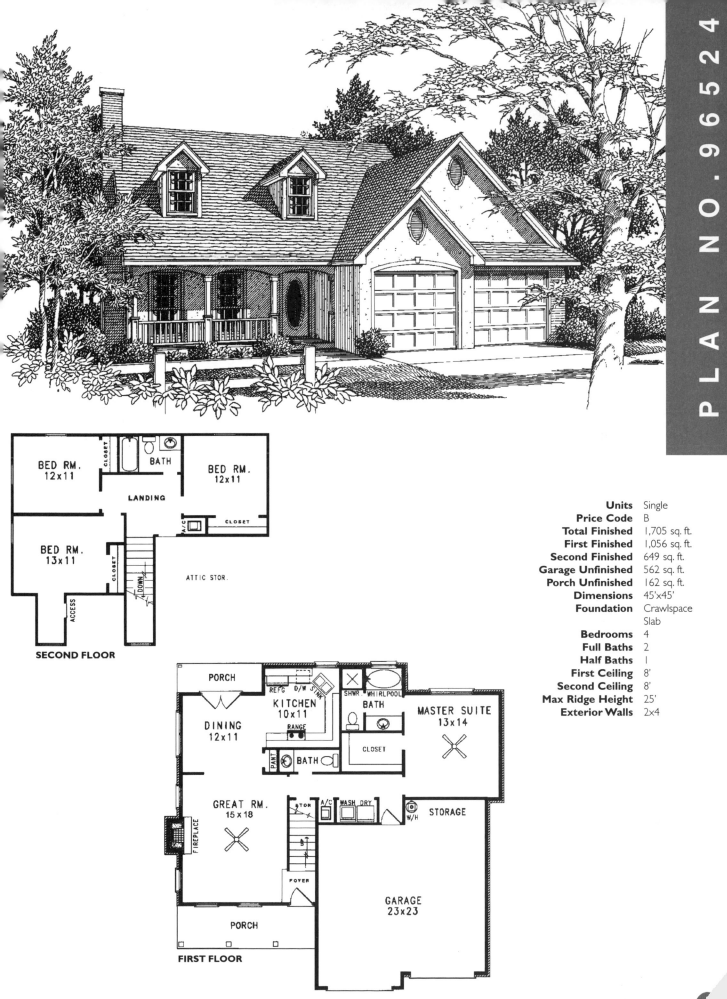

SECOND FLOOR

BED RM.
12x11

CLOSET

BATH

BED RM.
12x11

LANDING

A/C

CLOSET

BED RM.
13x11

CLOSET

DOWN

ATTIC STOR.

ACCESS

Units	Single
Price Code	B
Total Finished	1,705 sq. ft.
First Finished	1,056 sq. ft.
Second Finished	649 sq. ft.
Garage Unfinished	562 sq. ft.
Porch Unfinished	162 sq. ft.
Dimensions	45'x45'
Foundation	Crawlspace
	Slab
Bedrooms	4
Full Baths	2
Half Baths	1
First Ceiling	8'
Second Ceiling	8'
Max Ridge Height	25'
Exterior Walls	2x4

FIRST FLOOR

PORCH

REFG D/W SINK

KITCHEN
10x11

SHWR. WHIRLPOOL

BATH

MASTER SUITE
13x14

DINING
12x11

RANGE

PANT

BATH

CLOSET

GREAT RM.
15 x 18

FIREPLACE

STOR

A/C

WASH DRY

W/H

STORAGE

FOYER

GARAGE
23x23

PORCH

PLAN NO. 93407

Units	Single
Price Code	F
Total Finished	2,613 sq. ft.
First Finished	1,625 sq. ft.
Second Finished	988 sq. ft.
Basement Unfinished	1,625 sq. ft.
Garage Unfinished	491 sq. ft.
Dimensions	59'×50'
Foundation	Basement
Bedrooms	4
Full Baths	2
Half Baths	1
Max Ridge Height	32'
Roof Framing	Stick
Exterior Walls	2x4

FIRST FLOOR

SECOND FLOOR

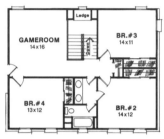

PLAN NO. 65151

FIRST FLOOR

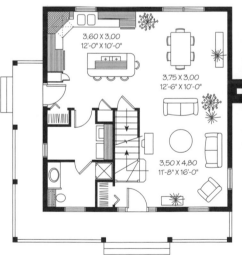

Units	Single
Price Code	A
Total Finished	1,456 sq. ft.
First Finished	728 sq. ft.
Second Finished	728 sq. ft.
Basement Unfinished	728 sq. ft.
Dimensions	26'×28'
Foundation	Basement
Bedrooms	3
Full Baths	2
First Ceiling	8'
Second Ceiling	8'
Max Ridge Height	26'
Roof Framing	Truss
Exterior Walls	2x6

SECOND FLOOR

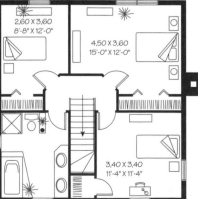

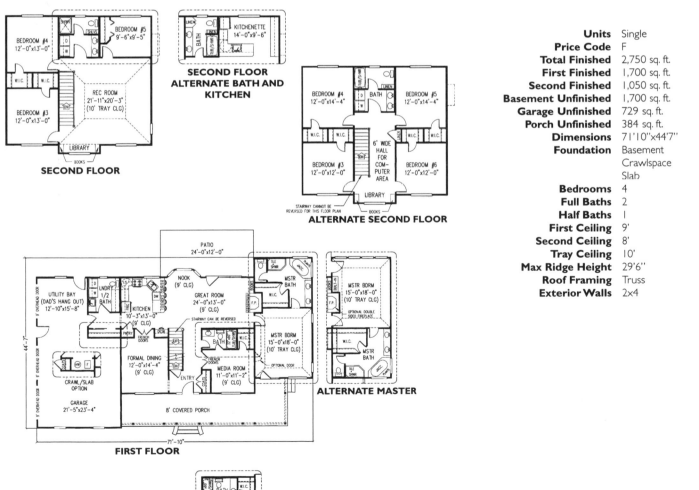

SECOND FLOOR

BEDROOM #4
12'-0"x13'-0"

BEDROOM #5
9'-6"x9'-5"

W.I.C.

W.I.C.

REC ROOM
21'-11"x20'-3"
(10' TRAY CLG)

BEDROOM #3
12'-0"x13'-0"

LIBRARY
BOOKS

SECOND FLOOR ALTERNATE BATH AND KITCHEN

LINEN

BATH

KITCHENETTE
14'-0"x9'-6"

ALTERNATE SECOND FLOOR

BEDROOM #4
12'-0"x14'-4"

BATH

LINEN

BEDROOM #5
12'-0"x14'-4"

W.I.C.

W.I.C.

6' WIDE HALL FOR COMPUTER AREA

W.I.C.

W.I.C.

BEDROOM #3
12'-0"x12'-0"

BEDROOM #6
12'-0"x12'-0"

LIBRARY

STAIRWAY CANNOT BE REVERSED FOR THIS FLOOR PLAN

BOOKS

FIRST FLOOR

PATIO
24'-0"x12'-0"

UTILITY BAY
(DAD'S HANG OUT)
12'-10"x15'-8"

LNDRY

1/2 BATH

KITCHEN
10'-3"x13'-0"
(9' CLG)

NOOK
(9' CLG)

GREAT ROOM
24'-0"x13'-0"
(9' CLG)

MSTR BATH

W.I.C.

MSTR BDRM
15'-0"x18'-0"
(10' TRAY CLG)

FORMAL DINING
12'-0"x14'-4"
(9' CLG)

MEDIA ROOM
11'-0"x11'-2"
(9' CLG)

BATH

W.I.C.

STAIRWAY CAN BE REVERSED

FRENCH DOORS

CRAWL/SLAB OPTION

GARAGE
21'-5"x23'-4"

ENTRY

8' COVERED PORCH

71'-10"

44'-7"

ALTERNATE MASTER

MSTR BDRM
15'-0"x18'-0"
(10' TRAY CLG)

OPTIONAL DOUBLE SIDED FIREPLACE

W.I.C.

MSTR BATH

TILE & SHWR

ALTERNATE MEDIA ROOM BATH

BATH

W.I.C.

Units	Single
Price Code	F
Total Finished	2,750 sq. ft.
First Finished	1,700 sq. ft.
Second Finished	1,050 sq. ft.
Basement Unfinished	1,700 sq. ft.
Garage Unfinished	729 sq. ft.
Porch Unfinished	384 sq. ft.
Dimensions	71'10"x44'7"
Foundation	Basement Crawlspace Slab
Bedrooms	4
Full Baths	2
Half Baths	1
First Ceiling	9'
Second Ceiling	8'
Tray Ceiling	10'
Max Ridge Height	29'6"
Roof Framing	Truss
Exterior Walls	2x4

Units	Single
Price Code	C
Total Finished	1,840 sq. ft.
First Finished	1,014 sq. ft.
Second Finished	826 sq. ft.
Garage Unfinished	690 sq. ft.
Dimensions	62'7"x45'
Foundation	Basement
	Crawlspace
	Slab
Bedrooms	4
Full Baths	3
First Ceiling	9'
Roof Framing	Stick
Exterior Walls	2x4

SECOND FLOOR

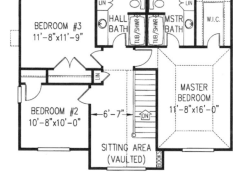

- BEDROOM #3 11'-8"x11'-9"
- HALL BATH
- MSTR BATH
- W.I.C.
- BEDROOM #2 10'-8"x10'-0"
- 6'-7"
- MASTER BEDROOM 11'-8"x16'-0"
- SITTING AREA (VAULTED)

FIRST FLOOR

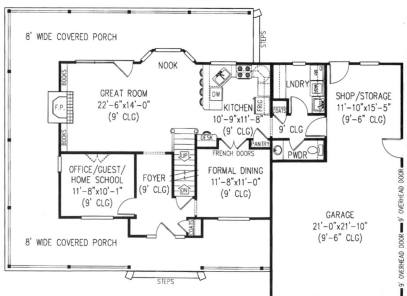

- 8' WIDE COVERED PORCH
- NOOK
- GREAT ROOM 22'-6"x14'-0" (9' CLG)
- KITCHEN 10'-9"x11'-8" (9' CLG)
- LNDRY
- SHOP/STORAGE 11'-10"x15'-5" (9'-6" CLG)
- 9' CLG
- F.P.
- DESK
- PANTRY
- PWDR
- OFFICE/GUEST/ HOME SCHOOL 11'-8"x10'-1" (9' CLG)
- FOYER (9' CLG)
- FORMAL DINING 11'-8"x11'-0" (9' CLG)
- FRENCH DOORS
- GARAGE 21'-0"x21'-10" (9'-6" CLG)
- 8' WIDE COVERED PORCH
- STEPS
- 9' OVERHEAD DOOR

To order your Blueprints, call 1-800-235-5700

FIRST FLOOR

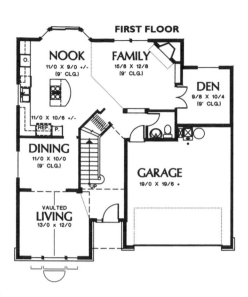

NOOK
11/0 X 9/0 +/-
(9' CLG.)

FAMILY
15/8 X 12/8
(9' CLG.)

DEN
9/8 X 10/4
(9' CLG.)

11/0 x 10/6 +/-
REF. P.

DINING
11/0 X 10/0
(9' CLG.)

GARAGE
19/0 X 19/6 +

VAULTED
LIVING
13/0 x 12/0

UP

SECOND FLOOR

VAULTED
MASTER
14/4 X 12/8

BR. 2
11/4 X 10/0 +/-

LINEN

DN.

W.
D.

PLANT
SHELF

VAULTED
BR. 3
10/0 X 11/0

Units	Single
Price Code	C
Total Finished	1,994 sq. ft.
First Finished	1,112 sq. ft.
Second Finished	882 sq. ft.
Dimensions	40'x43'
Foundation	Crawlspace
Bedrooms	3
Full Baths	2
Half Baths	1
First Ceiling	9'
Second Ceiling	8'
Max Ridge Height	29'
Roof Framing	Truss
Exterior Walls	2x6

FIRST FLOOR

Garage & Storage
22 x 25/10

Rear Porch
18 x 7/10

W
D

Kitchen
11/10 x 10/5

Breakfast
14/3 x 10/5
9' Clg.

Pantry

Stairs Up

Stairs Down

Desk

Family Room
14 x 18/8
9' Clg.

Dining
11 x 11/5
9' Clg.

Master Bedroom
13/9 x 16/8
9' Clg.

Foyer
8/9 x 5/10

Front Porch
40 x 7/10

SECOND FLOOR

Attic Storage

Stairs Down

Bedroom #3
14 x 12
8' Clg.

Linen

Bedroom #2
13/9 x 11/5
8' Clg.
Sloped Clg.

Units	Single
Price Code	C
Total Finished	1,966 sq. ft.
First Finished	1,409 sq. ft.
Second Finished	557 sq. ft.
Garage Unfinished	548 sq. ft.
Porch Unfinished	316 sq. ft.
Dimensions	48'2"x67'5"
Foundation	Basement
Bedrooms	3
Full Baths	2
Half Baths	1
Max Ridge Height	25'8"
Roof Framing	Stick
Exterior Walls	2x4

Units	Single
Price Code	E
Total Finished	2,404 sq. ft.
First Finished	1,468 sq. ft.
Second Finished	936 sq. ft.
Garage Unfinished	276 sq. ft.
Dimensions	54'x44'
Foundation	Basement
Bedrooms	3
Full Baths	1
Half Baths	1

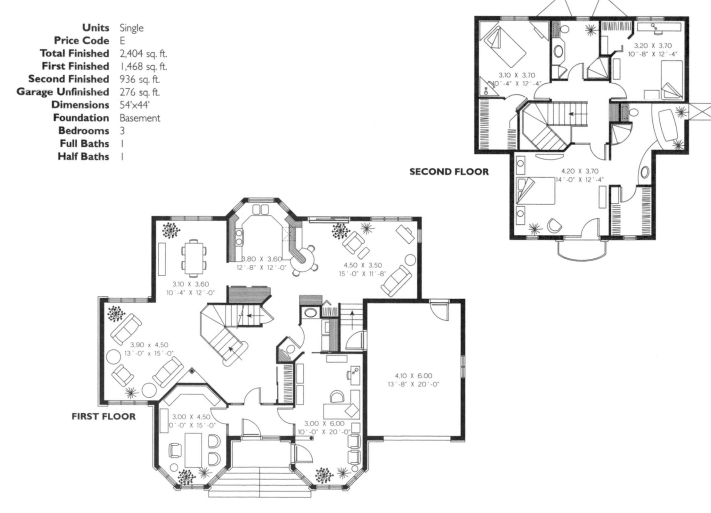

SECOND FLOOR

FIRST FLOOR

To order your Blueprints, call 1-800-235-5700

Photography supplied by Design Basics, Inc.

FIRST FLOOR

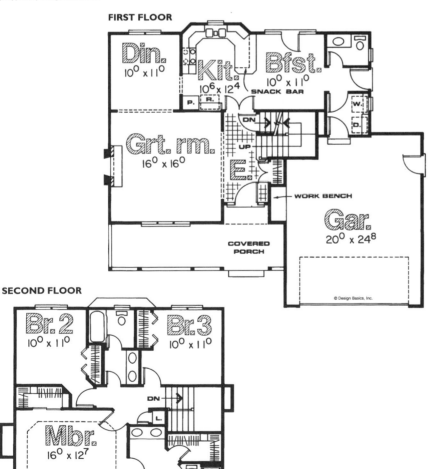

Din.
10⁰ x 11⁰

Kit.
10⁶ x 12⁴

Bfst.
10⁰ x 11⁰
SNACK BAR

P. R.

DN

UP

Grt. rm.
16⁰ x 16⁰

W.

WORK BENCH

COVERED PORCH

Gar.
20⁰ x 24⁸

© Design Basics, Inc.

SECOND FLOOR

Br. 2
10⁰ x 11⁰

Br. 3
10⁰ x 11⁰

DN

Mbr.
16⁰ x 12⁷
9'- 0" CEILING

WHIRLPOOL

Units	Single
Price Code	B
Total Finished	1,700 sq. ft.
First Finished	904 sq. ft.
Second Finished	796 sq. ft.
Garage Unfinished	509 sq. ft.
Dimensions	46'x41'4"
Foundation	Basement
	Crawlspace
	Slab
Bedrooms	3
Full Baths	2
Half Baths	1
First Ceiling	8'
Max Ridge Height	25'6"
Roof Framing	Stick
Exterior Walls	2x4,2x6

* Alternate foundation options available at an additional charge.
Please call 1-800-235-5700 for more information.

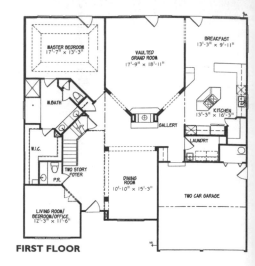

FIRST FLOOR

Units	Single
Price Code	G
Total Finished	2,864 sq. ft.
First Finished	2,062 sq. ft.
Second Finished	802 sq. ft.
Garage Unfinished	400 sq. ft.
Dimensions	50'×53'
Foundation	Slab
Bedrooms	4
Full Baths	2
Half Baths	1
Max Ridge Height	32'
Roof Framing	Stick
Exterior Walls	2x4

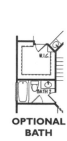

OPTIONAL BATH

SECOND FLOOR

FIRST FLOOR

Units	Single
Price Code	L
Total Finished	6,312 sq. ft.
First Finished	4,760 sq. ft.
Second Finished	1,552 sq. ft.
Garage Unfinished	802 sq. ft.
Porch Unfinished	483 sq. ft.
Dimensions	98'×103'8''
Foundation	Slab
Bedrooms	5
Full Baths	4
Half Baths	1
3/4 Baths	2
First Ceiling	10'
Max Ridge Height	42'8''
Roof Framing	Stick
Exterior Walls	2x6, 2x8

SECOND FLOOR

* Alternate foundation options available at an additional charge.
  Please call 1-800-235-5700 for more information.

To order your Blueprints, call 1-800-235-5700

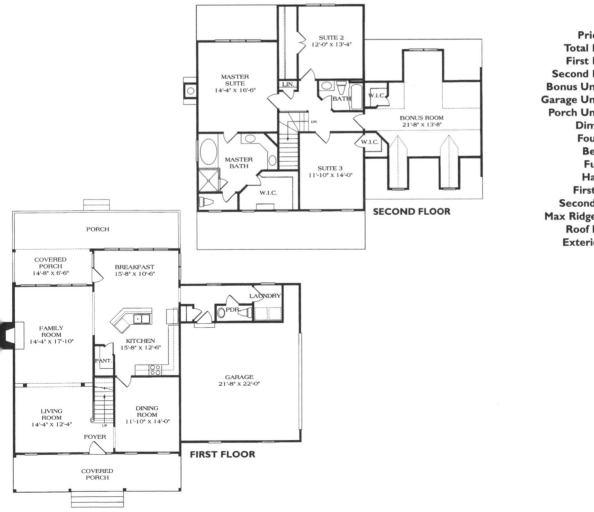

SECOND FLOOR

SUITE 2
12'-0" x 13'-4"

MASTER SUITE
14'-4" x 16'-6"

LIN.

BATH

W.I.C.

BONUS ROOM
21'-8" x 13'-8"

W.I.C.

DN

MASTER BATH

SUITE 3
11'-10" x 14'-0"

W.I.C.

PORCH

COVERED PORCH
14'-8" x 6'-6"

BREAKFAST
15'-8" x 10'-6"

LAUNDRY

FAMILY ROOM
14'-4" x 17'-10"

KITCHEN
15'-8" x 12'-6"

PDR.

PANT.

GARAGE
21'-8" x 22'-0"

LIVING ROOM
14'-4" x 12'-4"

DINING ROOM
11'-10" x 14'-0"

UP

FOYER

FIRST FLOOR

COVERED PORCH

Units	Single
Price Code	D
Total Finished	2,203 sq. ft.
First Finished	1,169 sq. ft.
Second Finished	1,034 sq. ft.
Bonus Unfinished	347 sq. ft.
Garage Unfinished	561 sq. ft.
Porch Unfinished	312 sq. ft.
Dimensions	55'4"x52'
Foundation	Crawlspace
Bedrooms	3
Full Baths	2
Half Baths	1
First Ceiling	9'
Second Ceiling	8'
Max Ridge Height	32'6"
Roof Framing	Stick
Exterior Walls	2x4

Units	Single
Price Code	C
Total Finished	1,765 sq. ft.
First Finished	1,210 sq. ft.
Second Finished	555 sq. ft.
Garage Unfinished	612 sq. ft.
Porch Unfinished	144 sq. ft.
Dimensions	43'4''x37'
Foundation	Basement
Bedrooms	3
Full Baths	2
Half Baths	1
Max Ridge Height	27'
Roof Framing	Stick
Exterior Walls	2x6

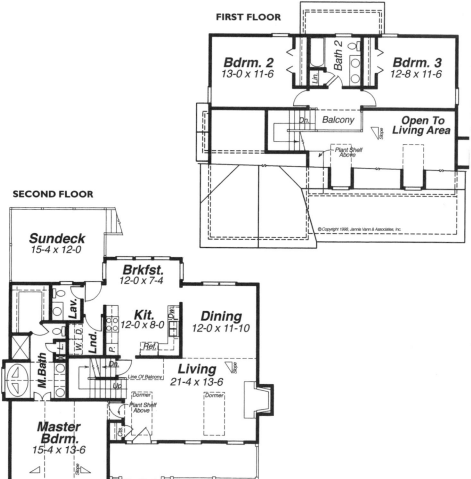

FIRST FLOOR

Bdrm. 2
13-0 x 11-6

Bath 2

Bdrm. 3
12-8 x 11-6

Lin.

Dn. Balcony

Open To
Living Area

Slope

Plant Shelf
Above

© Copyright 1998, Jannie Vann & Associates, Inc.

SECOND FLOOR

Sundeck
15-4 x 12-0

Brkfst.
12-0 x 7-4

Lav.

Kit.
12-0 x 8-0

Dining
12-0 x 11-10

Dw.

W. D.

Lnd.

P.

Ref.

M.Bath

Dn.

Living
21-4 x 13-6

Line Of Balcony

Slope

Up

Dormer

Dormer

Plant Shelf
Above

Cls.

Master
Bdrm.
15-4 x 13-6

Slope

To order your Blueprints, call 1-800-235-5700

Units	Single
Price Code	A
Total Finished	1,258 sq. ft.
First Finished	753 sq. ft.
Second Finished	505 sq. ft.
Basement Unfinished	753 sq. ft.
Dimensions	30'x28'
Foundation	Basement
Bedrooms	3
Full Baths	1
Half Baths	1
First Ceiling	8'
Second Ceiling	8'
Max Ridge Height	24'10''
Roof Framing	Truss
Exterior Walls	2x6

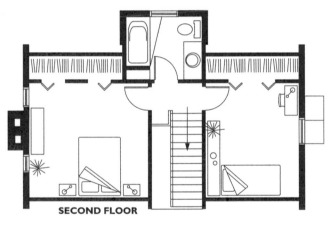

SECOND FLOOR

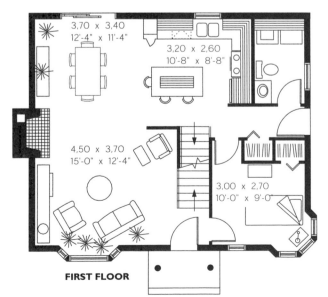

3,70 x 3,40
12'-4" x 11'-4"

3,20 x 2,60
10'-8" x 8'-8"

4,50 x 3,70
15'-0" x 12'-4"

3,00 x 2,70
10'-0" x 9'-0"

FIRST FLOOR

To order your Blueprints, call 1-800-235-5700

151

Units	Single
Price Code	E
Total Finished	2,497 sq. ft.
First Finished	1,706 sq. ft.
Second Finished	791 sq. ft.
Bonus Unfinished	366 sq. ft.
Basement Unfinished	1,365 sq. ft.
Garage Unfinished	546 sq. ft.
Porch Unfinished	35 sq. ft.
Dimensions	53'4''x63'4''
Foundation	Crawlspace
	Combo
	Basement/
	Crawlspace
Bedrooms	3
Full Baths	2
Half Baths	I
First Ceiling	9'
Second Ceiling	8'
Max Ridge Height	31'6''
Roof Framing	Truss
Exterior Walls	2x4

SECOND FLOOR

SUITE 2
16'-0" x 12'-0"

W.I.C.

W.I.C.

OPEN TO BELOW

OPT. SUITE 4 & BATH
12'-4" x 19'-4"

BATH

LOFT

OPT. BALCONY

SUITE 3
14'-0" x 12'-0"

DN

DN

PLANT LEDGE

W.I.C

BONUS ROOM
13'-6" x 19'-8"

FIRST FLOOR

DECK/ TERRACE

MASTER SUITE
16'-0" x 16'-0"

GRAND ROOM
16'-6" x 18'-8"

MORNING ROOM
12'-4" x 9'-6"

KITCHEN
12'-4" x 12'-0"

W.I.C.

MASTER BATH

PDR.

FOYER

DINING ROOM
12'-4" x 13'-6"

LAUNDRY

LOGGIA

STOR.

GARAGE
21'-4" x 21'-4"

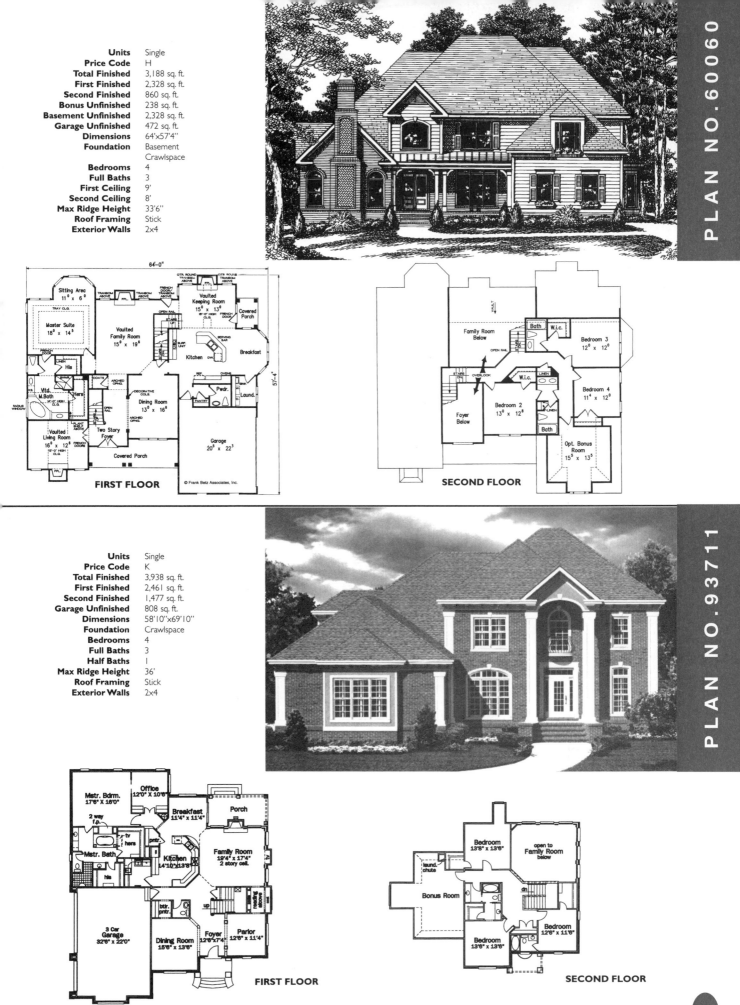

Units	Single
Price Code	H
Total Finished	3,188 sq. ft.
First Finished	2,328 sq. ft.
Second Finished	860 sq. ft.
Bonus Unfinished	238 sq. ft.
Basement Unfinished	2,328 sq. ft.
Garage Unfinished	472 sq. ft.
Dimensions	64'x57'4"
Foundation	Basement
	Crawlspace
Bedrooms	4
Full Baths	3
First Ceiling	9'
Second Ceiling	8'
Max Ridge Height	33'6"
Roof Framing	Stick
Exterior Walls	2x4

FIRST FLOOR

© Frank Betz Associates, Inc.

SECOND FLOOR

Units	Single
Price Code	K
Total Finished	3,938 sq. ft.
First Finished	2,461 sq. ft.
Second Finished	1,477 sq. ft.
Garage Unfinished	808 sq. ft.
Dimensions	58'10"x69'10"
Foundation	Crawlspace
Bedrooms	4
Full Baths	3
Half Baths	1
Max Ridge Height	36'
Roof Framing	Stick
Exterior Walls	2x4

FIRST FLOOR

SECOND FLOOR

To order your Blueprints, call 1-800-235-5700

Units	Single
Price Code	I
Total Finished	3,462 sq. ft.
First Finished	2,894 sq. ft.
Second Finished	568 sq. ft.
Garage Unfinished	598 sq. ft.
Porch Unfinished	899 sq. ft.
Dimensions	67'x102'
Foundation	Slab
Bedrooms	3
Full Baths	3
Half Baths	1
Max Ridge Height	33'
Roof Framing	Truss

* Alternate foundation options available at an additional charge.
Please call 1-800-235-5700 for more information.

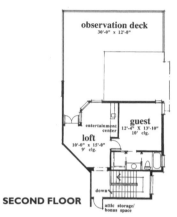

SECOND FLOOR

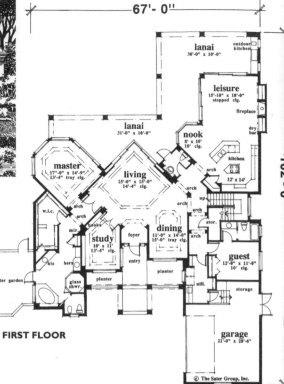

FIRST FLOOR

© The Sater Group, Inc.

67'- 0''

102'- 0''

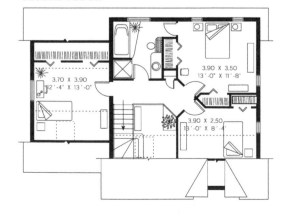

Units	Single
Price Code	A
Total Finished	1,417 sq. ft.
First Finished	702 sq. ft.
Second Finished	715 sq. ft.
Garage Unfinished	279 sq. ft.
Porch Unfinished	32 sq. ft.
Dimensions	38'x28'
Foundation	Basement
Bedrooms	3
Full Baths	1
Half Baths	1
First Ceiling	8'
Second Ceiling	8'
Max Ridge Height	26'2''
Roof Framing	Truss

FIRST FLOOR

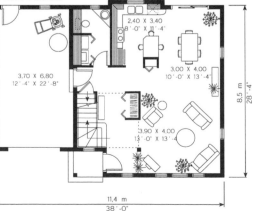

SECOND FLOOR

154

To order your Blueprints, call 1-800-235-5700

SECOND FLOOR

BED 3
10⁰×11²

BED 4
10⁰×11²

MASTER
13⁰×15⁶

COMPUTER LOFT

LINEN

DN
UP

OPEN

BED 2
10⁸×12⁸

FIRST FLOOR

FAMILY
17⁰×14⁰

MORN.
12⁰×10⁰

KTCH.
10⁰×12²

UP

LIVING/STUDY
10⁰×12⁰

DINING
11⁰×13⁰

GARAGE
20⁰×25⁰

COVERED PORCH

© Design Basics, Inc.

Units	Single
Price Code	E
Total Finished	2,336 sq. ft.
First Finished	1,189 sq. ft.
Second Finished	1,147 sq. ft.
Garage Unfinished	530 sq. ft.
Dimensions	48'x49'
Foundation	Basement
Bedrooms	4
Full Baths	3
Half Baths	1
First Ceiling	9'
Second Ceiling	8'
Max Ridge Height	30'8''
Roof Framing	Stick
Exterior Walls	2x4

* Alternate foundation options available at an additional charge.
Please call 1-800-235-5700 for more information.

Units	Single
Price Code	B
Total Finished	1,551 sq. ft.
First Finished	946 sq. ft.
Second Finished	604 sq. ft.
Dimensions	37'x30'8''
Foundation	Basement
Bedrooms	3
Full Baths	2

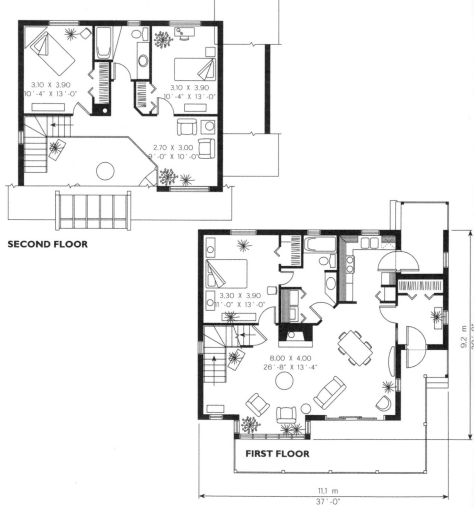

3.10 X 3.90
10'-4" X 13'-0"

3.10 X 3.90
10'-4" X 13'-0"

2.70 X 3.00
9'-0" X 10'-0"

SECOND FLOOR

3.30 X 3.90
11'-0" X 13'-0"

8.00 X 4.00
26'-8" X 13'-4"

9.2 m

FIRST FLOOR

11,1 m
37'-0"

To order your Blueprints, call 1-800-235-5700

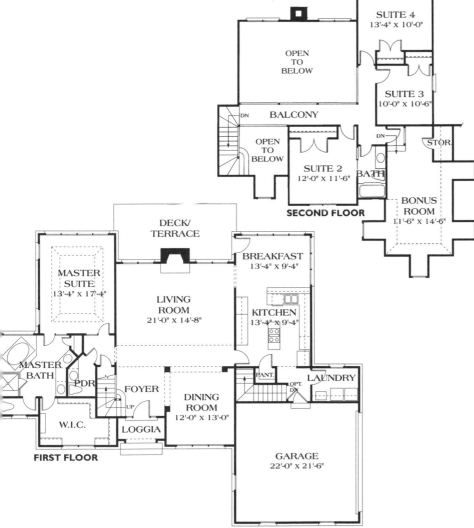

SUITE 4
13'-4" x 10'-0"

OPEN
TO
BELOW

SUITE 3
10'-0" x 10'-6"

DN   BALCONY

OPEN
TO
BELOW

SUITE 2
12'-0" x 11'-6"

DN

STOR.

BATH

SECOND FLOOR

BONUS
ROOM
11'-6" x 14'-6"

DECK/
TERRACE

MASTER
SUITE
13'-4" x 17'-4"

BREAKFAST
13'-4" x 9'-4"

LIVING
ROOM
21'-0" x 14'-8"

KITCHEN
13'-4" x 9'-4"

MASTER
BATH

PDR

FOYER

UP

DINING
ROOM
12'-0" x 13'-0"

PANT.

OPT.
D.

LAUNDRY

W.I.C.

LOGGIA

FIRST FLOOR

GARAGE
22'-0" x 21'-6"

Units	Single
Price Code	E
Total Finished	2,464 sq. ft.
First Finished	1,737 sq. ft.
Second Finished	727 sq. ft.
Bonus Unfinished	376 sq. ft.
Basement Unfinished	1,737 sq. ft.
Garage Unfinished	534 sq. ft.
Porch Unfinished	33 sq. ft.
Dimensions	65'6"x53'
Foundation	Basement Crawlspace
Bedrooms	4
Full Baths	2
Half Baths	1
First Ceiling	9'
Second Ceiling	8'
Vaulted Ceiling	18'6"
Tray Ceiling	10'6"
Max Ridge Height	31'6"
Exterior Walls	2x4

Units	Single
Price Code	F
Total Finished	2,553 sq. ft.
First Finished	1,202 sq. ft.
Second Finished	1,351 sq. ft.
Basement Unfinished	1,202 sq. ft.
Porch Unfinished	120 sq. ft.
Dimensions	71'6" x 28'2"
Foundation	Basement
Bedrooms	4
Full Baths	2
Half Baths	1
Max Ridge Height	27'6"
Roof Framing	Stick
Exterior Walls	2x4

SECOND FLOOR

SUN DECK

BEDROOM 1
20' x 13'

BEDROOM 2
20' x 11'

BATH

BATH

BEDROOM 4
14'-2" x 10'-6"

BEDROOM 3
14'-2" x 13'-4"

open foyer below

balcony

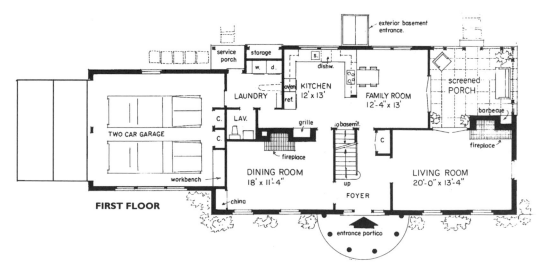

FIRST FLOOR

TWO CAR GARAGE

LAUNDRY

KITCHEN
12' x 13'

FAMILY ROOM
12'-4" x 13'

screened PORCH

DINING ROOM
18' x 11'-4"

FOYER

LIVING ROOM
20'-0" x 13'-4"

entrance portico

To order your Blueprints, call 1-800-235-5700

FIRST FLOOR

80'-0"

96'-0"

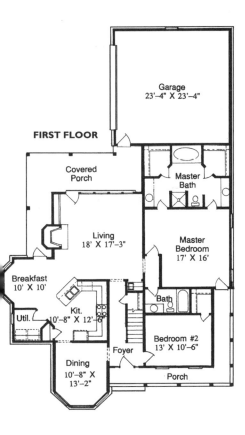

master
20'-4" x 22'-0"
14' step clg.

grand salon
18'-8" x 19'-8"
17'-8" coffered clg.

dining
11'-8" x 13'-6"
10' clg.

lanai

lanai

hers

tv niche

study
14'-0" x 14'-0"
13' step clg.

nook
10'-0" x 12'-0"
10' clg.

kitchen

14' x 16'

entry

foyer

utility

serv.

desk

planter

planter

planter

optional pool

leisure
18'-4" x 21'-4"
14'-6" step clg.

garage
11'-6" x 16'-6"

opt.
fireplace

entertainment center

lanai

planter

© Sater Design Collection

grill

lanai

portico entry

garage
22'-0" x 23'-6"

motorcourt

guest house
14'-0" x 13'-2"
10' clg.

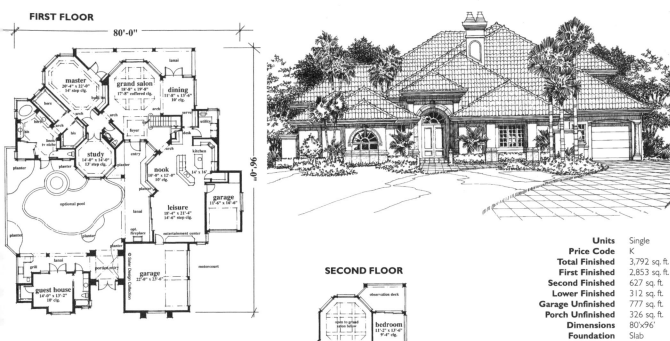

SECOND FLOOR

observation deck

bedroom
11'-2" x 13'-6"
9'-4" clg.

open to grand
salon below

overlook

observation deck

bedroom
15'-2" x 11'-8"
9'-4" clg.

Units	Single
Price Code	K
Total Finished	3,792 sq. ft.
First Finished	2,853 sq. ft.
Second Finished	627 sq. ft.
Lower Finished	312 sq. ft.
Garage Unfinished	777 sq. ft.
Porch Unfinished	326 sq. ft.
Dimensions	80'x96'
Foundation	Slab
Bedrooms	4
Full Baths	3
Half Baths	1
First Ceiling	10'
Second Ceiling	9'4"
Vaulted Ceiling	17'8"
Max Ridge Height	31'
Roof Framing	Truss

*Alternate foundation options available at an additional charge.
Please call 1-800-235-5700 for more information.

FIRST FLOOR

Garage
23'-4" X 23'-4"

Covered
Porch

Master
Bath

Living
18' X 17'-3"

Master
Bedroom
17' X 16'

Breakfast
10' X 10'

Bath

Util.

Kit.
10'-8" X 12'-6"

Bedroom #2
13' X 10'-6"

Foyer

Dining
10'-8" X
13'-2"

Porch

SECOND FLOOR

Bedroom #3

Gameroom
17' X 10'-10"

Ba.

Bedroom #4
14'-4" X 13'

Bedroom #5
17' X 12'

Units	Single
Price Code	G
Total Finished	2,801 sq. ft.
First Finished	1,651 sq. ft.
Second Finished	1,150 sq. ft.
Dimensions	46'4"x79'1"
Foundation	Crawlspace Slab
Bedrooms	5
Full Baths	3
First Ceiling	9'
Second Ceiling	8'
Roof Framing	Stick
Exterior Walls	2x4

Units	Single
Price Code	J
Total Finished	3,622 sq. ft.
First Finished	2,646 sq. ft.
Second Finished	976 sq. ft.
Basement Unfinished	2,646 sq. ft.
Dimensions	93'x59'2''
Foundation	Basement
Bedrooms	4
Full Baths	3
Half Baths	1
Max Ridge Height	33'
Roof Framing	Truss
Exterior Walls	2x6

SECOND FLOOR

FIRST FLOOR

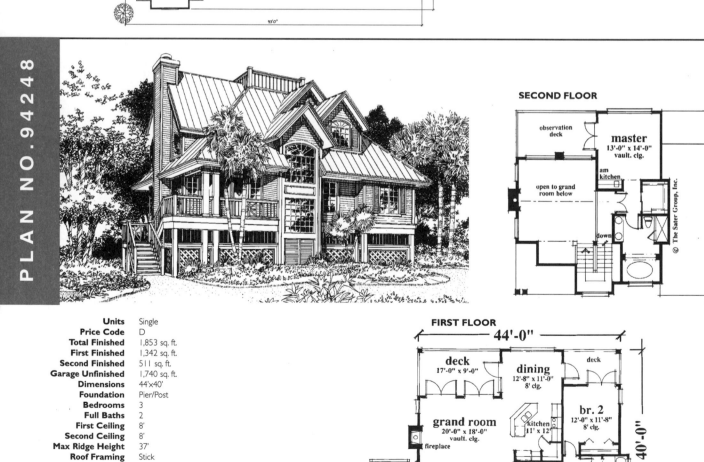

SECOND FLOOR

FIRST FLOOR

Units	Single
Price Code	D
Total Finished	1,853 sq. ft.
First Finished	1,342 sq. ft.
Second Finished	511 sq. ft.
Garage Unfinished	1,740 sq. ft.
Dimensions	44'x40'
Foundation	Pier/Post
Bedrooms	3
Full Baths	2
First Ceiling	8'
Second Ceiling	8'
Max Ridge Height	37'
Roof Framing	Stick
Exterior Walls	2x6

* Alternate foundation options available at an additional charge.
Please call 1-800-235-5700 for more information.

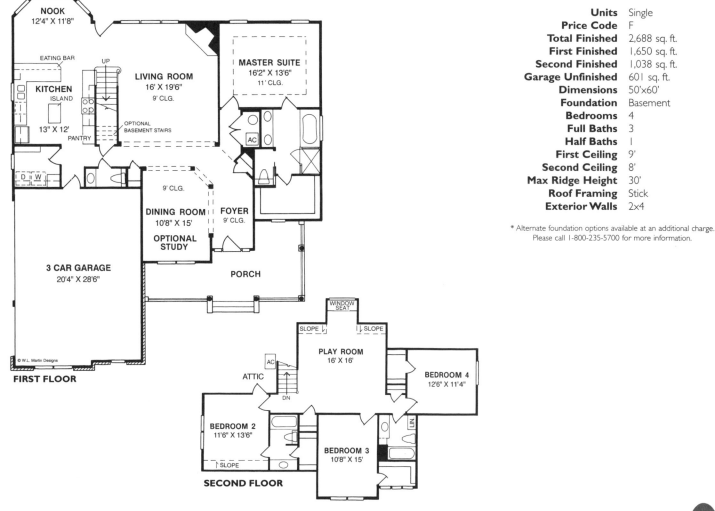

NOOK
12'4" X 11'8"

EATING BAR

KITCHEN
ISLAND
13" X 12'

PANTRY

UP

**OPTIONAL
BASEMENT STAIRS**

LIVING ROOM
16' X 19'6"
9' CLG.

MASTER SUITE
16'2" X 13'6"
11' CLG.

AC

D W

9' CLG.

DINING ROOM
10'8" X 15'

**OPTIONAL
STUDY**

FOYER
9' CLG.

3 CAR GARAGE
20'4" X 28'6"

PORCH

© W.L. Martin Designs

FIRST FLOOR

WINDOW SEAT

SLOPE   SLOPE

PLAY ROOM
16' X 16'

AC

ATTIC

DN

BEDROOM 4
12'6" X 11'4"

BEDROOM 2
11'6" X 13'6"

LIN

BEDROOM 3
10'8" X 15'

SLOPE

SECOND FLOOR

Units	Single
Price Code	F
Total Finished	2,688 sq. ft.
First Finished	1,650 sq. ft.
Second Finished	1,038 sq. ft.
Garage Unfinished	601 sq. ft.
Dimensions	50'x60'
Foundation	Basement
Bedrooms	4
Full Baths	3
Half Baths	1
First Ceiling	9'
Second Ceiling	8'
Max Ridge Height	30'
Roof Framing	Stick
Exterior Walls	2x4

* Alternate foundation options available at an additional charge.
Please call 1-800-235-5700 for more information.

To order your Blueprints, call 1-800-235-5700

Units	Single
Price Code	H
Total Finished	3,058 sq. ft.
First Finished	2,167 sq. ft.
Second Finished	891 sq. ft.
Bonus Unfinished	252 sq. ft.
Garage Unfinished	725 sq. ft.
Porch Unfinished	159 sq. ft.
Dimensions	64'x73'7"
Foundation	Crawlspace
Bedrooms	4
Full Baths	3
Max Ridge Height	33'6"
Roof Framing	Stick
Exterior Walls	2x4

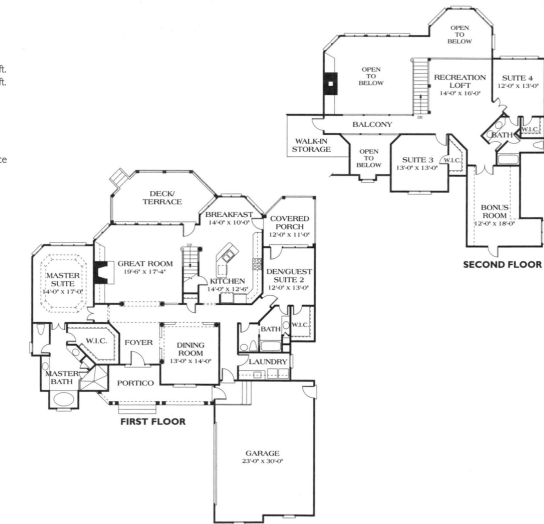

SECOND FLOOR

OPEN TO BELOW

RECREATION LOFT
14'-0" x 16'-0"

SUITE 4
12'-0" x 13'-0"

OPEN TO BELOW

BALCONY

WALK-IN STORAGE

W.I.C.

BATH

SUITE 3
13'-0" x 13'-0"

W.I.C.

OPEN TO BELOW

BONUS ROOM
12'-0" x 18'-0"

FIRST FLOOR

DECK/ TERRACE

BREAKFAST
14'-0" x 10'-0"

COVERED PORCH
12'-0" x 11'-0"

GREAT ROOM
19'-6" x 17'-4"

KITCHEN
14'-0" x 12'-6"

DEN/GUEST SUITE 2
12'-0" x 13'-0"

MASTER SUITE
14'-0" x 17'-0"

W.I.C.

FOYER

DINING ROOM
13'-0" x 14'-0"

BATH

W.I.C.

LAUNDRY

MASTER BATH

PORTICO

GARAGE
23'-0" x 30'-0"

To order your Blueprints, call 1-800-235-5700

FIRST FLOOR

KIT.
14'0" X 11'0"

EAT. BAR

PAN.

NK.
11'4" X 15'0"

GRT. RM.
10'1 1/8" CEILING
19'4" X 17'0"

DESK

DOWN

UP

LIN.

DIN.
12'0" X 12'8"

E.
10'1 1/8" CEILING

BUILT-IN CABINETS

DEN
10'1 1/8" CEILING
11'8" X 16'0"

ARCH.

2 CAR GAR.
22'4" X 24'0"

SECOND FLOOR

BR. #3
12'0" X 10'0"

BR. #4
10'4" X 12'8"

LIN.

DOWN

MBR.
CATHEDRAL CEILING
13'4" X 16'0"

BR. #2
11'0" X 11'4"

Units	Single
Price Code	E
Total Finished	2,416 sq. ft.
First Finished	1,356 sq. ft.
Second Finished	1,060 sq. ft.
Basement Unfinished	1,356 sq. ft.
Dimensions	56'x45'8"
Foundation	Basement
Bedrooms	4
Full Baths	2
Half Baths	1
Max Ridge Height	28'8"
Roof Framing	Truss
Exterior Walls	2x6

Units	Single
Price Code	A
Total Finished	1,311 sq. ft.
First Finished	713 sq. ft.
Second Finished	598 sq. ft.
Basement Unfinished	713 sq. ft.
Porch Unfinished	158 sq. ft.
Dimensions	30'8"x26'
Foundation	Basement
Bedrooms	2
Full Baths	2
First Ceiling	8'
Second Ceiling	8'
Roof Framing	Truss
Exterior Walls	2x6

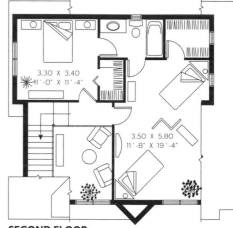

SECOND FLOOR

FIRST FLOOR

To order your Blueprints, call 1-800-235-5700

Units	Single
Price Code	I
Total Finished	3,274 sq. ft.
First Finished	2,332 sq. ft.
Second Finished	942 sq. ft.
Bonus Unfinished	305 sq. ft.
Basement Unfinished	2,332 sq. ft.
Garage Unfinished	617 sq. ft.
Dimensions	60'x64'6''
Foundation	Basement
	Crawlspace
Bedrooms	4
Full Baths	3
Half Baths	1
Max Ridge Height	29'10''
Roof Framing	Stick
Exterior Walls	2x4

FIRST FLOOR

SECOND FLOOR

Units	Single
Price Code	C
Total Finished	1,938 sq. ft.
First Finished	1,044 sq. ft.
Second Finished	894 sq. ft.
Garage Unfinished	487 sq. ft.
Dimensions	58'x43'6''
Foundation	Basement
Bedrooms	3
Full Baths	2
Half Baths	1
Roof Framing	Truss
Exterior Walls	2x6

FIRST FLOOR

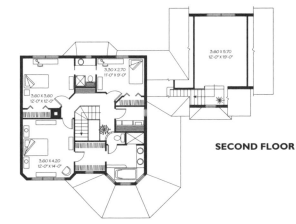

SECOND FLOOR

To order your Blueprints, call 1-800-235-5700

Units	Single
Price Code	G
Total Finished	2,988 sq. ft.
Main Finished	2,096 sq. ft.
Upper Finished	892 sq. ft.
Basement Unfinished	1,948 sq. ft.
Dimensions	56'x54'
Foundation	Basement
Bedrooms	3
Full Baths	3
Half Baths	1
Main Ceiling	9'
Max Ridge Height	36'
Exterior Walls	2x6

* Alternate foundation options available at an additional charge.
Please call 1-800-235-5700 for more information.

LOWER FLOOR

MAIN FLOOR

UPPER LEVEL

FIRST FLOOR

Units	Single
Price Code	F
Total Finished	2,603 sq. ft.
First Finished	1,836 sq. ft.
Second Finished	767 sq. ft.
Basement Unfinished	1,836 sq. ft.
Dimensions	58'6''x61'
Foundation	Basement
Bedrooms	4
Full Baths	3
Half Baths	1
Max Ridge Height	29'
Roof Framing	Truss
Exterior Walls	2x4

SECOND FLOOR

To order your Blueprints, call 1-800-235-5700

Units	Single
Price Code	F
Total Finished	2,674 sq. ft.
First Finished	2,022 sq. ft.
Second Finished	652 sq. ft.
Bonus Unfinished	285 sq. ft.
Garage Unfinished	488 sq. ft.
Dimensions	58'4''×54'5''
Foundation	Crawlspace
Bedrooms	3
Full Baths	2
Half Baths	1
First Ceiling	9'
Second Ceiling	9'
Max Ridge Height	34'6''
Roof Framing	Stick
Exterior Walls	2x4

SECOND FLOOR

SUITE 2
13'-0" x 12'-2"

OPEN TO BELOW

BATH

LIN.

DN

BALCONY

SUITE 3
12'-4" x 13'-10"

OPEN TO BELOW

UNFIN. BONUS ROOM
11'-8" x 19'-8"

FIRST FLOOR

PATIO

BREAKFAST
13'-0" x 10'-8"

MASTER SUITE
14'-6" x 18'-8"

KITCHEN
13'-0" x 12'-6"

GREAT ROOM
19'-0" x 19'-6"

LIN.

LAUNDRY

P.

PDR.

MASTER BATH

W.I.C.

DINING ROOM
12'-0" x 13'-6"

FOYER

GARAGE
21'-8" x 21'-8"

PORCH

OFFICE
12'-0" x 13'-6"

REAR ELEVATION

Units	Single
Price Code	A
Total Finished	1,342 sq. ft.
First Finished	927 sq. ft.
Second Finished	415 sq. ft.
Basement Unfinished	927 sq. ft.
Garage Unfinished	440 sq. ft.
Dimensions	42'x44'
Foundation	Basement
Bedrooms	3
Full Baths	2
Half Baths	1
First Ceiling	8'
Second Ceiling	8'
Max Ridge Height	25'6''
Roof Framing	Truss
Exterior Walls	2x6

MBR.
14'0" X 12'0"

KIT.
9'0" X 12'0"

DIN.
10'0" X 12'0"

LIV.
10'-1 1/8" CEILING HGT.
15'0" X 15'0"

2 CAR GARAGE
20'0" X 22'0"

FIRST FLOOR

BR. #2
10'0" X 12'0"

LIN.

BR. #3
11'0" X 11'0"

SECOND FLOOR

To order your Blueprints, call 1-800-235-5700

3,00 X 3,00
10'-0" X 10'-0"

3,60 X 3,60
12'-0" X 12'-0"

3,00 X 3,00
10'-0" X 10'-0"

SECOND FLOOR

Units	Single
Price Code	A
Total Finished	1,352 sq. ft.
First Finished	676 sq. ft.
Second Finished	676 sq. ft.
Dimensions	26'x26'
Foundation	Basement
Bedrooms	3
Full Baths	2
First Ceiling	8'
Second Ceiling	8'
Max Ridge Height	28'1"
Roof Framing	Truss
Exterior Walls	2x6

3,20 X 3,00
10'-8" X 10'-0"

4,20 X 3,70
14'-0" X 12'-4"

2,40 X 4,20
8'-0" X 14'-0"

7,8 m
26'-0"

7,8 m
26'-0"

FIRST FLOOR

To order your Blueprints, call 1-800-235-5700

Units	Single
Price Code	L
Total Finished	4,500 sq. ft.
First Finished	2,897 sq. ft.
Second Finished	1,603 sq. ft.
Basement Unfinished	2,897 sq. ft.
Garage Unfinished	793 sq. ft.
Dimensions	74'7''×77'3''
Foundation	Basement
	Slab
Bedrooms	4
Full Baths	3
Half Baths	1
3/4 Baths	1
First Ceiling	10'
Second Ceiling	9'
Max Ridge Height	33'6''
Roof Framing	Stick
Exterior Walls	2x4

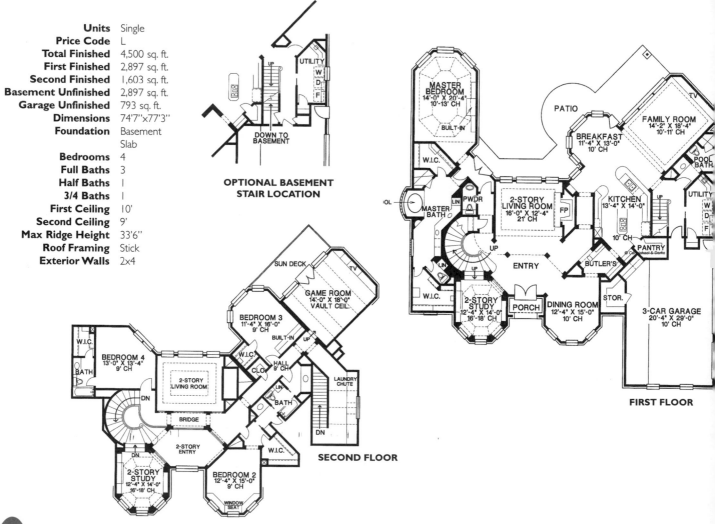

OPTIONAL BASEMENT STAIR LOCATION

SECOND FLOOR

FIRST FLOOR

To order your Blueprints, call 1-800-235-5700

FIRST FLOOR

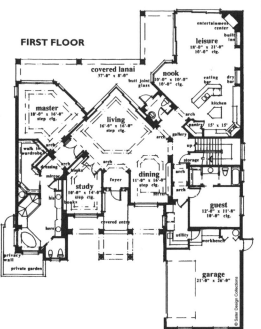

covered lanai
37'-0" x 8'-0"
butt joint glass

entertainment center
built in

leisure
18'-0" x 21'-0"
10'-0" clg.

nook
10'-0" x 10'-0"
10'-0" clg.

eating bar

dry bar

master
18'-0" x 16'-0"
step clg.

living
16'-0" x 16'-0"
step clg.

kitchen

arch

pantry
15' x 15'

walk in wardrobe

dressing

mirror

arch

hooks

arch

foyer

dining
11'-0" x 16'-0"
step clg.

gallery

up

storage

study
18'-0" x 14'-0"
step clg.

hooks

guest
12'-0" x 11'-8"
10'-0" clg.

hers

covered entry

server

utility

workbench

privacy wall

private garden

garage
21'-0" x 26'-0"

© Sater Design Collections

SECOND FLOOR

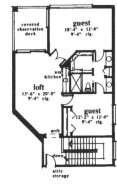

covered observation deck

guest
18'-4" x 12'-0"
9'-4" clg.

am kitchen

loft
13'-6" x 20'-0"
9'-4" clg.

guest
12'-2" x 12'-0"
9'-4" clg.

arch

down

attic storage

Units	Single
Price Code	K
Total Finished	3,958 sq. ft.
First Finished	3,010 sq. ft.
Second Finished	948 sq. ft.
Garage Unfinished	604 sq. ft.
Dimensions	65'x91'
Foundation	Slab
Bedrooms	4
Full Baths	3
Half Baths	1
First Ceiling	14'
Second Ceiling	10'
Max Ridge Height	35'6"
Roof Framing	Truss
Exterior Walls	2x8

* Alternate foundation options available at an additional charge.
Please call 1-800-235-5700 for more information.

Units	Single
Price Code	G
Total Finished	2,832 sq. ft.
First Finished	2,032 sq. ft.
Second Finished	800 sq. ft.
Bonus Unfinished	405 sq. ft.
Dimensions	74'x57'
Foundation	Basement
Bedrooms	4
Full Baths	2
Max Ridge Height	31'
Roof Framing	Truss
Exterior Walls	2x6

FIRST FLOOR

SUN RM.
14'8" x 9'8"

WD. DECK
19'8" x 25'6"

GRT. RM.
2-STORY CEILING
18'8" x 15'4"

NK.
13'0" x 13'0"

KIT.
12'2" x 12'0"

ISLAND

MBR
CATHEDRAL CEILING
13'0" x 16'10"

DIN.
13'0" x 13'0"

3 CAR GARAGE
23'8" x 33'8"

SECOND FLOOR

OPEN TO
GRT. RM.

BR. #3
12'4" x 10'4"

BR. #2
12'4" x 11'4"

BR. #4
CATHEDRAL CEILING
11'0" x 11'0"

BONUS RM.
11'0" x 26'6"

Units	Single
Price Code	D
Total Finished	2,120 sq. ft.
First Finished	995 sq. ft.
Second Finished	1,125 sq. ft.
Basement Unfinished	995 sq. ft.
Dimensions	56'4"x35'8"
Foundation	Basement
Bedrooms	4
Full Baths	2
Half Baths	1
Max Ridge Height	28'4"
Roof Framing	Truss
Exterior Walls	2x6

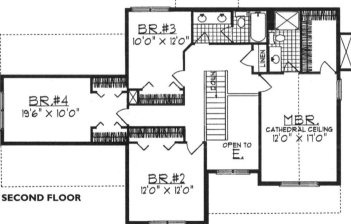

SECOND FLOOR

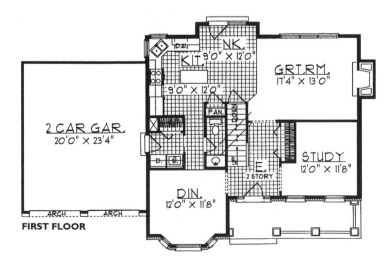

FIRST FLOOR

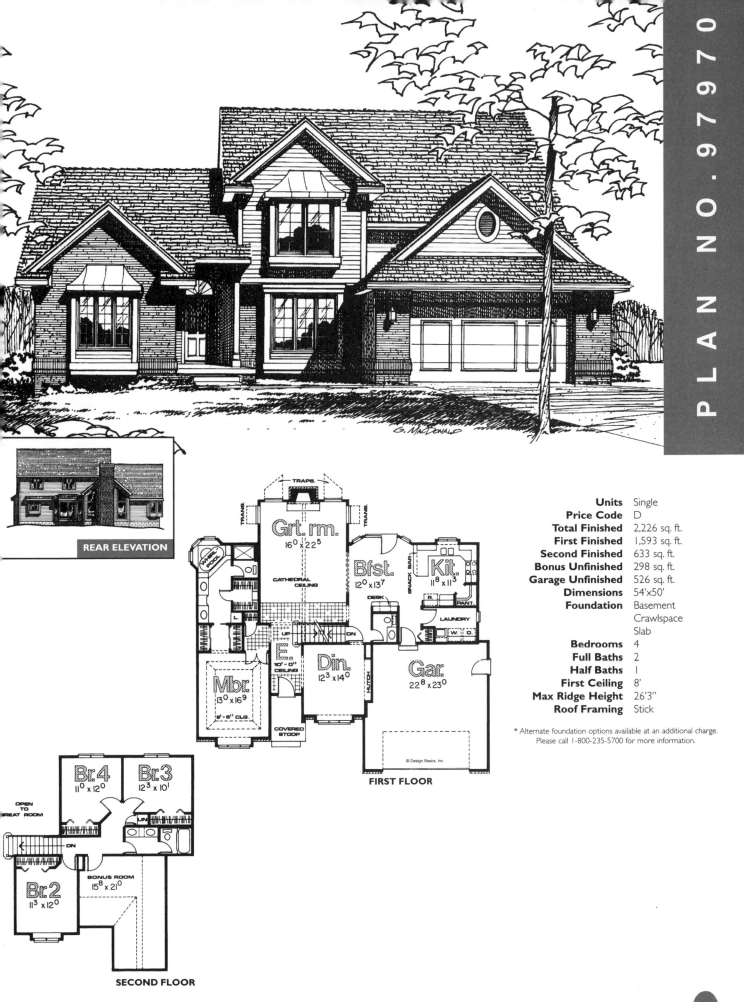

G. MacDONALD

REAR ELEVATION

TRAPS.

Grt. rm.
16⁰ x 22⁵

CATHEDRAL CEILING

Bfst.
12⁰ x 13⁷

SNACK BAR

Kit.
11⁸ x 11³

DESK

PANT.

LAUNDRY

W. D.

UP

DN

10' - 0" CEILING

Mbr.
13⁰ x 16⁹

9'-6" CLG.

Din.
12³ x 14⁰

HUTCH

Gar.
22⁸ x 23⁰

COVERED STOOP

© Design Basics, Inc.

FIRST FLOOR

Br. 4
11⁰ x 12⁰

Br. 3
12³ x 10¹

OPEN TO GREAT ROOM

DN

Br. 2
11³ x 12⁰

BONUS ROOM
15⁸ x 21⁰

SECOND FLOOR

Units	Single
Price Code	D
Total Finished	2,226 sq. ft.
First Finished	1,593 sq. ft.
Second Finished	633 sq. ft.
Bonus Unfinished	298 sq. ft.
Garage Unfinished	526 sq. ft.
Dimensions	54'x50'
Foundation	Basement
	Crawlspace
	Slab
Bedrooms	4
Full Baths	2
Half Baths	1
First Ceiling	8'
Max Ridge Height	26'3"
Roof Framing	Stick

* Alternate foundation options available at an additional charge. Please call 1-800-235-5700 for more information.

Units	Single
Price Code	I
Total Finished	3,384 sq. ft.
First Finished	1,653 sq. ft.
Second Finished	1,734 sq. ft.
Bonus Unfinished	788 sq. ft.
Basement Unfinished	1,653 sq. ft.
Dimensions	68'x48'
Foundation	Basement
	Crawlspace
Bedrooms	5
Full Baths	4
Half Baths	1
First Ceiling	9'
Second Ceiling	8'
Max Ridge Height	33'8"
Roof Framing	Stick
Exterior Walls	2x4

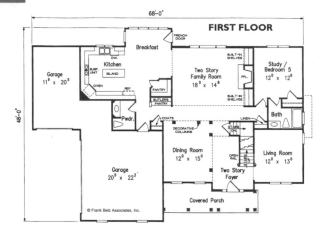

FIRST FLOOR

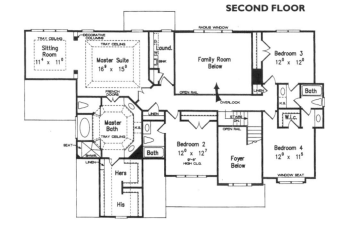

SECOND FLOOR

Units	Single
Price Code	L
Total Finished	3,893 sq. ft.
First Finished	2,841 sq. ft.
Second Finished	1,052 sq. ft.
Garage Unfinished	800 sq. ft.
Deck Unfinished	213 sq. ft.
Porch Unfinished	935 sq. ft.
Dimensions	82'x76'1.5"
Foundation	Crawlspace
Bedrooms	4
Full Baths	3
Half Baths	1
First Ceiling	10'
Second Ceiling	8'
Roof Framing	Truss

* Alternate foundation options available at an additional charge.
Please call 1-800-235-5700 for more information.

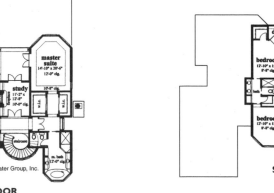

FIRST FLOOR

SECOND FLOOR

To order your Blueprints, call 1-800-235-5700

SECOND FLOOR

OPEN TO FAMILY ROOM BELOW

BEDROOM #2
13'4" X 11'0"

BATH

CLO.

TORAGE

OPEN RAILING

DN

UPPER FOYER

BEDROOM #4
11'8" X 16'8"

W.I.C.

CLO.

BEDROOM #3
11'8" X 16'8"

FIRST FLOOR

MASTER BEDROOM
13'4" X 21'0"

BOOKSHELVES

FAMILY ROOM
18'0" X 15'4"

BREAKFAST AREA
13'4" X 10'0"

PANTRY

KITCHEN
13'6" X 12'0"

LAUNDRY
11'9" X 5'10"

PORCH

MASTER CLO.

MSTR. BATH

SEAT

MIRROR

P.R.

CLO.

UP

HALL

DN

FOYER

DINING ROOM
11'8" X 14'0"

GARAGE
21'3" X 22'4"

PARLOR
13'4" X 12'0"

PORCH

Units	Single
Price Code	F
Total Finished	2,551 sq. ft.
First Finished	1,803 sq. ft.
Second Finished	748 sq. ft.
Basement Unfinished	1,803 sq. ft.
Dimensions	60'6"x53'4"
Foundation	Basement
Bedrooms	4
Full Baths	2
Half Baths	1
First Ceiling	9'
Second Ceiling	8'
Max Ridge Height	33'6"
Roof Framing	Stick
Exterior Walls	2x4

Units	Single
Price Code	A
Total Finished	1,450 sq. ft.
First Finished	918 sq. ft.
Second Finished	532 sq. ft.
Dimensions	26'4''x37'
Foundation	Basement
Bedrooms	2
Full Baths	I
3/4 Baths	I

13'-8" X 13'-8"
4,10 X 4,10

10'-0" X 10'-0"
3,00 X 3,00

SECOND FLOOR

12'-0" X 12'-0"
3,60 X 3,60

12'-4" X 8'-0"
3,70 X 2,40

13'-8" X 24'-0"
4,10 X 7,20

FIRST FLOOR

To order your Blueprints, call 1-800-235-5700

SECOND FLOOR

BEDROOM # 3
14' x 10'

CLOSET

BATH # 2
5' x 12'

A/C | DESK

STOR

DOWN

BEDROOM # 2
14' x 14'

CLOSET

FIRST FLOOR

WHIRLPOOL

MASTER BATH
12' x 14'

LINEN

BATH

CLOSET
8' x 8'

MASTER SUITE
15' x 15'
(11' CEILING)

HVAC

PORCH
23' x 8'

DINING
12' x 11'

REFG

KITCHEN
12' x 12'

RANGE

SNACK BAR

UTILITY
6' x 7'

DRY | WASH

GARAGE
21' x 25'

GREAT ROOM
18' x 21'
(9' CEILINGS)

FIREPLACE

STOR
4' x 5'

PORCH
22' x 6'

46'-0"

64'-0"

Units	Single
Price Code	C
Total Finished	1,925 sq. ft.
First Finished	1,329 sq. ft.
Second Finished	596 sq. ft.
Garage Unfinished	316 sq. ft.
Porch Unfinished	533 sq. ft.
Dimensions	64'x46'
Foundation	Crawlspace
	Slab
Bedrooms	3
Full Baths	2
Half Baths	1
First Ceiling	9'
Tray Ceiling	12'
Max Ridge Height	27'
Roof Framing	Stick
Exterior Walls	2x4

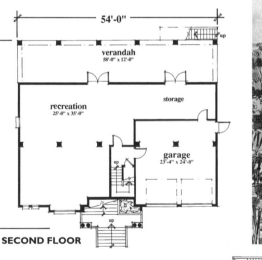

54'-0"

up

verandah
58'-0" x 12'-0"

recreation
25'-0" x 35'-0"

storage

garage
23'-4" x 24'-0"

up

up

58'-0"

SECOND FLOOR

©The Sater Group, Inc.

down

lanai
58'-0" x 10'-8"

master
suite
13'-0" x 15'-0"
9'-4" stepped clg.

built ins

grand room
20'-0" x 18'-0" avg.
tray ceiling

fireplace

built ins

hers | his

arch

arch

arch

nook
11'-0" x 9'-4"

kitchen
11' x 11'

eating
bar

br. 2
12'-0" x 11'-4"
9'-4" flat clg.

utility

study
11'-0" x 11'-0"
9'-4" flat clg.

foyer

down

dn.

dining
10'-10" x 15'-0"
9'-4" flat clg.

br. 3
12'-0" x 11'-0"
9'-4" flat clg.

entry porch

planter

FIRST FLOOR

Units	Single
Price Code	F
Total Finished	2,068 sq. ft.
First Finished	2,068 sq. ft.
Bonus Unfinished	1,402 sq. ft.
Garage Unfinished	560 sq. ft.
Porch Unfinished	696 sq. ft.
Dimensions	54'x58'
Foundation	Post
Bedrooms	3
Full Baths	2
Max Ridge Height	37'
Roof Framing	Truss
Exterior Walls	2x6

* Alternate foundation options available at an additional charge.
Please call 1-800-235-5700 for more information.

Units	Single
Price Code	F
Total Finished	2,717 sq. ft.
First Finished	1,614 sq. ft.
Second Finished	1,103 sq. ft.
Bonus Unfinished	318 sq. ft.
Dimensions	63'8''×42'4''
Foundation	Basement
Bedrooms	3
Full Baths	2
Half Baths	1
Max Ridge Height	35'10''
Roof Framing	Truss
Exterior Walls	2x6

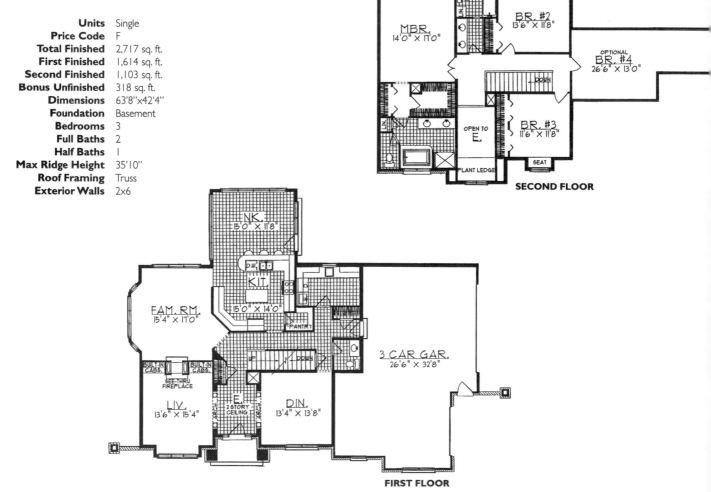

SECOND FLOOR

FIRST FLOOR

FIRST FLOOR

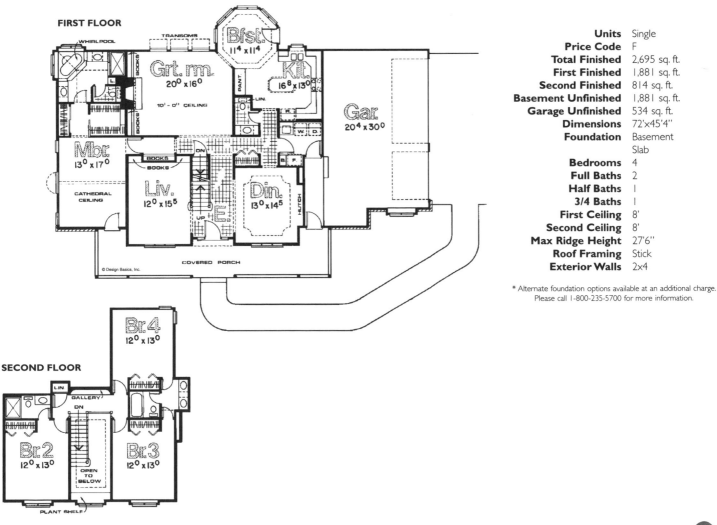

WHIRL POOL

TRANSOMS

Bfst.
11⁴ x11⁴

Grt. rm.
20⁰ x 16⁰

Kit.
16⁸ x 13⁰

10'-0" CEILING

PANT.

LIN.

Gar.
20⁴ x 30⁰

W. D.

Mbr.
13⁰ x 17⁰

BOOKS

BOOKS

DN

CATHEDRAL CEILING

Liv.
12⁰ x 15⁵

Din.
13⁰ x 14⁵

B. F.

HUTCH

UP

© Design Basics, Inc.

COVERED PORCH

Br. 4
12⁰ x 13⁰

SECOND FLOOR

LIN

GALLERY

DN

Br. 2
12⁰ x 13⁰

OPEN TO BELOW

Br. 3
12⁰ x 13⁰

PLANT SHELF

Units	Single
Price Code	F
Total Finished	2,695 sq. ft.
First Finished	1,881 sq. ft.
Second Finished	814 sq. ft.
Basement Unfinished	1,881 sq. ft.
Garage Unfinished	534 sq. ft.
Dimensions	72'x45'4''
Foundation	Basement
	Slab
Bedrooms	4
Full Baths	2
Half Baths	1
3/4 Baths	1
First Ceiling	8'
Second Ceiling	8'
Max Ridge Height	27'6''
Roof Framing	Stick
Exterior Walls	2x4

* Alternate foundation options available at an additional charge. Please call 1-800-235-5700 for more information.

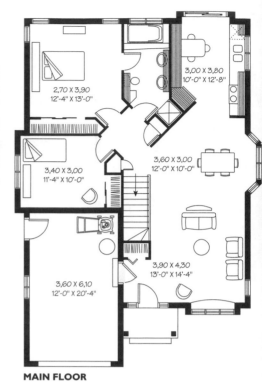

Units	Single
Price Code	A
Total Finished	1,068 sq. ft.
Main Finished	1,068 sq. ft.
Garage Unfinished	245 sq. ft.
Dimensions	30'8''x48'
Foundation	Basement
Bedrooms	2
Full Baths	1

2,70 X 3,90
12'-4" X 13'-0"

3,00 X 3,80
10'-0" X 12'-8"

3,40 X 3,00
11'-4" X 10'-0"

3,60 X 3,00
12'-0" X 10'-0"

3,90 X 4,30
13'-0" X 14'-4"

3,60 X 6,10
12'-0" X 20'-4"

MAIN FLOOR

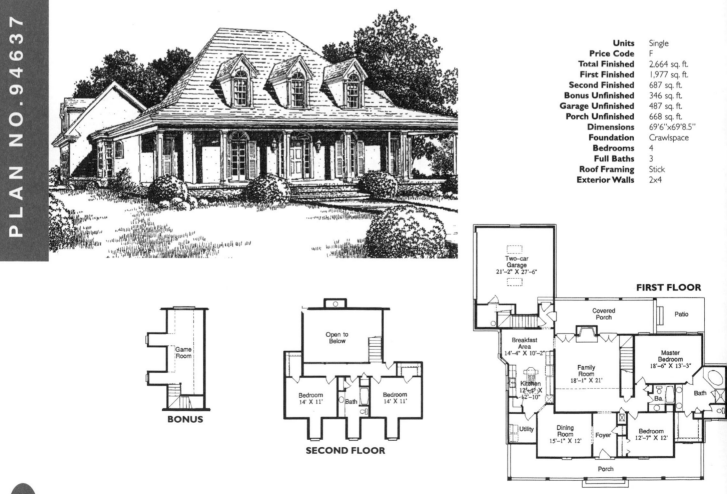

Units	Single
Price Code	F
Total Finished	2,664 sq. ft.
First Finished	1,977 sq. ft.
Second Finished	687 sq. ft.
Bonus Unfinished	346 sq. ft.
Garage Unfinished	487 sq. ft.
Porch Unfinished	668 sq. ft.
Dimensions	69'6''x69'8.5''
Foundation	Crawlspace
Bedrooms	4
Full Baths	3
Roof Framing	Stick
Exterior Walls	2x4

Game Room

BONUS

Open to Below

Bedroom
14' X 11'

Bath

Bedroom
14' X 11'

SECOND FLOOR

Two-car Garage
21'-2" X 27'-6"

FIRST FLOOR

Covered Porch

Patio

Breakfast Area
14'-4" X 10'-2"

Family Room
18'-1" X 21'

Master Bedroom
18'-6" X 13'-3"

Kitchen
12'-4" X 12'-10"

Ba.

Bath

Utility

Dining Room
15'-1" X 12'

Foyer

Bedroom
12'-7" X 12'

Porch

To order your Blueprints, call 1-800-235-5700

SECOND FLOOR

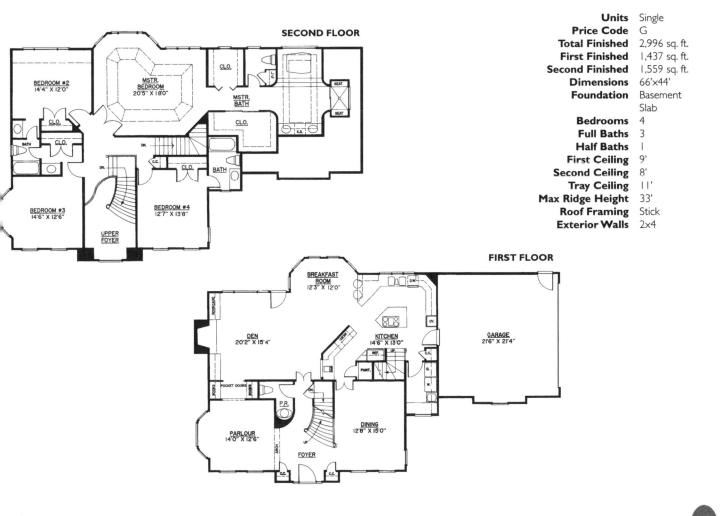

BEDROOM #2
14'4" X 12'0"

MSTR.
BEDROOM
20'5" X 18'0"

CLO.

MSTR.
BATH

CLO.

CLO.

SEAT

SEAT

BATH

CLO.

DN.

CLO.

BEDROOM #3
14'6" X 12'6"

DN.

C.C.

CLO.

BATH

UPPER
FOYER

BEDROOM #4
12'7" X 13'8"

Units	Single
Price Code	G
Total Finished	2,996 sq. ft.
First Finished	1,437 sq. ft.
Second Finished	1,559 sq. ft.
Dimensions	66'x44'
Foundation	Basement
	Slab
Bedrooms	4
Full Baths	3
Half Baths	1
First Ceiling	9'
Second Ceiling	8'
Tray Ceiling	11'
Max Ridge Height	33'
Roof Framing	Stick
Exterior Walls	2x4

FIRST FLOOR

BREAKFAST
ROOM
12'3" X 12'0"

DEN
20'2" X 15'4"

KITCHEN
14'6" X 13'0"

GARAGE
21'6" X 21'4"

REF.

PANT.

POCKET DOORS

P.R.

PARLOUR
14'0" X 12'6"

DINING
12'8" X 15'0"

FOYER

ARCH

Units	Single
Price Code	B
Total Finished	1,519 sq. ft.
First Finished	788 sq. ft.
Second Finished	731 sq. ft.
Garage Unfinished	266 sq. ft.
Foundation	Basement
Bedrooms	3
Full Baths	1
Half Baths	1

SECOND FLOOR

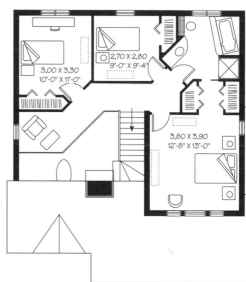

3,00 X 3,30
10'-0" X 11'-0"

2,70 X 2,80
9'-0" X 9'-4"

3,80 X 3,90
12'-8" X 13'-0"

FIRST FLOOR

3,30 X 3,90
11'-0" X 13'-0"

3,1 X 2,70
10'-4" X 9'-0"

2,70 X 2,00
9'-0" X 6'-8"

4,20 X 5,10
14'-0" X 17'-0"

3,80 X 6,20
12'-8" X 20'-8"

10,8 m
36'-0"

9,6 m
32'-0"

To order your Blueprints, call 1-800-235-5700

Units	Single
Price Code	F
Total Finished	2,616 sq. ft.
First Finished	1,992 sq. ft.
Second Finished	624 sq. ft.
Bonus Unfinished	314 sq. ft.
Basement Unfinished	1,992 sq. ft.
Garage Unfinished	460 sq. ft.
Dimensions	55'x51'6"
Foundation	Basement
	Crawlspace
Bedrooms	4
Full Baths	3
First Ceiling	9'
Second Ceiling	8'
Max Ridge Height	29'
Roof Framing	Stick
Exterior Walls	2x4

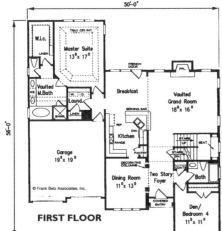

FIRST FLOOR

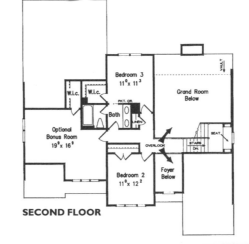

SECOND FLOOR

Units	Single
Price Code	G
Total Finished	2,875 sq. ft.
First Finished	2,079 sq. ft.
Second Finished	796 sq. ft.
Porch Unfinished	234 sq. ft.
Dimensions	63'x68'
Foundation	Basement
Bedrooms	4
Full Baths	2
Half Baths	1
First Ceiling	9'1 1/8"
Second Ceiling	8'1 1/8"
Max Ridge Height	33'2"
Roof Framing	Truss
Exterior Walls	2x6

FIRST FLOOR

SECOND FLOOR

To order your Blueprints, call 1-800-235-5700

Units	Single
Price Code	E
Total Finished	2,270 sq. ft.
First Finished	1,150 sq. ft.
Second Finished	1,120 sq. ft.
Basement Unfinished	1,150 sq. ft.
Garage Unfinished	457 sq. ft.
Dimensions	46'x48'
Foundation	Basement
Bedrooms	4
Full Baths	2
Half Baths	1
First Ceiling	8'
Second Ceiling	8'
Tray Ceiling	9'4"
Max Ridge Height	28'
Roof Framing	Stick
Exterior Walls	2x4

* Alternate foundation options available at an additional charge.
Please call 1-800-235-5700 for more information.

FIRST FLOOR

Bfst.
11⁰ x 11⁰

DESK

Grt. rm.
20⁰ x 16⁰

Hrth.
11⁸ x 10⁰

Kit.
10⁰ x 11³

ENT.
CENTER

DN

UP

Din.
12⁰ x 13⁰

HUTCH

Gar.
20⁷ x 21⁸

COVERED PORCH

SECOND FLOOR

WHIRLPOOL

Mbr.
16⁰ x 14⁰
9' - 4" CEILING

LIN.

Br 2
11² x 11⁶

LINEN

DN

PLANT
SHELF

Br 4
11⁰ x 11⁴

OPEN
TO
BELOW

Br 3
11⁰ x 12⁰
10' - 0" CEILING

DESK

To order your Blueprints, call 1-800-235-5700

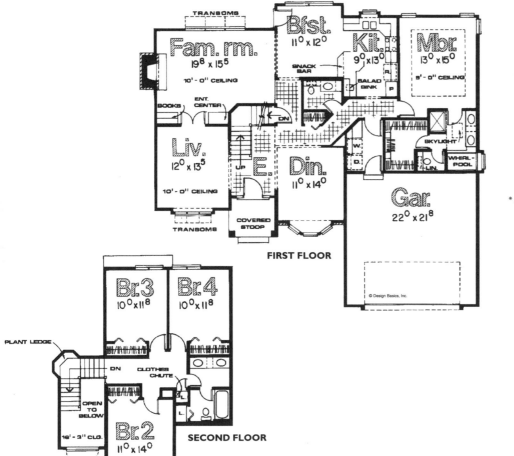

FIRST FLOOR

Fam. rm. 19⁸ x 15⁵ / 10'-0" CEILING

Bfst. 11⁰ x 12⁰

Kit. 9⁰ x 13⁰

Mbr. 13⁰ x 15⁰ / 9'-0" CEILING

Liv. 12⁰ x 13⁵ / 10'-0" CEILING

Din. 11⁰ x 14⁰

Gar. 22⁰ x 21⁸

COVERED STOOP

TRANSOMS

© Design Basics, Inc.

SECOND FLOOR

Br.3 10⁰ x 11⁸

Br.4 10⁰ x 11⁸

Br.2 11⁰ x 14⁰

PLANT LEDGE

OPEN TO BELOW

16'-3" CLG.

TRANSOM

Units	Single
Price Code	E
Total Finished	2,256 sq. ft.
First Finished	1,602 sq. ft.
Second Finished	654 sq. ft.
Dimensions	54'x50'
Foundation	Basement
Bedrooms	4
Full Baths	2
Half Baths	1
Max Ridge Height	26'
Roof Framing	Stick/ Truss
Exterior Walls	2x4

* Alternate foundation options available at an additional charge.
Please call 1-800-235-5700 for more information.

SECOND FLOOR

Units	Single
Price Code	A
Total Finished	1,152 sq. ft.
First Finished	576 sq. ft.
Second Finished	576 sq. ft.
Dimensions	24'x24'
Foundation	Basement
Bedrooms	3
Full Baths	1
Half Baths	2

FIRST FLOOR

7,2 m
24'-0"

Units	Single
Price Code	D
Total Finished	2,200 sq. ft.
First Finished	1,688 sq. ft.
Second Finished	512 sq. ft.
Bonus Unfinished	238 sq. ft.
Basement Unfinished	1,688 sq. ft.
Garage Unfinished	471 sq. ft.
Dimensions	52'x48'
Foundation	Basement
	Crawlspace
Bedrooms	3
Full Baths	2
First Ceiling	9'
Second Ceiling	8'
Roof Framing	Stick
Exterior Walls	2x4

FIRST FLOOR

SECOND FLOOR

copyright © 1997 frank betz associates, inc.

To order your Blueprints, call 1-800-235-5700

FIRST FLOOR

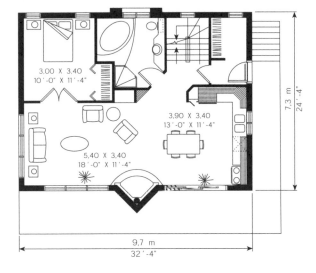

3,00 X 3,40
10'-0" X 11'-4"

3,90 X 3,40
13'-0" X 11'-4"

5,40 X 3,40
18'-0" X 11'-4"

7,3 m
24'-4"

9,7 m
32'-4"

Units	Single
Price Code	C
Total Finished	1,864 sq. ft.
First Finished	790 sq. ft.
Second Finished	287 sq. ft.
Lower Finished	787 sq. ft.
Dimensions	32'4''×24'4''
Foundation	Basement
Bedrooms	3
Full Baths	2
Max Ridge Height	29'6'
Roof Framing	Truss

LOWER FLOOR

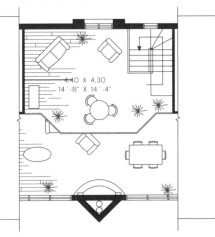

4,40 X 4,30
14'-8" X 14'-4"

SECOND FLOOR

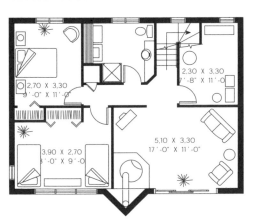

2,70 X 3,30
9'-0" X 11'-0"

2,30 X 3,30
7'-8" X 11'-0"

3,90 X 2,70
13'-0" X 9'-0"

5,10 X 3,30
17'-0" X 11'-0"

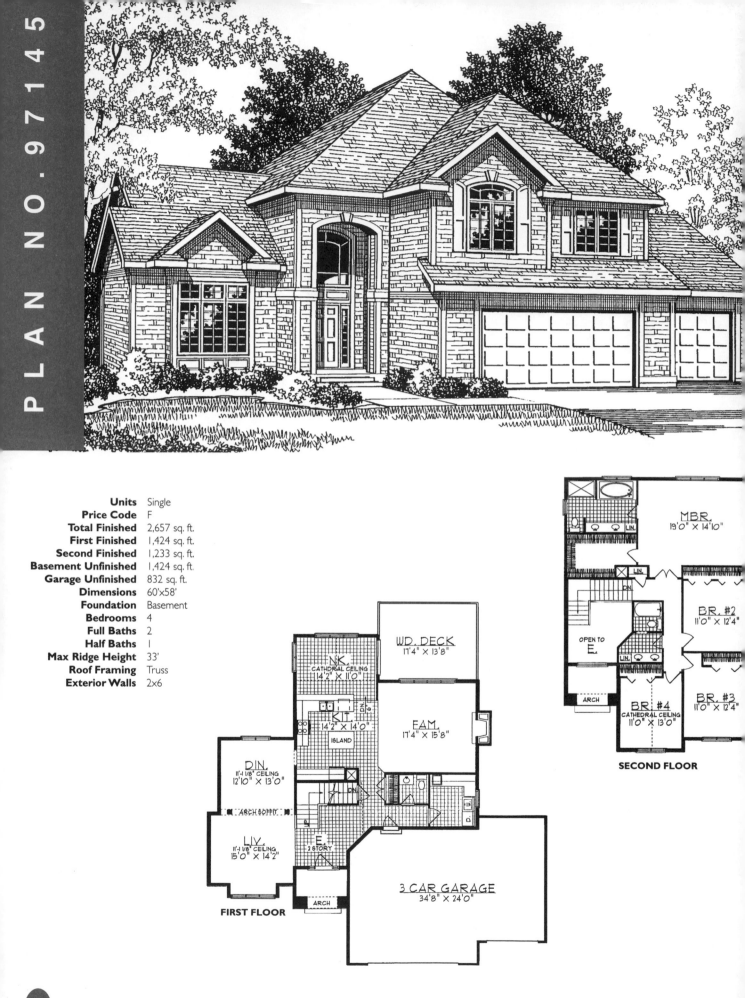

Units	Single
Price Code	F
Total Finished	2,657 sq. ft.
First Finished	1,424 sq. ft.
Second Finished	1,233 sq. ft.
Basement Unfinished	1,424 sq. ft.
Garage Unfinished	832 sq. ft.
Dimensions	60'x58'
Foundation	Basement
Bedrooms	4
Full Baths	2
Half Baths	1
Max Ridge Height	33'
Roof Framing	Truss
Exterior Walls	2x6

SECOND FLOOR

MBR.
19'0" X 14'10"

BR. #2
11'0" X 12'4"

OPEN TO
E.

BR. #4
CATHEDRAL CEILING
11'0" X 13'0"

BR. #3
11'0" X 12'4"

ARCH

FIRST FLOOR

N.K.
CATHEDRAL CEILING
14'2" X 11'0"

WD. DECK
17'4" X 13'8"

KIT.
14'2" X 14'0"

ISLAND

FAM.
17'4" X 15'8"

DIN.
11'-1 1/8" CEILING
12'10" X 13'0"

ARCH SOFFIT

LIV.
11'-1 1/8" CEILING
15'0" X 14'2"

E.
2 STORY

ARCH

3 CAR GARAGE
34'8" X 24'0"

To order your Blueprints, call 1-800-235-5700

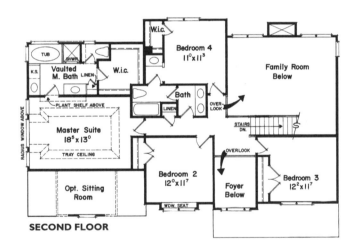

SECOND FLOOR

- W.i.c.
- Bedroom 4 11⁰x11⁵
- Family Room Below
- TUB
- SHWR.
- Vaulted M. Bath
- K.S.
- LINEN
- W.i.c.
- Bath
- LINEN
- OVER-LOOK
- PLANT SHELF ABOVE
- STAIRS DN.
- RADIUS WINDOW ABOVE
- Master Suite 18⁵x13⁰
- TRAY CEILING
- Bedroom 2 12⁰x11⁷
- OVERLOOK
- Foyer Below
- Bedroom 3 12²x11⁷
- Opt. Sitting Room
- WDW. SEAT

Units	Single
Price Code	E
Total Finished	2,368 sq. ft.
First Finished	1,200 sq. ft.
Second Finished	1,168 sq. ft.
Basement Unfinished	1,200 sq. ft.
Garage Unfinished	527 sq. ft.
Dimensions	56'x39'
Foundation	Basement
	Crawlspace
	Slab
Bedrooms	4
Full Baths	2
Half Baths	I
First Ceiling	9'
Second Ceiling	8'
Max Ridge Height	31'6"
Roof Framing	Stick
Exterior Walls	2x4

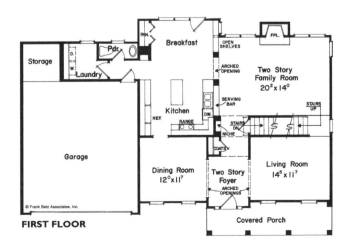

FIRST FLOOR

- Storage
- PAN.
- Breakfast
- OPEN SHELVES
- FPL.
- Pdr.
- D.
- W.
- Laundry
- Kitchen
- ARCHED OPENING
- Two Story Family Room 20²x14⁰
- SERVING BAR
- STAIRS UP
- REF.
- RANGE
- D.W.
- STAIRS DN.
- NICHE
- Garage
- COATS
- Dining Room 12⁰x11⁷
- Two Story Foyer
- Living Room 14⁵x11⁷
- ARCHED OPENINGS
- © Frank Betz Associates, Inc.
- Covered Porch

Units	Single
Price Code	G
Total Finished	2,914 sq. ft.
First Finished	1,583 sq. ft.
Second Finished	1,331 sq. ft.
Garage Unfinished	676 sq. ft.
Dimensions	58'x59'4''
Foundation	Basement
Bedrooms	4
Full Baths	2
Half Baths	1
3/4 Baths	1
Max Ridge Height	29'
Roof Framing	Stick
Exterior Walls	2x4

* Alternate foundation options available at an additional charge.
Please call 1-800-235-5700 for more information.

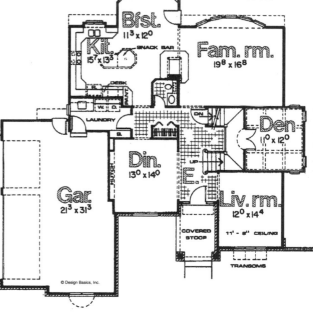

FIRST FLOOR

Bfst. 11³ x 12⁰

Kit. 15⁷ x 13³

SNACK BAR

Fam. rm. 19⁸ x 16⁸

Den 11⁰ x 12⁰

LAUNDRY

Din. 13⁰ x 14⁰

Gar. 21³ x 31³

Liv. rm. 12⁰ x 14⁴

COVERED STOOP

11' - 8" CEILING

TRANSOMS

© Design Basics, Inc.

SECOND FLOOR

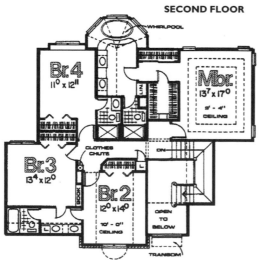

WHIRLPOOL

Br. 4 11⁰ x 12¹¹

Mbr. 13⁷ x 17⁰
9' - 4" CEILING

CLOTHES CHUTE

Br. 3 13⁴ x 12⁰

Br. 2 12⁰ x 14⁰
10' - 0" CEILING

OPEN TO BELOW

TRANSOM

190

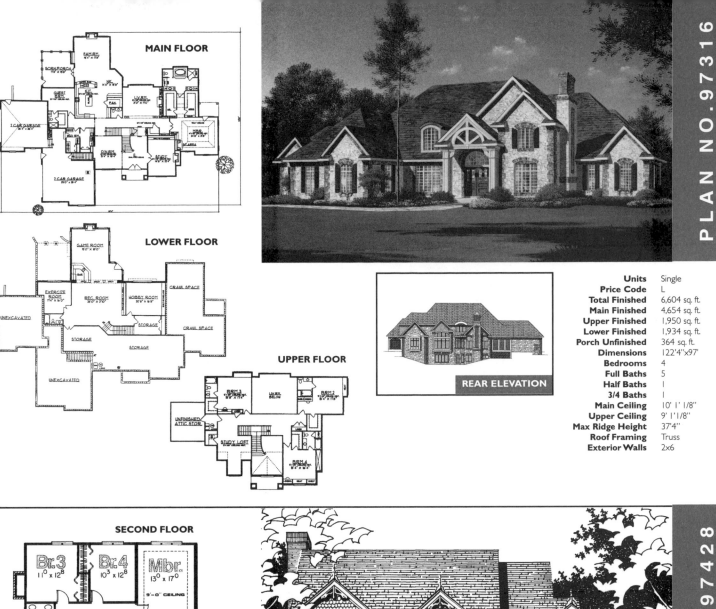

MAIN FLOOR

2 CAR GARAGE

2 CAR GARAGE

LOWER FLOOR

GAME ROOM
15'0" x 16'0"

EXERCIZE ROOM

REC. ROOM

HOBBY ROOM

CRAWL SPACE

CRAWL SPACE

UNEXCAVATED

STORAGE

STORAGE

STORAGE

UNEXCAVATED

UPPER FLOOR

BRM 3

LV. RM. BELOW

BRM 2

UNFINISHED ATTIC STOR.

STUDY LOFT

BRM 4

REAR ELEVATION

Units	Single
Price Code	L
Total Finished	6,604 sq. ft.
Main Finished	4,654 sq. ft.
Upper Finished	1,950 sq. ft.
Lower Finished	1,934 sq. ft.
Porch Unfinished	364 sq. ft.
Dimensions	122'4"x97'
Bedrooms	4
Full Baths	5
Half Baths	I
3/4 Baths	I
Main Ceiling	10' 1' 1/8''
Upper Ceiling	9' 1'1/8''
Max Ridge Height	37'4''
Roof Framing	Truss
Exterior Walls	2x6

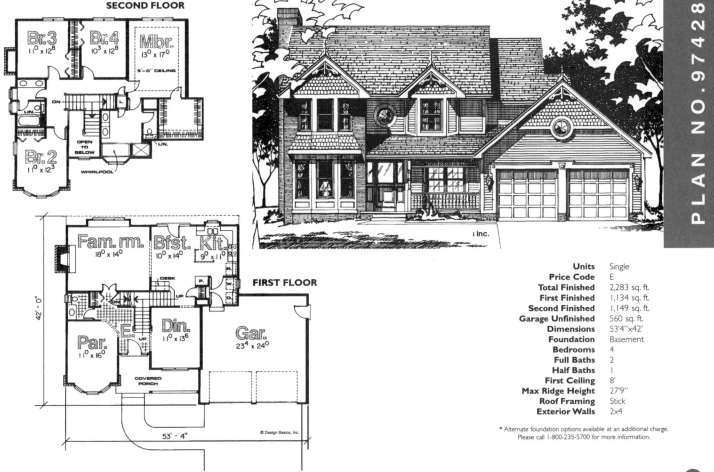

SECOND FLOOR

Br. 3
11'0" x 12'8"

Br. 4
10'3" x 12'8"

Mbr.
13'0" x 17'0"

9'-0" CEILING

LIN.

ON

LIN.

OPEN TO BELOW

Br. 2
11'0" x 12'3"

WHIRLPOOL

FIRST FLOOR

Fam. rm.
18'0 x 14'0

Bfst.
10'0 x 14'0

Kit.
9'0 x 11'0

DESK

UP

ON

Par.
11'0 x 16'0

UP

Din.
11'0 x 13'6

Gar.
23'4 x 24'0

COVERED PORCH

42'-0"

53'-4"

© Design Basics, Inc.

Units	Single
Price Code	E
Total Finished	2,283 sq. ft.
First Finished	1,134 sq. ft.
Second Finished	1,149 sq. ft.
Garage Unfinished	560 sq. ft.
Dimensions	53'4"x42'
Foundation	Basement
Bedrooms	4
Full Baths	2
Half Baths	I
First Ceiling	8'
Max Ridge Height	27'9''
Roof Framing	Stick
Exterior Walls	2x4

* Alternate foundation options available at an additional charge.
Please call 1-800-235-5700 for more information.

Units Single
Price Code C
Total Finished 1,976 sq. ft.
First Finished 924 sq. ft.
Second Finished 1,052 sq. ft.
Dimensions 44'8"x36'
Foundation Basement
Bedrooms 3
Full Baths 2
Half Baths 1

FIRST FLOOR

4,20 X 2,80
14'-0" X 9'-4"

5,60 X 3,50
18'-8" X 11'-8"

3,70 X 6,80
12'-4" X 22'-8"

5,90 X 6,60
19'-8" X 22'-0"

SECOND FLOOR

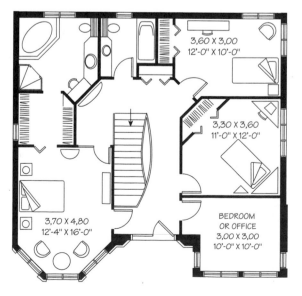

3,60 X 3,00
12'-0" X 10'-0"

3,30 X 3,60
11'-0" X 12'-0"

3,70 X 4,80
12'-4" X 16'-0"

BEDROOM
OR OFFICE
3,00 X 3,00
10'-0" X 10'-0"

To order your Blueprints, call 1-800-235-5700

3,40 X 4,40
11'-4" X 14'-8"

3,80 X 3,30
12'-8" X 11'-0"

4,00 X 3,30
13'-4" X 11'-0"

3,90 X 5,60
13'-0" X 18'-8"

4,10 X 6,20
13'-8" X 20'-8"

2,10 X 1,80
7'-0" X 6'-0"

2,00 X 3,10
6'-8" X 10'-4"

12,2 m
40'-8"

12,9 m
43'-0"

FIRST FLOOR

3,20 X 3,30
10'-8" X 11'-0"

3,60 X 3,00
12'-0" X 10'-0"

2,00 X 3,40
6'-8" X 11'-4"

5,10 X 3,40
17'-0" X 11'-4"

SECOND FLOOR

Units	Single
Price Code	D
Total Finished	2,089 sq. ft.
First Finished	1,204 sq. ft.
Second Finished	885 sq. ft.
Garage Unfinished	287 sq. ft.
Dimensions	43'x40'
Foundation	Basement
Bedrooms	3
Full Baths	1
Half Baths	1

Deck

Breakfast
12'10" x 10'6"

Great Room
18'2" x 16'4"

Kitchen
12'10" x 10'

Dining Room
14'6" x 10'

Foyer

Bath

Two-car Garage
19'6" x 22'

Porch

FIRST FLOOR

Bedroom
10'6" x 12'4"

Bath

Master Bedroom
11'8" x 16'4"

walk-in closet

Bath

Balcony

Bedroom
10' x 10'9"

Laun.

Foyer Below

Plant Ledge

Bonus Room
11'2" x 21'10"

SECOND FLOOR

Units	Single
Price Code	B
Total Finished	1,727 sq. ft.
First Finished	939 sq. ft.
Second Finished	788 sq. ft.
Bonus Unfinished	210 sq. ft.
Basement Unfinished	939 sq. ft.
Garage Unfinished	401 sq. ft.
Porch Unfinished	65 sq. ft.
Dimensions	34'x52'2''
Foundation	Basement
Bedrooms	3
Full Baths	2
Half Baths	1
First Ceiling	8'
Second Ceiling	8'
Max Ridge Height	27'10''
Roof Framing	Truss
Exterior Walls	2x4

To order your Blueprints, call 1-800-235-5700

Rear Elevation

Units	Single
Price Code	I
Total Finished	3,489 sq. ft.
First Finished	2,514 sq. ft.
Second Finished	975 sq. ft.
Basement Unfinished	2,514 sq. ft.
Garage Unfinished	854 sq. ft.
Dimensions	74'8''x64'8''
Foundation	Basement
Bedrooms	4
Full Baths	2
Half Baths	I
3/4 Baths	I
Roof Framing	Truss
Exterior Walls	2x6

SECOND FLOOR

BR. #2
14'6"x14'4"

OPEN TO BELOW

BR. #3
17'4"x19'0"

OPEN TO BELOW

BR. #4
14'0"x16'0"

PLANT LEDGE

FIRST FLOOR

3 CAR GAR.
23'10"x35'10"

NK
VAULTED CEILING
14'4"x13'0"

WOOD DECK
20'4"x11'8"

GR. RM.
2-STORY CEILING
22'8"x18'0"

KIT.
14'4"x11'4"

STUDY
13'8"x14'2"

DIN.
14'2"x15'0"

2-STORY CEILING

MBR.
15'8"x17'8"

194

To order your Blueprints, call 1-800-235-5700

FIRST FLOOR

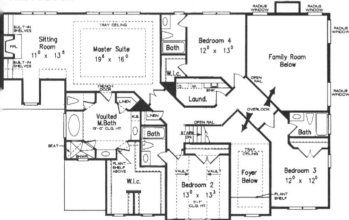

Units	Single
Price Code	J
Total Finished	3,698 sq. ft.
First Finished	1,802 sq. ft.
Second Finished	1,896 sq. ft.
Dimensions	68'x45'4''
Foundation	Basement
	Crawlspace
Bedrooms	5
Full Baths	5
Half Baths	1
First Ceiling	9'
Second Ceiling	9'
Max Ridge Height	36'8''
Roof Framing	Stick
Exterior Walls	2x4

SECOND FLOOR

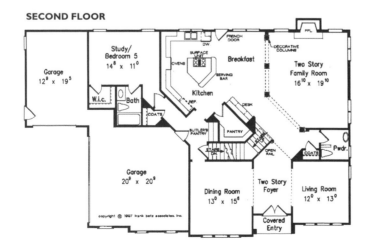

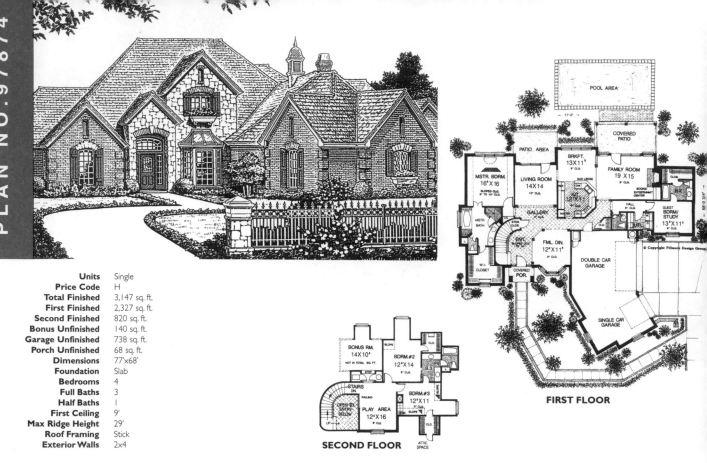

Units	Single
Price Code	H
Total Finished	3,147 sq. ft.
First Finished	2,327 sq. ft.
Second Finished	820 sq. ft.
Bonus Unfinished	140 sq. ft.
Garage Unfinished	738 sq. ft.
Porch Unfinished	68 sq. ft.
Dimensions	77'x68'
Foundation	Slab
Bedrooms	4
Full Baths	3
Half Baths	1
First Ceiling	9'
Max Ridge Height	29'
Roof Framing	Stick
Exterior Walls	2x4

SECOND FLOOR

FIRST FLOOR

Units	Single
Price Code	H
Total Finished	2,374 sq. ft.
Main Finished	1,510 sq. ft.
Upper Finished	864 sq. ft.
Basement Unfinished	1,290 sq. ft.
Porch Unfinished	275 sq. ft.
Dimensions	44'x49'
Foundation	Basement
Bedrooms	3
Full Baths	3
Half Baths	1
Max Ridge Height	43'4''
Roof Framing	Truss
Exterior Walls	2x6

* Alternate foundation options available at an additional charge.
Please call 1-800-235-5700 for more information.

MAIN FLOOR

UPPER FLOOR

LOWER LOWER

To order your Blueprints, call 1-800-235-5700

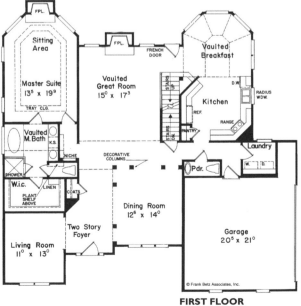

SECOND FLOOR

Family Room Below

Bedroom 2
13⁰ x 11⁴

Storage

OVERLOOK

STAIRS DN.

W.i.c. | Bath

LINEN

Bedroom 3
12⁶ x 14⁰

W.i.c.

Foyer
Below

Optional
Bonus Room
10⁵ x 18⁷

FIRST FLOOR

FPL.

Sitting
Area

FPL.

FRENCH
DOOR

Vaulted
Breakfast

Master Suite
13⁵ x 19⁹

Vaulted
Great Room
15⁰ x 17³

D.W.

Kitchen

STAIRS UP

RADIUS
WDW.

TRAY CLG.

Vaulted
M. Bath

K.S.

REF.

PANTRY

STAIRS DN.

RANGE

NICHE

DECORATIVE
COLUMNS

Laundry

W. | D.

SHOWER

Pdr.

W.i.c. | LINEN

COATS

PLANT
SHELF
ABOVE

Dining Room
12⁶ x 14⁰

Living Room
11⁰ x 13⁰

Two Story
Foyer

Garage
20⁵ x 21⁰

© Frank Betz Associates, Inc.

Units	Single
Price Code	E
Total Finished	2,425 sq. ft.
First Finished	1,796 sq. ft.
Second Finished	629 sq. ft.
Bonus Unfinished	208 sq. ft.
Basement Unfinished	1,796 sq. ft.
Garage Unfinished	588 sq. ft.
Dimensions	54'x53'10''
Foundation	Basement
	Crawlspace
	Slab
Bedrooms	3
Full Baths	2
Half Baths	1
First Ceiling	9'
Second Ceiling	8'
Max Ridge Height	32'
Roof Framing	Stick
Exterior Walls	2x4

Units	Single
Price Code	F
Total Finished	2,673 sq. ft.
First Finished	2,018 sq. ft.
Second Finished	655 sq. ft.
Basement Unfinished	2,018 sq. ft.
Porch Unfinished	224 sq. ft.
Dimensions	81'x53'
Foundation	Basement
Bedrooms	3
Full Baths	2
Half Baths	1
Max Ridge Height	30'
Roof Framing	Truss
Exterior Walls	2x6

SECOND FLOOR

OPEN TO
GRT.RM.

BR.#2
12'0" X 14'4"

LOFT
8'0" X 14'4"

DN

OPEN TO
E.

BR.#3
12'4" X 14'4"

BRICK
ARCH

FIRST FLOOR

SCREEN
PORCH
16'0" X 14'0"

GRT.RM.
2 STORY
17'0" X 19'0"

KIT.

NK.
13'0" X 14'6"

13'0" X 14'6"

MBR.
16'8" X 13'8"

PAN.

DN

UP

3 CAR GAR.
34'4" X 23'8"

DIN.
12'4" X 12'4"

E.
2 STORY

DEN
CATHEDRAL CEILING
12'4" X 14'2"

BRICK
ARCH

Units	Single
Price Code	I
Total Finished	3,300 sq. ft.
First Finished	1,679 sq. ft.
Second Finished	1,621 sq. ft.
Basement Unfinished	1,679 sq. ft.
Garage Unfinished	485 sq. ft.
Dimensions	65'4"x52'6"
Foundation	Basement
	Crawlspace
Bedrooms	5
Full Baths	4
Half Baths	I
First Ceiling	9'
Second Ceiling	8'
Max Ridge Height	33'6"
Roof Framing	Stick
Exterior Walls	2x4

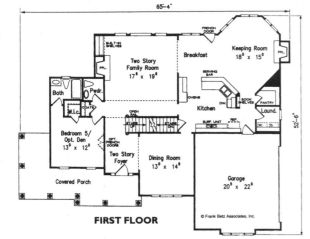

FIRST FLOOR

© Frank Betz Associates, Inc.

SECOND FLOOR

Units	Single
Price Code	D
Total Finished	2,089 sq. ft.
First Finished	1,146 sq. ft.
Second Finished	943 sq. ft.
Garage Unfinished	403 sq. ft.
Dimensions	56'x38'
Foundation	Basement
Bedrooms	3
Full Baths	2
Half Baths	I

FIRST FLOOR

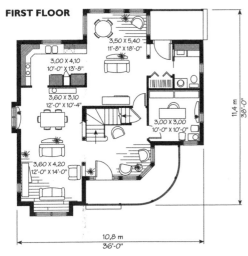

SECOND FLOOR

To order your Blueprints, call 1-800-235-5700

199

Units	Single
Price Code	I
Total Finished	3,460 sq. ft.
First Finished	2,497 sq. ft.
Second Finished	963 sq. ft.
Bonus Unfinished	307 sq. ft.
Basement Unfinished	2,497 sq. ft.
Garage Unfinished	654 sq. ft.
Dimensions	65'x62'9''
Foundation	Basement
	Crawlspace
Bedrooms	4
Full Baths	3
Half Baths	I
First Ceiling	9'
Second Ceiling	8'
Max Ridge Height	30'8''
Roof Framing	Stick
Exterior Walls	2x4

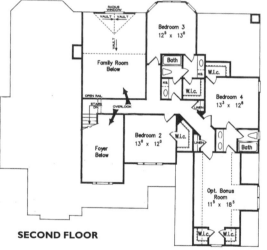

SECOND FLOOR

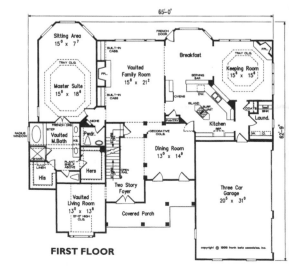

FIRST FLOOR

200

Rear Elevation

SECOND FLOOR

3,00 X 3,30
10'-0" X 11'-0"

OPEN TO BELOW

3,30 X 3,60
11'-0" X 12'-0"

BONUS ROOM
6,10 X 4,20
20'-4" X 14'-0"

4,20 X 3,00
14'-0" X 10'-0"

Units	Single
Price Code	E
Total Finished	2,300 sq. ft.
First Finished	1,620 sq. ft.
Second Finished	680 sq. ft.
Garage Unfinished	595 sq. ft.
Dimensions	56'x53'2''
Foundation	Basement
Bedrooms	3
Full Baths	2
Half Baths	1
Exterior Walls	2x6

FIRST FLOOR

4,50 X 4,50
15'-0" X 15'-0"

1,90 X 4,00
6'-4" X 13'-4"

3,30 X 3,60
11'-0" X 12'-0"

3,60 X 4,50
12'-0" X 15'-0"

4,10 X 3,00
13'-8" X 10'-0"

3,00 X 3,00
10'-0" X 10'-0"

6,90 X 6,30
23'-0" X 21'-0"

To order your Blueprints, call 1-800-235-5700

Units	Single
Price Code	E
Total Finished	2,478 sq. ft.
Main Finished	1,883 sq. ft.
Upper Finished	595 sq. ft.
Basement Unfinished	617 sq. ft.
Garage Unfinished	675 sq. ft.
Porch Unfinished	429 sq. ft.
Dimensions	48'x42'
Foundation	Basement
Bedrooms	3
Full Baths	2
Max Ridge Height	36'
Exterior Walls	2x6

* Alternate foundation options available at an additional charge.
Please call 1-800-235-5700 for more information.

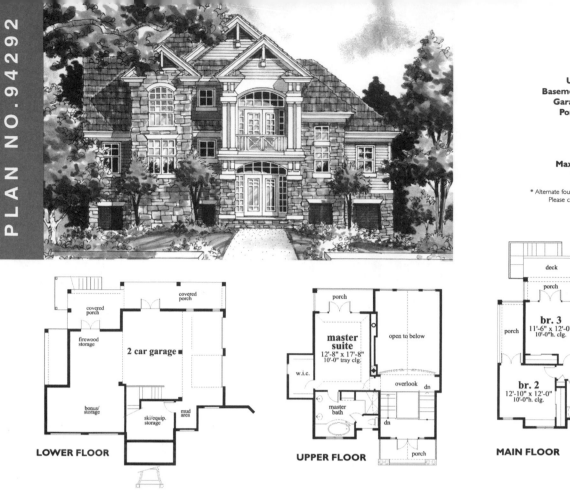

LOWER FLOOR

covered porch
covered porch
firewood storage
2 car garage
bonus/ storage
ski/equip. storage
mud area

UPPER FLOOR

porch
master suite
12'-8" x 17'-8"
10'-0" tray clg.
w.i.c.
open to below
overlook
dn
master bath
dn
porch

MAIN FLOOR

deck
covered porch
porch
br. 3
11'-6" x 12'-0"
10'-0"h. clg.
fireplace
great room
15'-0" x 19'-6"
vaulted clg.
dining
11'-0" x 12'-8"
11'-0" tray clg.
built ins
kitchen
11'-0" x 12'-0"
porch
br. 2
12'-10" x 12'-0"
10'-0"h. clg.
up
stor.
util.
up foyer
entry

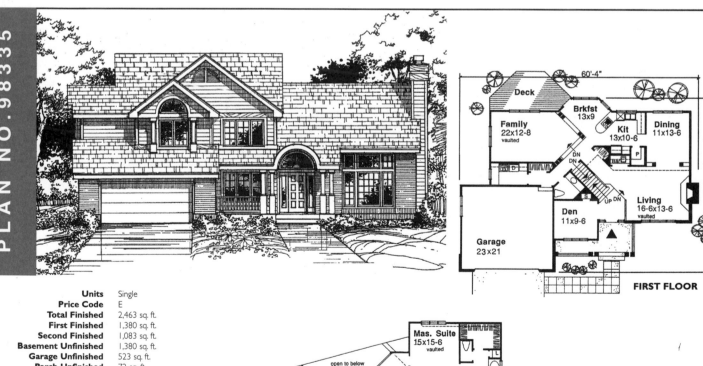

FIRST FLOOR

60'-4"
Deck
Brkfst 13x9
Family 22x12-8 vaulted
Kit 13x10-6
Dining 11x13-6
44'-0"
Den 11x9-6
Living 16-6x13-6 vaulted
Garage 23 x21

Units	Single
Price Code	E
Total Finished	2,463 sq. ft.
First Finished	1,380 sq. ft.
Second Finished	1,083 sq. ft.
Basement Unfinished	1,380 sq. ft.
Garage Unfinished	523 sq. ft.
Porch Unfinished	72 sq. ft.
Dimensions	60'4''x44'
Foundation	Basement
Bedrooms	4
Full Baths	2
Half Baths	1
Max Ridge Height	26'
Roof Framing	Truss
Exterior Walls	2x4

SECOND FLOOR

Mas. Suite 15x15-6 vaulted
open to below
DN
open to below
Br 4 10x11
Br 3 10x11-6
Br 2 11x15-6

To order your Blueprints, call 1-800-235-5700

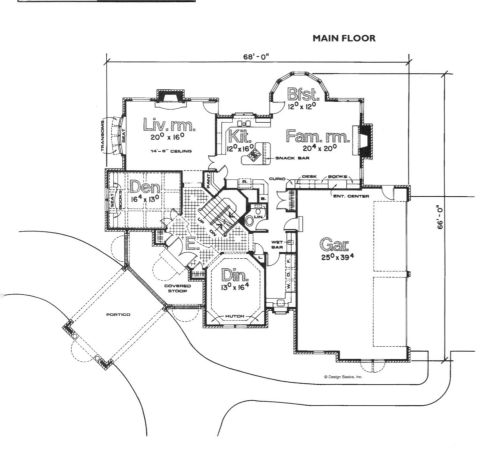

REAR ELEVATION

MAIN FLOOR

68'-0"

66'-0"

Liv. rm.
20⁰ x 16⁰
14'-8" CEILING

TRANSOMS

SEAT

Bfst.
12⁰ x 12⁰

Kit.
12⁰ x 16⁰

Fam. rm.
20⁴ x 20⁰

SNACK BAR

Den
16⁴ x 13⁰

SEAT

BOOKS

PANT.

CURIO   DESK   BOOKS

ENT. CENTER

LIN.

WET BAR

Gar.
25⁰ x 39⁴

Din.
13⁰ x 16⁴

COVERED
STOOP

HUTCH

PORTICO

© Design Basics, Inc.

Units	Single
Price Code	K
Total Finished	3,992 sq. ft.
Main Finished	2,040 sq. ft.
Second Finished	1,952 sq. ft.
Garage Unfinished	988 sq. ft.
Dimensions	68'x66'
Foundation	Basement
	Crawlspace
	Slab
Bedrooms	4
Full Baths	2
Half Baths	1
3/4 Baths	1
Main Ceiling	9'
Max Ridge Height	35'5"
Roof Framing	Stick
Exterior Walls	2x4

** Alternate foundation options available at an additional charge.
Please call 1-800-235-5700 for more information.*

Units	Single
Price Code	J
Total Finished	3,525 sq. ft.
First Finished	1,786 sq. ft.
Second Finished	1,739 sq. ft.
Basement Unfinished	1,786 sq. ft.
Garage Unfinished	704 sq. ft.
Dimensions	59'x53'
Foundation	Basement
	Crawlspace
Bedrooms	5
Full Baths	4
Half Baths	1
First Ceiling	9'
Second Ceiling	9'
Max Ridge Height	35'
Roof Framing	Stick
Exterior Walls	2x4

SECOND FLOOR

Sitting Room 10⁰ x 12⁰

Master Suite 18⁰ x 15⁰

Family Room Below

Bedroom 4 12⁰ x 12⁶

Vaulted M.Bath

Laund.

Bath

W.i.c.

Bedroom 2 13⁰ x 12⁴

Foyer Below

Bedroom 3 14⁴ x 12⁰

Hers

His

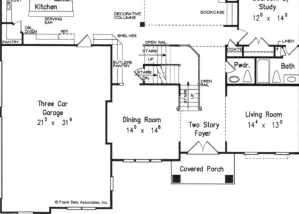

FIRST FLOOR

Breakfast

Kitchen

Two Story Family Room 16⁰ x 19³

Bedroom 5/ Study 12⁰ x 14⁰

Pantry

Three Car Garage 21⁵ x 31⁹

Dining Room 14⁰ x 14⁸

Two Story Foyer

Living Room 14⁴ x 13⁰

Pwdr.

Bath

Covered Porch

© Frank Betz Associates, Inc.

To order your Blueprints, call 1-800-235-5700

Rear Elevation

SECOND FLOOR

M.B.R.
TRAY CEILING
13'0" X 19'0"

OPEN TO BELOW

B.R. #2
21'10" X 13'0"

ART
NICHE

BR #3
CATHEDRAL CLG.
14'0" X 12'2"

BR #4
12'10" X 12'6"

OPEN TO BELOW

SHELVES

Units	Single
Price Code	J
Total Finished	3,688 sq. ft.
First Finished	2,065 sq. ft.
Second Finished	1,623 sq. ft.
Garage Unfinished	869 sq. ft.
Porch Unfinished	214 sq. ft.
Dimensions	82'x50'4"
Foundation	Basement
Bedrooms	4
Full Baths	2
Half Baths	2
3/4 Baths	1
First Ceiling	9'1 1/8"
Second Ceiling	9'1 1/8"
Max Ridge Height	27'
Roof Framing	Truss
Exterior Walls	2x6

FIRST FLOOR

SCREEN
PORCH
15'6" X 15'6"

NOOK
13'0" X 11'2"

FAM. RM.
2-STORY CEILING HGT.
21'0" X 14'4"

BUILT-IN
CABS.

DEN
14'6" X 13'0"

KIT.
21'0" X 14'4"

ISLAND

ARCH SOFFIT

BUILT-IN

DESK
BUILT-IN SHELVES

3 CAR GARAGE
23'0" X 40'0"

ART
NICH.

FAN.

LIV. RM.
12'-1 1/8" CEILING HGT.
13'4" X 15'4"

E.
2-STORY
CLG. HGT.

DIN. RM.
TRAY CEILING
13'0" X 16'2"

ARCH

Units	Single
Price Code	A
Total Finished	1,387 sq. ft.
Main Finished	1,387 sq. ft.
Porch	126 sq. ft.
Dimensions	44'8"x34'
Foundation	Basement
Bedrooms	2
Full Baths	1
Max Ridge Height	44'8"
Roof Framing	Truss
Exterior Walls	2x6

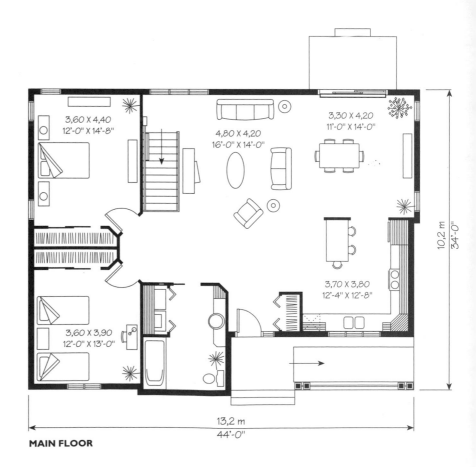

3,60 X 4,40
12'-0" X 14'-8"

4,80 X 4,20
16'-0" X 14'-0"

3,30 X 4,20
11'-0" X 14'-0"

3,70 X 3,80
12'-4" X 12'-8"

3,60 X 3,90
12'-0" X 13'-0"

10,2 m
34'-0"

13,2 m
44'-0"

MAIN FLOOR

Units	Single
Price Code	E
Total Finished	2,424 sq. ft.
First Finished	1,306 sq. ft.
Second Finished	1,118 sq. ft.
Garage Unfinished	576 sq. ft.
Dimensions	52'x46'
Foundation	Basement
Bedrooms	3
Full Baths	2
Half Baths	1

FIRST FLOOR

SECOND FLOOR

Units	Single
Price Code	I
Total Finished	3,395 sq. ft.
First Finished	2,467 sq. ft.
Second Finished	928 sq. ft.
Bonus Unfinished	296 sq. ft.
Basement Unfinished	2,467 sq. ft.
Garage Unfinished	566 sq. ft.
Dimensions	64'6"x62'10"
Foundation	Basement
	Crawlspace
	Slab
Bedrooms	4
Full Baths	3
Half Baths	1
First Ceiling	9'
Second Ceiling	8'
Max Ridge Height	32'8"
Roof Framing	Stick
Exterior Walls	2x4

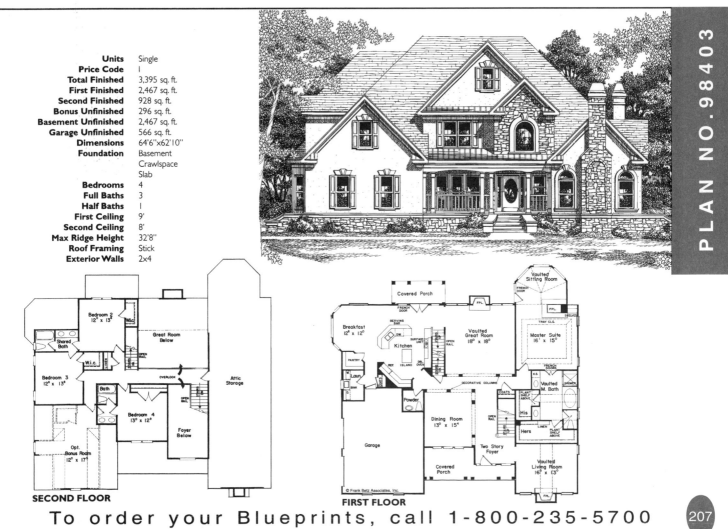

SECOND FLOOR

FIRST FLOOR

© Frank Betz Associates, Inc.

PLAN NO. 64147

Units	Single
Price Code	I
Total Finished	2,847 sq. ft.
First Finished	1,642 sq. ft.
Second Finished	1,205 sq. ft.
Bonus Unfinished	340 sq. ft.
Dimensions	53'7''x72'6''
Foundation	Crawlspace
Bedrooms	3
Full Baths	2
Half Baths	I
Exterior Walls	2x6

* Alternate foundation options available at an additional charge.
Please call 1-800-235-5700 for more information.

FIRST FLOOR

SECOND FLOOR

PLAN NO. 98406

Units	Single
Price Code	B
Total Finished	1,600 sq. ft.
First Finished	828 sq. ft.
Second Finished	772 sq. ft.
Basement Unfinished	828 sq. ft.
Garage Unfinished	473 sq. ft.
Dimensions	52'4''x34'
Foundation	Basement
	Crawlspace
	Slab
Bedrooms	3
Full Baths	2
Half Baths	I
First Ceiling	9'
Second Ceiling	8'
Max Ridge Height	28'
Roof Framing	Stick
Exterior Walls	2x4

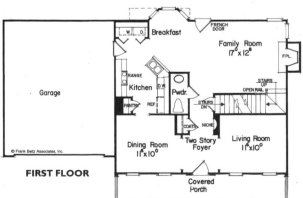

FIRST FLOOR

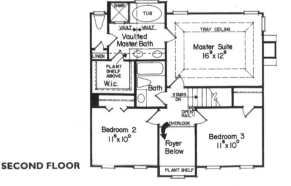

SECOND FLOOR

208

To order your Blueprints, call 1-800-235-5700

OPEN TO BELOW

BEDROOM 13'-0" x 16'-0"

BATH

DN

BONUS ROOM 13'-0" X 30'-0"

BALCONY

UPPER HALL

DN

LINEN

BATH

WIC

OPEN TO BELOW

BEDROOM 14'-0" x 13'-0"

SECOND FLOOR

Units	Single
Price Code	L
Total Finished	4,375 sq. ft.
First Finished	3,185 sq. ft.
Second Finished	1,190 sq. ft.
Bonus Unfinished	486 sq. ft.
Basement Unfinished	3,079 sq. ft.
Garage Unfinished	716 sq. ft.
Dimensions	102'x54'
Foundation	Basement
Bedrooms	3
Full Baths	3
Half Baths	2
First Ceiling	8'
Second Ceiling	8'
Max Ridge Height	36'
Roof Framing	Stick
Exterior Walls	2x6

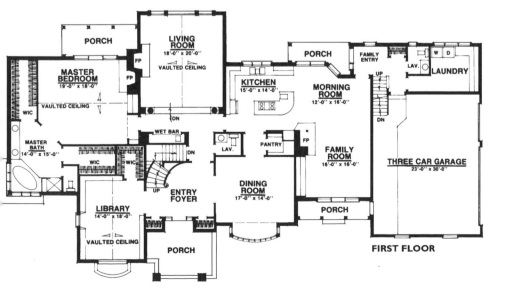

PORCH

LIVING ROOM 18'-0" x 20'-0" VAULTED CEILING

PORCH

FAMILY ENTRY

W D

LAV.

LAUNDRY

FP

MASTER BEDROOM 19'-0" x 18'-0"

KITCHEN 15'-0" x 14'-0"

MORNING ROOM 12'-0" x 16'-0"

UP

DN

VAULTED CEILING

WIC

DN

WET BAR

DN

LAV.

PANTRY

FP

MASTER BATH 14'-0" x 15'-0"

WIC

WIC

UP

ENTRY FOYER

FAMILY ROOM 16'-0" x 16'-0"

THREE CAR GARAGE 23'-0" x 30'-0"

DINING ROOM 17'-0" x 14'-0"

LIBRARY 14'-0" x 18'-0"

VAULTED CEILING

PORCH

PORCH

PORCH

FIRST FLOOR

Units	Single
Price Code	E
Total Finished	2,340 sq. ft.
First Finished	1,132 sq. ft.
Second Finished	1,208 sq. ft.
Basement Unfinished	1,132 sq. ft.
Garage Unfinished	514 sq. ft.
Dimensions	56'4"x39'6"
Foundation	Basement
	Crawlspace
	Slab
Bedrooms	4
Full Baths	2
Half Baths	1
First Ceiling	9'
Second Ceiling	8'
Primary Roof Pitch	12:12
Max Ridge Height	33'
Roof Framing	Stick
Exterior Walls	2x4

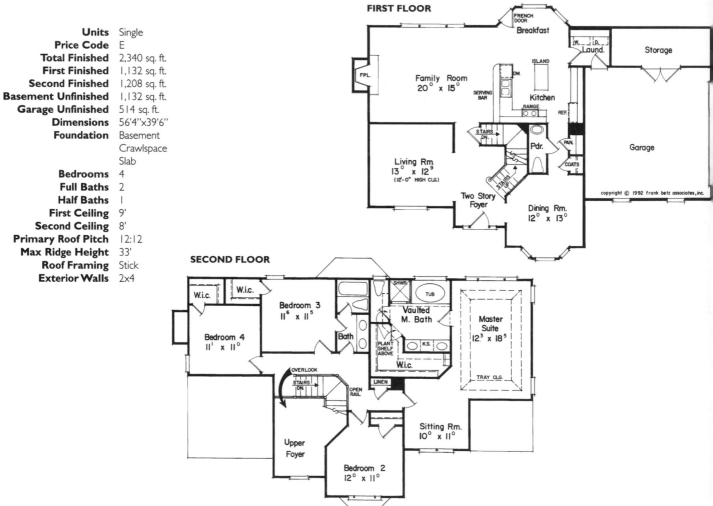

To order your Blueprints, call 1-800-235-5700

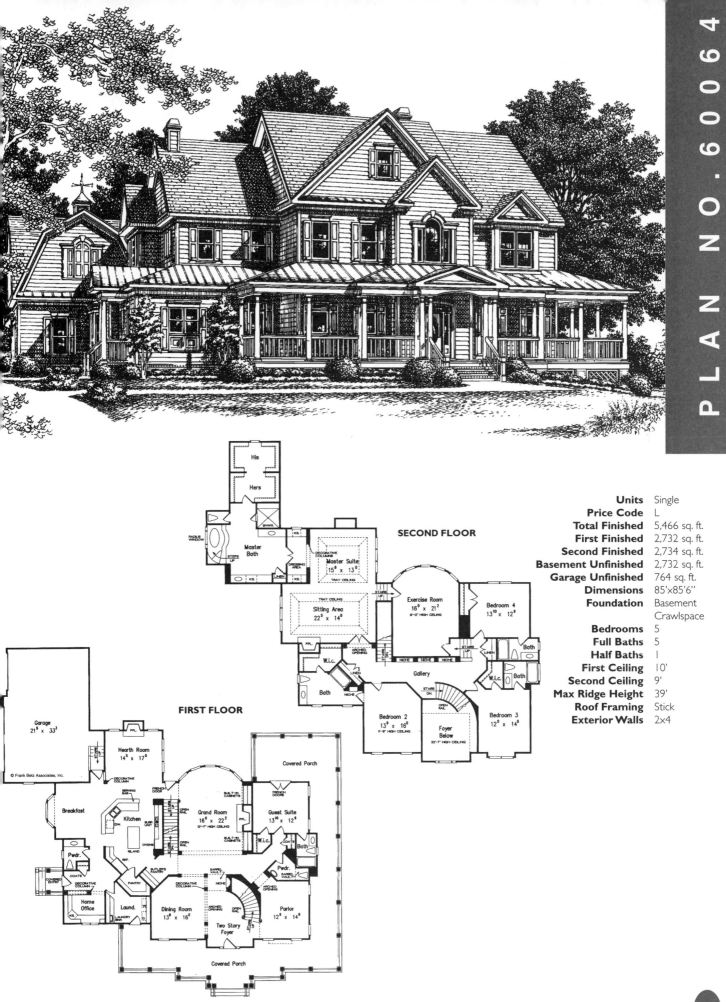

SECOND FLOOR

His

Hers

SHWR.

RADIUS WINDOW

Master Bath

STEPS UP

DRESSING AREA

KS.

KS.

KS.

LINEN

DECORATIVE COLUMNS

Master Suite
15⁹ x 13⁰
TRAY CEILING

TRAY CEILING

Sitting Area
22⁵ x 14⁰

FPL.

Exercise Room
16⁰ x 21²
9'-0" HIGH CEILING

STAIRS UP

Bedroom 4
13¹⁰ x 12⁰

Bath

W.I.c.

ARCHED OPENING

STAIRS DN.

NICHE NICHE NICHE

LINEN

STAIRS UP

Bath

W.I.c.

Bath

Gallery

LINEN

Bath

NICHE

STAIRS DN.

OPEN RAIL

Bedroom 2
13⁰ x 16⁰
11'-6" HIGH CEILING

Foyer Below
22'-7" HIGH CEILING

Bedroom 3
12⁰ x 14⁶

FIRST FLOOR

Garage
21⁸ x 33³

© Frank Betz Associates, Inc.

FPL.

Hearth Room
14⁵ x 17⁰

DECORATIVE COLUMN

Breakfast

SERVING BAR

FRENCH DOORS

DW.

Kitchen

ISLAND

OVENS

REF.

BUFF. UNIT

OPEN RAIL

OPEN RAIL

BUILT-IN CABINETS

Grand Room
16⁰ x 22²
12'-7" HIGH CEILING

FPL.

BUILT-IN CABINETS

FRENCH DOORS

Covered Porch

Guest Suite
13¹⁰ x 12⁰

W.i.c.

COATS

Bath

Pwdr.

COATS

BUTLER'S PANTRY

PANTRY

DECORATIVE COLUMN

BARREL VAULT

NICHE

Pwdr.

BARREL VAULT

ARCHED OPENING

COVERED ENTRY

Home Office

KS.

Laund.

LAUNDRY SINK

Dining Room
13⁰ x 16⁰

ARCHED OPENING

Two Story Foyer

OPEN RAIL

STAIRS

Parlor
12⁰ x 14⁶

Covered Porch

Units	Single
Price Code	L
Total Finished	5,466 sq. ft.
First Finished	2,732 sq. ft.
Second Finished	2,734 sq. ft.
Basement Unfinished	2,732 sq. ft.
Garage Unfinished	764 sq. ft.
Dimensions	85'x85'6''
Foundation	Basement
	Crawlspace
Bedrooms	5
Full Baths	5
Half Baths	1
First Ceiling	10'
Second Ceiling	9'
Max Ridge Height	39'
Roof Framing	Stick
Exterior Walls	2x4

To order your Blueprints, call 1-800-235-5700

211

Units	Single
Price Code	A
Total Finished	1,324 sq. ft.
First Finished	737 sq. ft.
Second Finished	587 sq. ft.
Dimensions	26'x33'
Foundation	Basement
Bedrooms	1
Full Baths	1
Half Baths	1

8.40 X 5.70
28'-0" X 19'-0"

**SECOND FLOOR
1 BEDROOM OPTION**

3,60 X 3,60
12'-0" X 12'-0"

3,60 X 4,20
12'-0" X 14'-0"

**SECOND FLOOR
2 BEDROOM OPTION**

2,40 X 2,70
8'-0" X 9'-0"

7.8 m
26'-0"

3,30 X 5,70
11'-0" X 19'-0"

4,20 X 4,80
14'-0" X 16'-0"

FIRST FLOOR

9,9 m
33'-0"

To order your Blueprints, call 1-800-235-5700

Units	Single
Price Code	J
Total Finished	3,618 sq. ft.
First Finished	2,602 sq. ft.
Second Finished	1,016 sq. ft.
Bonus Unfinished	238 sq. ft.
Basement Unfinished	2,602 sq. ft.
Garage Unfinished	680 sq. ft.
Dimensions	73'x61'6"
Foundation	Basement
	Crawlspace
Bedrooms	4
Full Baths	3
Half Baths	1
First Ceiling	9'
Second Ceiling	8'
Max Ridge Height	29'6"
Roof Framing	Stick
Exterior Walls	2x4

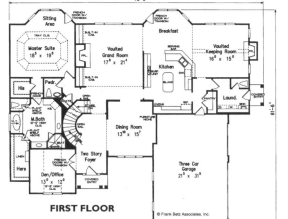

FIRST FLOOR

© Frank Betz Associates, Inc.

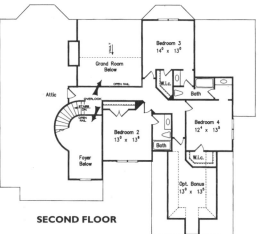

SECOND FLOOR

Units	Single
Price Code	H
Total Finished	2,374 sq. ft.
First Finished	1,510 sq. ft.
Second Finished	864 sq. ft.
Basement Unfinished	1,290 sq. ft.
Dimensions	44'x49'
Foundation	Basement
Bedrooms	3
Full Baths	3
Half Baths	1
Max Ridge Height	43'4"
Roof Framing	Truss
Exterior Walls	2x6

* Alternate foundation options available at an additional charge.
Please call 1-800-235-5700 for more information.

FIRST FLOOR

SECOND FLOOR

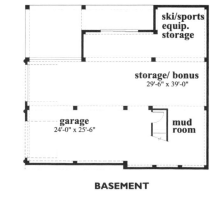

BASEMENT

To order your Blueprints, call 1-800-235-5700

Units	Single
Price Code	D
Total Finished	2,175 sq. ft.
First Finished	874 sq. ft.
Second Finished	1,301 sq. ft.
Garage Unfinished	528 sq. ft.
Dimensions	48'x40'
Foundation	Basement
Bedrooms	3
Full Baths	2
Half Baths	1

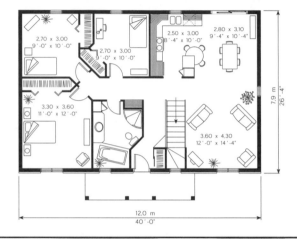

MAIN FLOOR

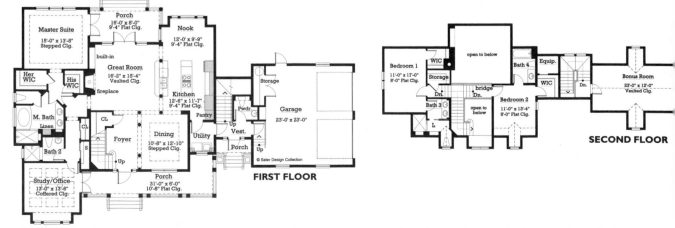

Units	Single
Price Code	I
Total Finished	2,581 sq. ft.
First Finished	1,842 sq. ft.
Second Finished	739 sq. ft.
Bonus Unfinished	379 sq. ft.
Porch Unfinished	241 sq. ft.
Dimensions	79'x50'
Foundation	Crawlspace
Bedrooms	3
Full Baths	4
Half Baths	1
Max Ridge Height	22'4''
Exterior Walls	2x6

* Alternate foundation options available at an additional charge.
Please call 1-800-235-5700 for more information.

FIRST FLOOR

SECOND FLOOR

To order your Blueprints, call 1-800-235-5700

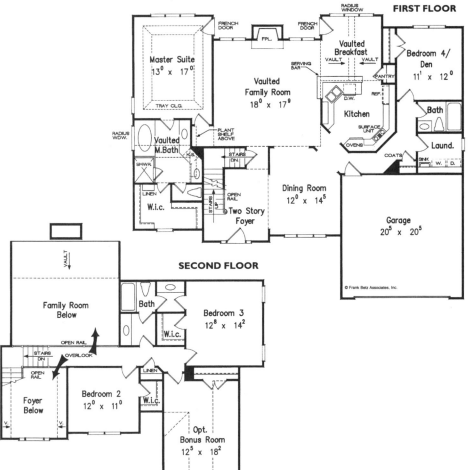

FIRST FLOOR

Master Suite
13⁰ x 17⁰

TRAY CLG.

FRENCH DOOR

FPL.

FRENCH DOOR

RADIUS WINDOW

Vaulted Breakfast

VAULT

VAULT

Bedroom 4/ Den
11¹ x 12⁰

SERVING BAR

PANTRY

Vaulted Family Room
18⁰ x 17⁹

Kitchen

D.W.

REF.

Bath

SURFACE UNIT

OVENS

Laund.

W. D.

COATS

SINK

RADIUS WDW.

Vaulted M.Bath

PLANT SHELF ABOVE

W.S.

STAIRS DN.

OPEN RAIL

SHWR.

LINEN

W.i.c.

STAIRS UP

Dining Room
12⁰ x 14⁵

Two Story Foyer

Garage
20⁵ x 20⁵

© Frank Betz Associates, Inc.

VAULT

SECOND FLOOR

Family Room Below

OPEN RAIL

OVERLOOK

STAIRS DN

OPEN RAIL

Foyer Below

V.

Bath

Bedroom 3
12⁸ x 14²

W.i.c.

LINEN

Bedroom 2
12⁰ x 11⁰

W.i.c.

Opt. Bonus Room
12⁵ x 18²

Units	Single
Price Code	E
Total Finished	2,349 sq. ft.
First Finished	1,761 sq. ft.
Second Finished	588 sq. ft.
Bonus Unfinished	267 sq. ft.
Basement Unfinished	1,761 sq. ft.
Garage Unfinished	435 sq. ft.
Dimensions	56'x47'6''
Foundation	Basement Crawlspace
Bedrooms	4
Full Baths	3
First Ceiling	9'
Second Ceiling	8'
Max Ridge Height	31'6''
Roof Framing	Stick
Exterior Walls	2x4

To order your Blueprints, call 1-800-235-5700

Units	Single
Price Code	A
Total Finished	1,257 sq. ft.
Garage Unfinished	384 sq. ft.
Dimensions	54'x35'8''
Foundation	Basement
Bedrooms	3
Full Baths	1
Half Baths	1
Roof Framing	Stick
Exterior Walls	2x6

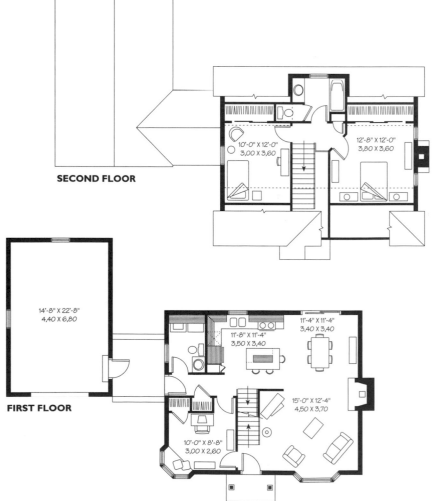

SECOND FLOOR

10'-0" X 12'-0"
3,00 X 3,60

12'-8" X 12'-0"
3,80 X 3,60

14'-8" X 22'-8"
4,40 X 6,80

FIRST FLOOR

11'-8" X 11'-4"
3,50 X 3,40

11'-4" X 11'-4"
3,40 X 3,40

10'-0" X 8'-8"
3,00 X 2,60

15'-0" X 12'-4"
4,50 X 3,70

To order your Blueprints, call 1-800-235-5700

SECOND FLOOR

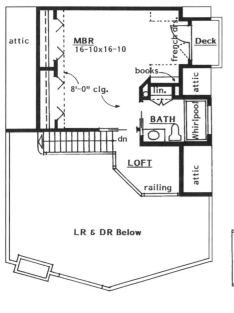

attic

MBR
16-10x16-10

Deck

books

french drs.

8'-0" clg.

lin.

attic

BATH

Whirlpool

dn

LOFT

attic

railing

LR & DR Below

FIRST FLOOR

BR 2
12-0x13-0

Pantry

frzr

Mud Rm/Utility

clos.

lt

W D

Bath

F

FOYER

Porch

up

stor

KITCHEN
12-4x12-0

dw

LR
15-0x18-6

DINING
12-0x12-0/9-9

Gas FP

Patio door

SUNDECK

Units	Single
Price Code	B
Total Finished	1,677 sq. ft.
First Finished	1,064 sq. ft.
Second Finished	613 sq. ft.
Porch Unfinished	32 sq. ft.
Dimensions	28'x40'
Foundation	Basement
	Crawlspace
Bedrooms	2
Full Baths	2
First Ceiling	8'
Second Ceiling	8'
Vaulted Ceiling	22'
Max Ridge Height	26'6"
Roof Framing	Stick
Exterior Walls	2x6

To order your Blueprints, call 1-800-235-5700

Units	Single
Price Code	G
Total Finished	2,940 sq. ft.
First Finished	2,044 sq. ft.
Second Finished	896 sq. ft.
Bonus Unfinished	197 sq. ft.
Basement Unfinished	2,044 sq. ft.
Garage Unfinished	544 sq. ft.
Dimensions	63'x54'
Foundation	Basement
	Crawlspace
	Slab
Bedrooms	4
Full Baths	3
Half Baths	1
First Ceiling	9'
Second Ceiling	8'
Max Ridge Height	31'4"
Roof Framing	Stick
Exterior Walls	2x4

SECOND FLOOR

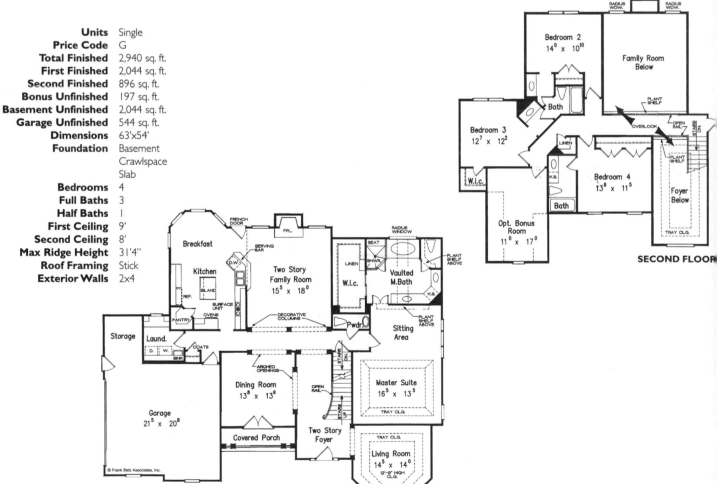

FIRST FLOOR

© Frank Betz Associates, Inc.

Units	Single
Price Code	D
Total Finished	2,044 sq. ft.
First Finished	1,203 sq. ft.
Second Finished	841 sq. ft.
Garage Unfinished	462 sq. ft.
Porch Unfinished	323 sq. ft.
Dimensions	56'x44'5''
Foundation	Slab
Bedrooms	3
Full Baths	3
First Ceiling	8'
Second Ceiling	8'
Vaulted Ceiling	16'
Max Ridge Height	28'9''
Roof Framing	Stick
Exterior Walls	2x4

SECOND FLOOR

CL **BEDR'M 2** 11'-9" X 10'-9" **BATH-2**

BEDR'M 3 12'-0" X 12'-7" CL

HALL **ATTIC** DN

PLAYROOM 18'-0" X 14'-0" CL

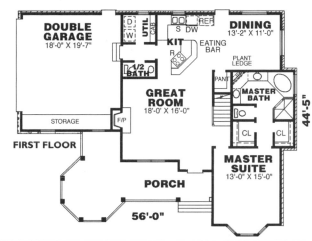

DOUBLE GARAGE 18'-0" X 19'-7"

UTIL D W · S DW REF · **DINING** 13'-2" X 11'-0"

KIT · EATING BAR · R · PLANT LEDGE

1/2 **BATH** · PANT

GREAT ROOM 18'-0" X 16'-0" · **MASTER BATH**

STORAGE · F/P · CL · CL

FIRST FLOOR · 44'-5"

MASTER SUITE 13'-0" X 15'-0"

PORCH

56'-0"

Units	Single
Price Code	G
Total Finished	1,928 sq. ft.
First Finished	1,383 sq. ft.
Second Finished	595 sq. ft.
Dimensions	48'x42'
Foundation	Basement
Bedrooms	3
Full Baths	2
Roof Pitch	10:12
Max Ridge Height	36'8''
Roof Framing	Truss
Exterior Walls	2x6

* Alternate foundation options available at an additional charge.
  Please call 1-800-235-5700 for more information.

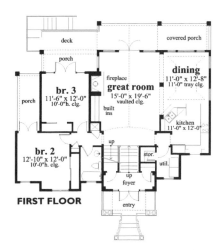

deck · covered porch

porch · fireplace · **dining** 11'-0" x 12'-8" 11'-0" tray clg.

br. 3 11'-6" x 12'-0" 10'-0"h. clg. · **great room** 15'-0" x 19'-6" vaulted clg. · built ins · **kitchen** 11'-0" x 12'-0"

porch · built ins

br. 2 12'-10" x 12'-0" 10'-0"h. clg. · up · stor. · util.

up foyer · entry

FIRST FLOOR

2 car garage

bonus/ storage · storage

© Sater Design Collection

LOWER FLOOR

porch

master suite 12'-8" x 17'-8" 10'-0" tray clg. · open to below

w.i.c. · overlook · dn

master bath · dn

porch

SECOND FLOOR

Units	Single
Price Code	D
Total Finished	2,082 sq. ft.
First Finished	1,218 sq. ft.
Second Finished	864 sq. ft.
Garage Unfinished	472 sq. ft.
Porch Unfinished	118 sq. ft.
Dimensions	44'x51'
Foundation	Crawlspace
	Slab
Bedrooms	3
Full Baths	2
Half Baths	1
First Ceiling	9'
Second Ceiling	8'
Max Ridge Height	28'
Roof Framing	Truss
Exterior Walls	2x4

SECOND FLOOR

ba 2

lin

br 2
11⁸ ×15

storage

plant shelf

br 3
16 ×12

dormers

9' ceiling

entertainment room
16⁸×20

FIRST FLOOR

morning rm
8 8×9

pan

mbr
15¹⁰×14

kitchen
8¹⁰ ×12¹⁰

lin

great room
15⁶×15¹⁰

oval tub

mba

w

coats

utility

9⁰ clgs

foyer

opt door

pwdr

dining
11⁶×10⁶

opt french door

opt wrap porch

garage
20×21⁴

porch

SECOND FLOOR

3,00 X 3,10
10'-0" X 10'-4"

2,80 X 3,90
9'-4" X 13'-0"

3,30 X 3,40
11'-0" X 11'-4"

3,90 X 4,30
13'-0" X 14'-4"

FIRST FLOOR

3,90 X 4,30
13'-0" X 14'-4"

3,50 X 3,90
11'-8" X 13'-0"

3,60 X 4,40
12'-0" X 14'-8"

2,20 X 4,40
7'-4" X 14'-8"

6,30 X 6,60
21'-0" X 22'-0"

3,90 X 4,30
13'-0" X 14'-4"

51'-0"

15,8 m
52'-8"

Units	Single
Price Code	E
Total Finished	2,333 sq. ft.
First Finished	1,472 sq. ft.
Second Finished	861 sq. ft.
Dimensions	52'8''x51'
Foundation	Basement
Bedrooms	4
Full Baths	2
Half Baths	I

To order your Blueprints, call 1-800-235-5700

221

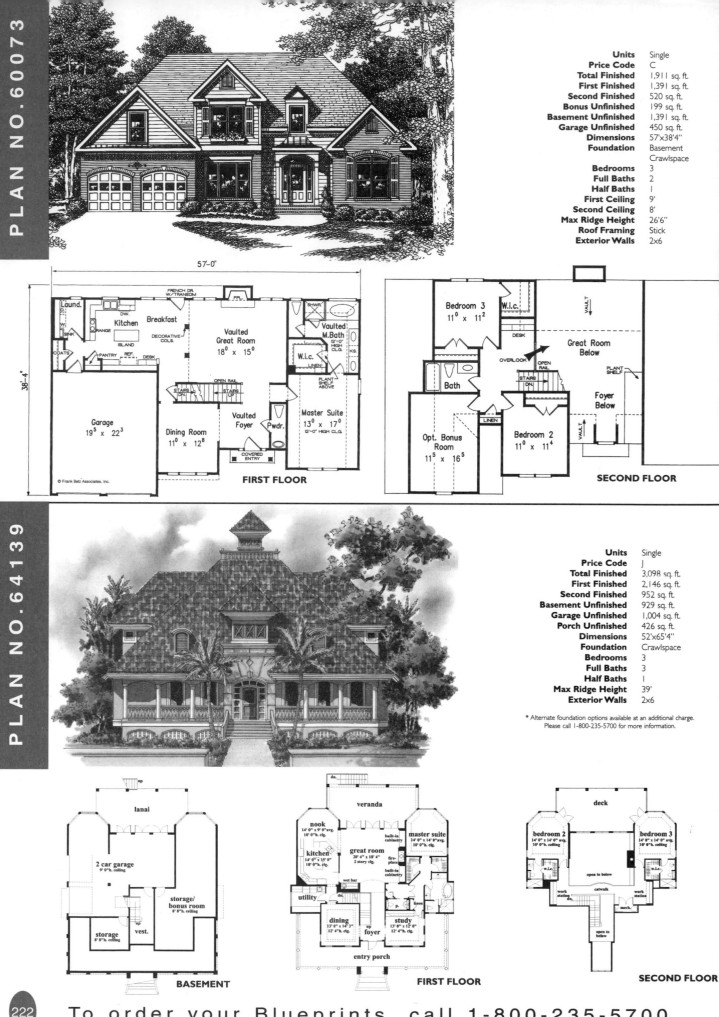

Units Single
Price Code C
Total Finished 1,911 sq. ft.
First Finished 1,391 sq. ft.
Second Finished 520 sq. ft.
Bonus Unfinished 199 sq. ft.
Basement Unfinished 1,391 sq. ft.
Garage Unfinished 450 sq. ft.
Dimensions 57'x38'4''
Foundation Basement
Crawlspace

Bedrooms 3
Full Baths 2
Half Baths 1
First Ceiling 9'
Second Ceiling 8'
Max Ridge Height 26'6''
Roof Framing Stick
Exterior Walls 2x6

57'-0"

38'-4"

Laund.
Kitchen
Breakfast
DW.
SINK RANGE
ISLAND
COATS PANTRY REF. DESK
FRENCH DR. W/TRANSOM
FP.
DECORATIVE COLS.
Vaulted Great Room 18⁰ x 15⁰
SHWR.
Vaulted M. Bath 12'-0" HIGH CLG.
KS.
W.i.c.
LINEN
PLANT SHELF ABOVE
OPEN RAIL
STAIRS DN STAIRS UP
Garage 19⁵ x 22³
Dining Room 11⁰ x 12⁸
Vaulted Foyer
Pwdr.
Master Suite 13⁰ x 17⁰ 12'-0" HIGH CLG.
COVERED ENTRY
© Frank Betz Associates, Inc.

FIRST FLOOR

Bedroom 3 11⁰ x 11²
W.i.c.
DESK
VAULT
Bath
OVERLOOK OPEN RAIL
STAIRS DN
Great Room Below
PLANT SHELF
Opt. Bonus Room 11⁵ x 16⁵
LINEN
Bedroom 2 11⁰ x 11⁴
VAULT
Foyer Below

SECOND FLOOR

Units Single
Price Code J
Total Finished 3,098 sq. ft.
First Finished 2,146 sq. ft.
Second Finished 952 sq. ft.
Basement Unfinished 929 sq. ft.
Garage Unfinished 1,004 sq. ft.
Porch Unfinished 426 sq. ft.
Dimensions 52'x65'4''
Foundation Crawlspace
Bedrooms 3
Full Baths 3
Half Baths 1
Max Ridge Height 39'
Exterior Walls 2x6

* Alternate foundation options available at an additional charge.
Please call 1-800-235-5700 for more information.

up
lanai
2 car garage 9' 0" h. ceiling
storage/ bonus room 8' 8" h. ceiling
storage 8' 8" h. ceiling
vest.

BASEMENT

dn.
veranda
nook 14' 0" x 9' 0" avg. 10' 0" h. clg.
kitchen 14' 0" x 15' 0" 10' 0" h. clg.
built-in cabinetry
master suite 14' 0" x 14' 0" avg. 10' 0" h. clg.
great room 20' 4" x 18' 4" 2 story clg.
fire-place
built-in cabinetry
wet bar
utility
dn.
dining 13' 0" x 14' 3" 12' 4" h. clg.
up foyer
study 13' 0" x 12' 0" 12' 4" h. clg.
p. linen
entry porch

FIRST FLOOR

deck
bedroom 2 14' 0" x 14' 0" avg. 10' 8" h. ceiling
bedroom 3 14' 0" x 14' 0" avg. 10' 8" h. ceiling
w.i.c.
w.i.c.
open to below
work station
catwalk
work station
stairs dn.
mech.
open to below

SECOND FLOOR

To order your Blueprints, call 1-800-235-5700

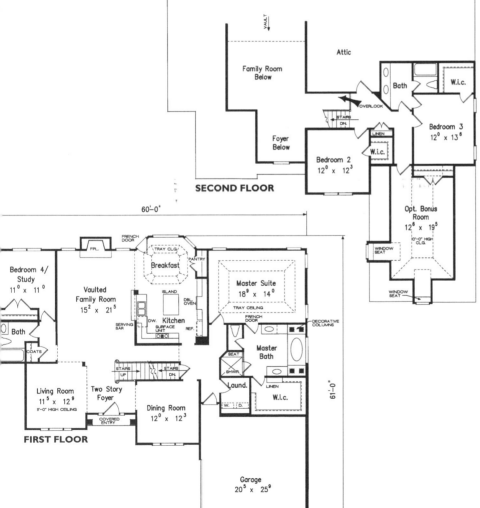

SECOND FLOOR

- Family Room Below
- Attic (VAULT)
- Bath
- W.i.c.
- Overlook
- STAIRS DN.
- Foyer Below
- LINEN
- W.i.c.
- Bedroom 2 12⁰ x 12³
- Bedroom 3 12⁰ x 13⁶
- Opt. Bonus Room 12⁶ x 19⁵ 10'-0" HIGH CLG.
- WINDOW SEAT

FIRST FLOOR

60'-0"

61'-0"

- Bedroom 4/ Study 11⁰ x 11⁰
- FRENCH DOOR
- FPL.
- TRAY CLG.
- PANTRY
- Breakfast
- ISLAND
- DBL. OVEN
- Vaulted Family Room 15² x 21⁵
- Master Suite 18⁹ x 14⁰
- TRAY CEILING
- Bath
- SERVING BAR
- DW.
- Kitchen SURFACE UNIT
- REF.
- FRENCH DOOR
- DECORATIVE COLUMNS
- COATS
- STAIRS UP
- STAIRS DN.
- Master Bath
- SEAT
- SHWR.
- Living Room 11⁵ x 12⁹ 11'-0" HIGH CEILING
- Two Story Foyer
- Laund.
- LINEN
- W.i.c.
- W. D.
- Dining Room 12⁰ x 13³
- COVERED ENTRY
- Garage 20⁵ x 25⁹

copyright © 1996 frank betz associates, inc.

Units	Single
Price Code	F
Total Finished	2,601 sq. ft.
First Finished	2,003 sq. ft.
Second Finished	598 sq. ft.
Bonus Unfinished	321 sq. ft.
Basement Unfinished	2,003 sq. ft.
Garage Unfinished	546 sq. ft.
Dimensions	60'x61'
Foundation	Basement
	Crawlspace
	Slab
Bedrooms	4
Full Baths	3
Max Ridge Height	31'6"
Roof Framing	Stick
Exterior Walls	2x4

Units	Single
Price Code	A
Total Finished	1,208 sq. ft.
First Finished	1,208 sq. ft.
Garage Unfinished	278 sq. ft.
Dimensions	41'x45'
Foundation	Basement
Bedrooms	1
Full Baths	1

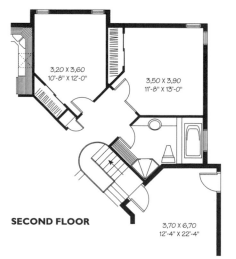

3,70 X 4,10
12'-4" X 13'-8"

4,20 X 3,90
14'-0" X 13'-0"

3,30 X 3,60
11'-0" X 12'-0"

4,10 X 4,80
13'-8" X 16'-0"

3,70 X 6,70
12'-4" X 22'-4"

FIRST FLOOR

3,20 X 3,60
10'-8" X 12'-0"

3,50 X 3,90
11'-8" X 13'-0"

SECOND FLOOR

3,70 X 6,70
12'-4" X 22'-4"

To order your Blueprints, call 1-800-235-5700

SECOND FLOOR

ATTIC

GREAT ROOM BELOW

ATTIC

BEDROOM-3
13'-5"
X 14'-5"

BALCONY

DN | LANDING | BATH-3

CL.

ENTRY BELOW

FUTURE GAME ROOM OR BEDROOM-4
20'-5" X 14'-5"

CL.

FIRST FLOOR

MASTER BATH (VAULTED)
S/L | S/L
CL. | CL.

MASTER SUITE
13'-0"
X 16'-0"

F/P

GREAT ROOM
21'-0" X 15'-0"
(VAULTED)

BRK.
10'-0"
X 12'-6"

OVENS
COOK TOP (ISLAND)
L/S
S.
D.W.

KIT.
10'-0". X 12'-6"
PANT | REF

LINE OF BALCONEY ABOVE

BATH-2

HALL

BEDROOM-2
10'-8"
X 11'-3"

CL.

COATS | LANDING

ENTRY (VAULTED)

UP

DINING
11'-0"
X 13'-0"

UTILITY
W | D | F

STORAGE

DOUBLE GARAGE
20'-0" X 20'-0"

PORCH

62'-4"

60'-10"

PLAN NO. 67004

Units	Single
Price Code	D
Total Finished	2,093 sq. ft.
First Finished	1,713 sq. ft.
Second Finished	381 sq. ft.
Bonus Unfinished	327 sq. ft.
Garage Unfinished	480 sq. ft.
Porch Unfinished	271 sq. ft.
Dimensions	62'4''x60'
Foundation	Crawlspace
	Slab
Bedrooms	3
Full Baths	2
Half Baths	I
First Ceiling	8'
Second Ceiling	8'
Max Ridge Height	20'
Roof Framing	Stick
Exterior Walls	2x4

PLAN NO. 98570

Units	Single
Price Code	H
Total Finished	3,115 sq. ft.
First Finished	2,132 sq. ft.
Second Finished	983 sq. ft.
Garage Unfinished	660 sq. ft.
Porch Unfinished	48 sq. ft.
Dimensions	69'x34'4''
Foundation	Slab
Bedrooms	3
Full Baths	2
Half Baths	I
Max Ridge Height	30'
Roof Framing	Stick
Exterior Walls	2x4

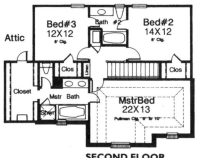

Attic

Bed#3
12X12
9' Clg.

Bath #2

Bed#2
14X12
8' Clg.

Clos | Linen | Clos

Closet

Mstr Bath

MstrBed
22X13
Pullman Clg. 9' to 10'

Shwr

SECOND FLOOR

3-Car Gar

Covered Patio

11X12
Kit

Brkfst
11X12
9' Clg.

Pwdr

LivRm
15X23
Hip Clg.

Pantry

Util
D | W

Study

FmlDin
14X14
9' Clg.

Ent

Cov Por

FIRST FLOOR

To order your Blueprints, call 1-800-235-5700

225

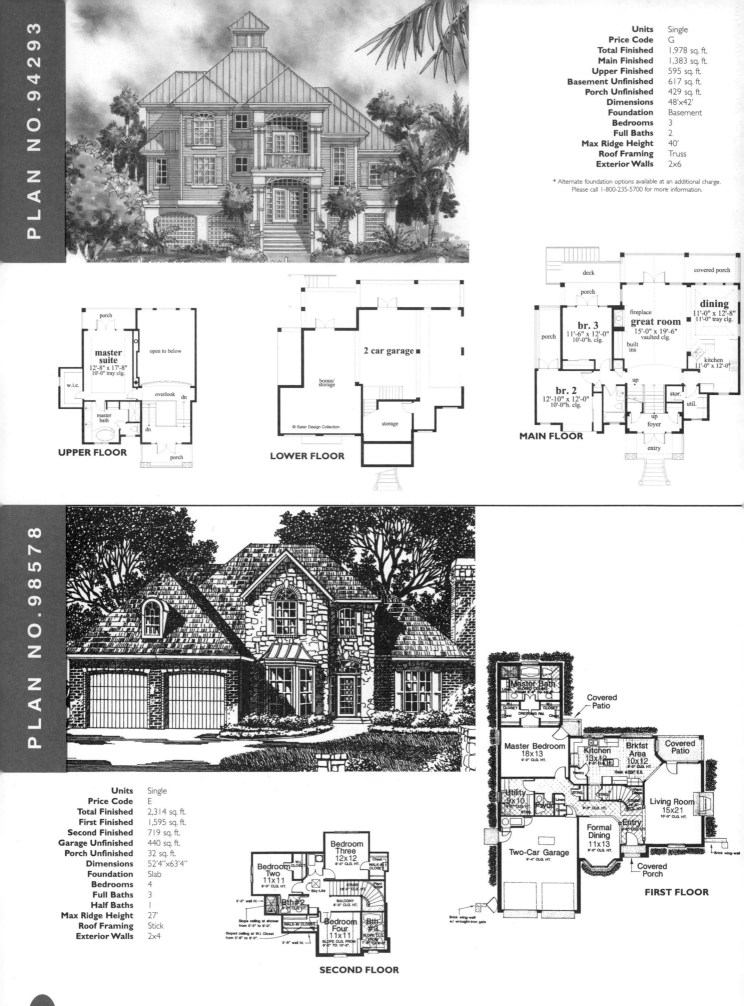

Units	Single
Price Code	G
Total Finished	1,978 sq. ft.
Main Finished	1,383 sq. ft.
Upper Finished	595 sq. ft.
Basement Unfinished	617 sq. ft.
Porch Unfinished	429 sq. ft.
Dimensions	48'x42'
Foundation	Basement
Bedrooms	3
Full Baths	2
Max Ridge Height	40'
Roof Framing	Truss
Exterior Walls	2x6

* Alternate foundation options available at an additional charge.
Please call 1-800-235-5700 for more information.

UPPER FLOOR

porch

master suite
12'-8" x 17'-8"
10'-0" tray clg.

w.i.c.

open to below

overlook

master bath

dn

dn

porch

LOWER FLOOR

2 car garage

bonus/ storage

storage

© Sater Design Collection

MAIN FLOOR

deck

covered porch

porch

fireplace

porch

br. 3
11'-6" x 12'-0"
10'-0"h. clg.

great room
15'-0" x 19'-6"
vaulted clg.

built ins

dining
11'-0" x 12'-8"
11'-0" tray clg.

kitchen
11'-0" x 12'-0"

br. 2
12'-10" x 12'-0"
10'-0"h. clg.

up

stor.

util.

up

foyer

entry

Units	Single
Price Code	E
Total Finished	2,314 sq. ft.
First Finished	1,595 sq. ft.
Second Finished	719 sq. ft.
Garage Unfinished	440 sq. ft.
Porch Unfinished	32 sq. ft.
Dimensions	52'4''x63'4''
Foundation	Slab
Bedrooms	4
Full Baths	3
Half Baths	1
Max Ridge Height	27'
Roof Framing	Stick
Exterior Walls	2x4

SECOND FLOOR

Bedroom Two
11x11
8'-0" CLG. HT.

Bedroom Three
12x12
8'-0" CLG. HT.

WALK-IN CLOSET

Bth#2

BALCONY
8'-0" CLG. HT.

Sky-Lite

5'-0" wall ht.

Slope ceiling at shower from 5'-0" to 8'-0".

Bedroom Four
11x11
SLOPE CLG. FROM 8'-0" to 10'-0".

Bth #3

Sloped ceiling at W.I. Closet from 5'-8" to 8'-0".

5'-8" wall ht.

FIRST FLOOR

Master Bath

Covered Patio

Master Bedroom
18x13
9'-0" CLG. HT.

Kitchen
13x12

Brkfst Area
10x12
8'-0" CLG. HT.

Covered Patio

Utility
9x10

Living Room
15x21
10'-0" CLG. HT.

Formal Dining
11x13
9'-0" CLG. HT.

Entry

Two-Car Garage
9'-4" CLG. HT.

Brick wing-wall

Covered Porch

Brick wing-wall w/ wrought-iron gate

To order your Blueprints, call 1-800-235-5700

SECOND FLOOR

Family Room Below

Bedroom 4
12⁰ x 13¹

PLANT SHELF ABOVE
SHWR
LINEN
Vaulted M. Bath
K.S.
W.c.
PLANT SHELF ABOVE

OPEN RAIL
STAIRS DN.
OPEN RAIL
Bath

Bedroom 2
13³ x 12⁵

OVERLOOK
Foyer Below

Bedroom 3
12³ x 11⁰

LIN.
W.c.

Master Suite
17⁹ x 13¹⁰

TRAY CLG.

ARCHED OPENING

Opt. Sitting Room

Units	Single
Price Code	F
Total Finished	2,608 sq. ft.
First Finished	1,351 sq. ft.
Second Finished	1,257 sq. ft.
Bonus Unfinished	115 sq. ft.
Basement Unfinished	1,351 sq. ft.
Garage Unfinished	511 sq. ft.
Dimensions	60'x46'4''
Foundation	Basement
Bedrooms	4
Full Baths	2
Half Baths	1
Max Ridge Height	36'
Roof Framing	Stick
Exterior Walls	2x4

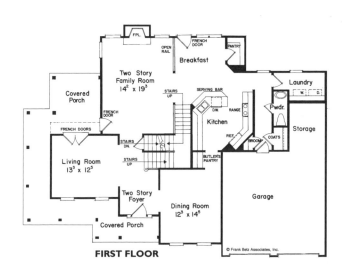

FIRST FLOOR

FPL
OPEN RAIL
FRENCH DOOR
Breakfast
PANTRY

Two Story Family Room
14² x 19³

Covered Porch

STAIRS UP
SERVING BAR
Laundry
W. D.

FRENCH DOOR
Kitchen
D.W.
RANGE
Pwdr.

FRENCH DOORS
Living Room
13³ x 12⁵

STAIRS DN.
STAIRS UP
BUTLER'S PANTRY
REF.
BROOM
COATS
Storage

Two Story Foyer

Dining Room
12³ x 14⁵

Garage

Covered Porch

© Frank Betz Associates, Inc.

Units	Single
Price Code	D
Total Finished	2,126 sq. ft.
First Finished	1,583 sq. ft.
Second Finished	543 sq. ft.
Bonus Unfinished	251 sq. ft.
Basement Unfinished	1,583 sq. ft.
Garage Unfinished	460 sq. ft.
Dimensions	53'x47'
Foundation	Basement
	Crawlspace
Bedrooms	4
Full Baths	3
First Ceiling	9'
Second Ceiling	8'
Max Ridge Height	31'6''
Roof Framing	Stick
Exterior Walls	2x4

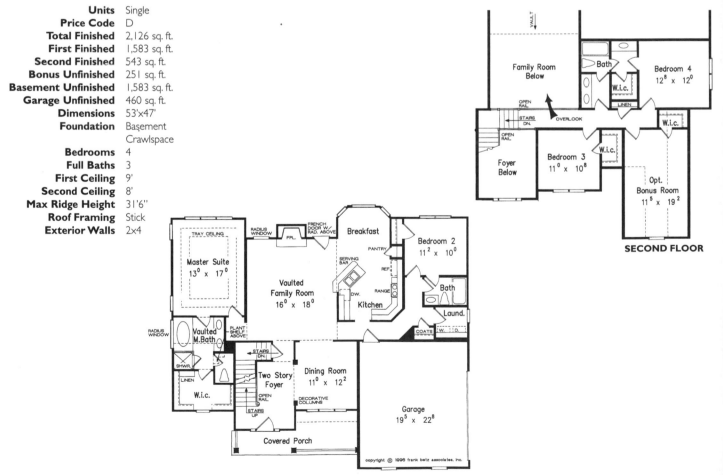

FIRST FLOOR

SECOND FLOOR

copyright © 1996 frank betz associates, inc.

To order your Blueprints, call 1-800-235-5700

FIRST FLOOR

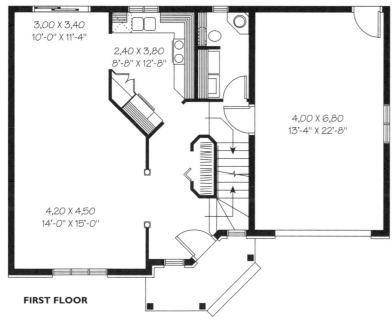

3,00 X 3,40
10'-0" X 11'-4"

2,40 X 3,80
8'-8" X 12'-8"

4,00 X 6,80
13'-4" X 22'-8"

4,20 X 4,50
14'-0" X 15'-0"

Units	Single
Price Code	A
Total Finished	1,404 sq. ft.
First Finished	702 sq. ft.
Second Finished	702 sq. ft.
Garage Unfinished	306 sq. ft.
Dimensions	40'x28'
Foundation	Basement
Bedrooms	3
Full Baths	1
Half Baths	1

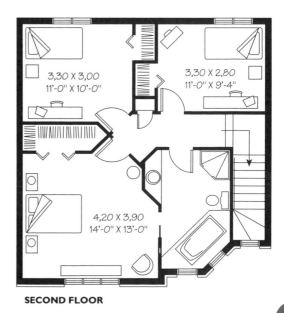

3,30 X 3,00
11'-0" X 10'-0"

3,30 X 2,80
11'-0" X 9'-4"

4,20 X 3,90
14'-0" X 13'-0"

SECOND FLOOR

To order your Blueprints, call 1-800-235-5700

Units	Single
Price Code	K
Total Finished	3,783 sq. ft.
First Finished	2,804 sq. ft.
Second Finished	979 sq. ft.
Basement Unfinished	2,804 sq. ft.
Garage Unfinished	802 sq. ft.
Dimensions	98'x45'10''
Foundation	Basement
	Slab
Bedrooms	4
Full Baths	3
Half Baths	1
Max Ridge Height	32'
Roof Framing	Stick
Exterior Walls	2x4

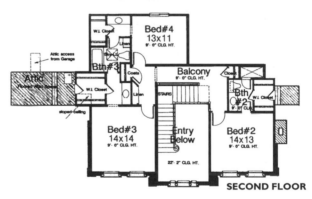

SECOND FLOOR

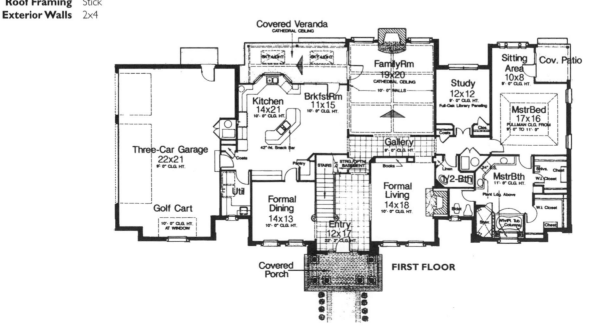

FIRST FLOOR

To order your Blueprints, call 1-800-235-5700

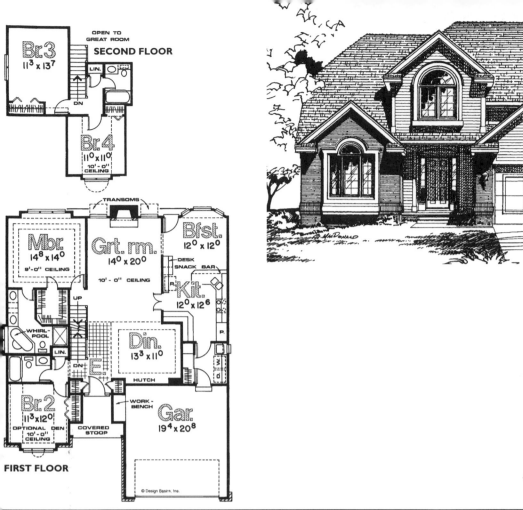

SECOND FLOOR

OPEN TO GREAT ROOM

Br. 3
11³ x 13⁷

Br. 4
11⁰ x 11⁰
10'-0" CEILING

LIN. DN

TRANSOMS

Mbr.
14⁸ x 14⁰
9'-0" CEILING

Grt. rm.
14⁰ x 20⁰
10'-0" CEILING

Bfst.
12⁰ x 12⁰

DESK
SNACK BAR

Kit.
12⁰ x 12⁶

UP

WHIRL-POOL

LIN.

Din.
13³ x 11⁰

DN

HUTCH

Br. 2
11³ x 12⁰
OPTIONAL DEN
10'-0" CEILING

WORK-BENCH

COVERED STOOP

Gar.
19⁴ x 20⁸

FIRST FLOOR

© Design Basics, Inc.

Units	Single
Price Code	C
Total Finished	1,948 sq. ft.
First Finished	1,517 sq. ft.
Second Finished	431 sq. ft.
Basement Unfinished	1,517 sq. ft.
Garage Unfinished	443 sq. ft.
Dimensions	42'x54'
Foundation	Basement
	Crawlspace
	Slab
Bedrooms	4
Full Baths	3
First Ceiling	8'
Second Ceiling	8'
Max Ridge Height	24'6"
Roof Framing	Stick
Exterior Walls	2x4

* Alternate foundation options available at an additional charge.
Please call 1-800-235-5700 for more information.

Units	Single
Price Code	I
Total Finished	2,513 sq. ft.
First Finished	1,542 sq. ft.
Second Finished	971 sq. ft.
Bonus Unfinished	747 sq. ft.
Garage Unfinished	663 sq. ft.
Porch Unfinished	330 sq. ft.
Dimensions	46'x51'
Foundation	Basement
Bedrooms	4
Full Baths	3
Max Ridge Height	39'4"
Roof Framing	Truss
Exterior Walls	2x6

* Alternate foundation options available at an additional charge.
Please call 1-800-235-5700 for more information.

bonus/storage

2 car garage

storage

storage

LOWER FLOOR

br. 2
11'-4" x 13'-0"
10'-0" h. clg.

covered porch

built ins

great room
19'-0" x 18'-0"
2-story clg.

fireplace

built ins

up

built ins

foyer

dining
12'-0" x 14'-0"
10'-0" h. clg.

kitchen
10'-8" x 13'-6"

butler pantry

util.

study
13'-4" x 12'-0"
vaulted clg.

entry porch

FIRST FLOOR

br. 3
11'-4" x 13'-0"
vaulted clg.

deck

open to below

sitting

overlook

dn

open

master suite
16'-0" x 14'-0"
vaulted clg.

dn

master bath

w.i.c.

© Sater Design Collection

SECOND FLOOR

To order your Blueprints, call 1-800-235-5700

231

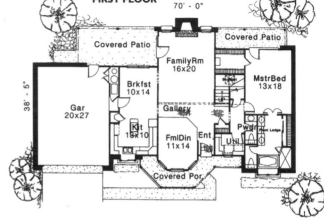

Units	Single
Price Code	E
Total Finished	2,272 sq. ft.
First Finished	1,572 sq. ft.
Second Finished	700 sq. ft.
Bonus Unfinished	202 sq. ft.
Dimensions	70'x38'5''
Foundation	Basement
	Crawlspace
	Slab
Bedrooms	3
Full Baths	2
Half Baths	1
First Ceiling	9'
Second Ceiling	8'
Max Ridge Height	26'
Roof Framing	Stick
Exterior Walls	2x4

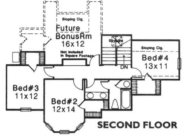

SECOND FLOOR

Future BonusRm 16x12
Not Included In Square Footage
Sloping Clg.
Bed #4 13x11
Sloping Clg.
DN
Bed#3 11x12
Bed#2 12x14

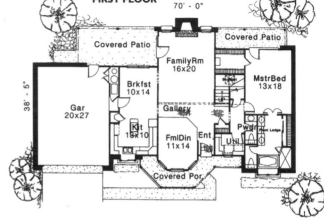

FIRST FLOOR 70' - 0"

38' - 5"

Covered Patio
Covered Patio
FamilyRm 16x20
MstrBed 13x18
Brkfst 10x14
Gar 20x27
Gallery
Kit 13x10
FmlDin 11x14
Ent
Pwdr
Covered Por.

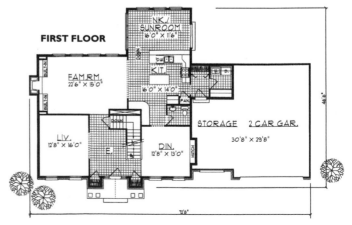

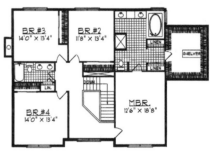

SECOND FLOOR

BR.#3 14'0" X 13'4"
BR.#2 11'8" X 13'4"
SHELVES
LINEN
LINEN
LIN.
BR.#4 14'0" X 13'4"
M.B.R. 12'6" X 18'8"

Units	Single
Price Code	H
Total Finished	3,124 sq. ft.
First Finished	1,632 sq. ft.
Second Finished	1,492 sq. ft.
Basement Unfinished	1,632 sq. ft.
Dimensions	72'8''x46'6''
Foundation	Basement
Bedrooms	4
Full Baths	2
Half Baths	1
Max Ridge Height	31'
Roof Framing	Truss
Exterior Walls	2x4

FIRST FLOOR

NK./ SUNROOM 16'0" X 11'6"
FAM.RM. 22'6" X 15'0"
KIT. 16'0" X 14'0"
PAN.
STORAGE
2 CAR GAR. 30'8" X 29'8"
LIV. 12'8" X 16'0"
DIN. 12'8" X 13'0"
72'8"

To order your Blueprints, call 1-800-235-5700

SECOND FLOOR

RAD. WDW.   RAD. WDW.
RAD. WDW.

Family Room Below

TRAY CEILING

W.i.c.
LINEN

Opt. Loft
12⁰ x 13⁰

Master Suite
18⁰ x 13⁰

SHELVES

PLANT SHELF ABOVE

OPEN RAIL
FRENCH DOORS

STAIRS DN.   STAIRS DN.   OVERLOOK

Foyer Below

LINEN

Vaulted Master Bath

SHWR.

Bath

K.S.

W.i.c.

RAD. WDW.

Bedroom 2
12⁰ x 13⁴

Bedroom 3
11⁰ x 13⁵

PLANT SHELF

FIRST FLOOR

FPL.

Den/Bedroom 4
12⁰ x 11²

Two Story Family Room
14⁰ x 18⁰

FRENCH DOOR

Breakfast

Kitchen

DW.

Laund. W.
D.

ISLAND

REF.

Bath   W.i.c.

STAIRS DN.

Pwdr.

COATS

SURFACE UNIT

DBL. OVENS

PANTRY

Vaulted Living Room
12⁰ x 12⁰

VLT.

Two Story Foyer

STAIRS

Dining Room
12⁰ x 13⁴

Garage
20⁵ x 22²

VLT.

Covered Porch

© Frank Betz Associates, Inc.

Units	Single
Price Code	E
Total Finished	2,430 sq. ft.
First Finished	1,415 sq. ft.
Second Finished	1,015 sq. ft.
Bonus Unfinished	169 sq. ft.
Basement Unfinished	1,415 sq. ft.
Garage Unfinished	471 sq. ft.
Dimensions	54'x43'4''
Foundation	Basement Crawlspace
Bedrooms	4
Full Baths	3
Half Baths	1
Max Ridge Height	30'
Roof Framing	Stick
Exterior Walls	2x4

Units	Single
Price Code	A
Total Finished	1,148 sq. ft.
First Finished	726 sq. ft.
Second Finished	420 sq. ft.
Bonus Unfinished	728 sq. ft.
Porch Unfinished	187 sq. ft.
Dimensions	28'x26'
Foundation	Basement
Bedrooms	1
Full Baths	1
Half Baths	1
First Ceiling	8'
Second Ceiling	8'
Max Ridge Height	29'8"
Exterior Walls	2x6

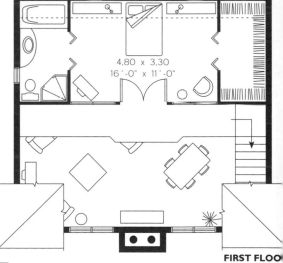

FIRST FLOOR

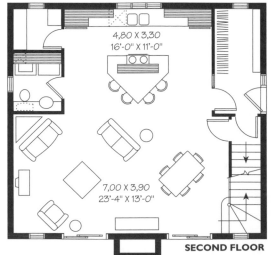

SECOND FLOOR

To order your Blueprints, call 1-800-235-5700

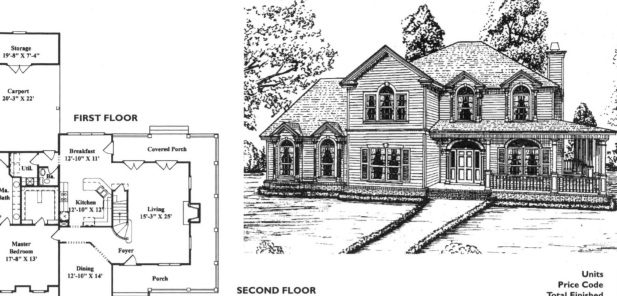

FIRST FLOOR

Storage 19'-8" X 7'-4"

Carport 20'-3" X 22'

Breakfast 12'-10" X 11'

Covered Porch

Util.

Ba.

Ma. Bath

Kitchen 12'-10" X 12'

Living 15'-3" X 25'

Master Bedroom 17'-8" X 13'

Foyer

Dining 12'-10" X 14'

Porch

SECOND FLOOR

Bedroom #2 12'-10" X 12'

Balcony

Bath

Bedroom #4 11'-6" X 14'

Unfinished Gameroom 17'-8" X 14'-8"

Bedroom #3 12'-10" X 13'

Bath

Units	Single
Price Code	G
Total Finished	2,852 sq. ft.
First Finished	1,730 sq. ft.
Second Finished	1,122 sq. ft.
Bonus Unfinished	270 sq. ft.
Porch Unfinished	553 sq. ft.
Dimensions	60'x67'6"
Foundation	Crawlspace
	Slab
Bedrooms	4
Full Baths	2
Half Baths	1
Max Ridge Height	32'10"
Roof Framing	Stick
Exterior Walls	2x4

SECOND FLOOR

M. Bath

Two Story Family Rm.

Bdrm.4 13-2 x 11-8

Bath 3

Master Bdrm. 15-8 x 15-8

Bdrm.2 11-6 x 13-6

Two Story Foyer

Bdrm.3 11-6 x 13-8

Bath 2

Sitting 6-0 x 9-8

FIRST FLOOR

Sundeck 18-0 x 12-0

Guest Bdrm. 12-2 x 10-0

Two Story Family Rm. 18-8 x 15-4

Brkfst. 10-10 x 11-10

Kit. 12-6 x 14-0

Ref.

Guest Bath

Pantry

Dbl. Garage 21-8 x 21-8

Living 11-4 x 13-4

Two Story Foyer 11-8 x 11-6

Dining 11-4 x 13-6

Oven

W. D.

©1998, Jannis Vann & Associates, Inc.

58-0

Units	Single
Price Code	H
Total Finished	3,140 sq. ft.
First Finished	1,553 sq. ft.
Second Finished	1,587 sq. ft.
Basement Unfinished	1,553 sq. ft.
Garage Unfinished	485 sq. ft.
Porch Unfinished	73 sq. ft.
Dimensions	58'x40'4"
Foundation	Basement
Bedrooms	5
Full Baths	4
First Ceiling	9'
Second Ceiling	8'
Max Ridge Height	34'
Roof Framing	Stick
Exterior Walls	2x4

Units	Single
Price Code	I
Total Finished	3,494 sq. ft.
First Finished	2,469 sq. ft.
Second Finished	1,025 sq. ft.
Bonus Unfinished	320 sq. ft.
Garage Unfinished	795 sq. ft.
Porch Unfinished	249 sq. ft.
Dimensions	67'8''x74'2''
Foundation	Basement
	Crawlspace
	Slab
Bedrooms	4
Full Baths	3
Half Baths	1
Max Ridge Height	31'
Roof Framing	Stick
Exterior Walls	2x4

Rear Elevation

SECOND FLOOR

FIRST FLOOR

To order your Blueprints, call 1-800-235-5700

SECOND FLOOR

Family Room Below

Bath

W.i.c.

Bedroom 3
12⁰ x 12⁰

STAIRS DN.

OPEN RAIL

OVERLOOK

STAIRS DN.

LINEN

W.i.c.

KS. DESK

Foyer Below

Bedroom 2
13⁰ x 12⁸

Bath

Bedroom 4
11⁴ x 12⁰

W.i.c.

Opt. Bonus
13⁰ x 16⁰

FIRST FLOOR

Sitting Area

TRAY CLG.

Master Suite
17¹⁰ x 20³

RAD. WDW.   FPL.   RAD. WDW.

FRENCH DOOR

VAULT   VAULT

Vaulted Keeping Room
15⁰ x 13⁰

Porch

FRENCH DOOR

FPL.

Vaulted Family Room
15⁰ x 19⁶

STAIRS UP

OPEN RAIL

SURFACE UNIT

SERVING BAR

Breakfast

PLANT SHELF ABOVE   LINEN   His

SHWR

KS.

BARREL VAULT

COATS

NICHE

Kitchen

DW

Vaulted M.Bath

Hers

STAIRS DN.

OPEN RAIL

DECORATIVE COLUMNS

Dining Room
13⁰ x 15⁵

REF.   OVEN

PANTRY   Pwdr.   SINK   W.   Laund.

Living Room
13⁰ x 13⁰
12'-0" HIGH CLG.

Two Story Foyer

ARCHED OPENINGS

Garage
20⁵ x 22³

© Frank Betz Associates, Inc.

Units	Single
Price Code	H
Total Finished	3,147 sq. ft.
First Finished	2,302 sq. ft.
Second Finished	845 sq. ft.
Bonus Unfinished	247 sq. ft.
Basement Unfinished	2,302 sq. ft.
Garage Unfinished	500 sq. ft.
Dimensions	64'x59'4''
Foundation	Basement
	Crawlspace
Bedrooms	4
Full Baths	3
Half Baths	1
First Ceiling	9'
Second Ceiling	8'
Max Ridge Height	34'
Roof Framing	Stick
Exterior Walls	2x4

Units	Single
Price Code	F
Total Finished	2,560 sq. ft.
First Finished	1,250 sq. ft.
Second Finished	1,166 sq. ft.
Lower Finished	144 sq. ft.
Basement Unfinished	1,106 sq. ft.
Garage Unfinished	528 sq. ft.
Dimensions	64'x52'
Foundation	Basement
Bedrooms	4
Full Baths	2
Half Baths	1
First Ceiling	9'
Second Ceiling	8'
Max Ridge Height	30'
Roof Framing	Stick
Exterior Walls	2x4

FIRST FLOOR

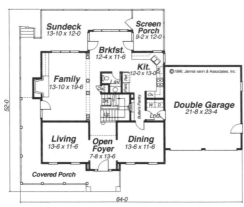

SECOND FLOOR

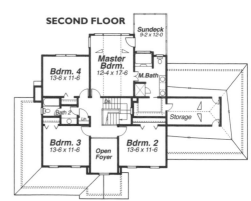

FIRST FLOOR

Units	Single
Price Code	F
Total Finished	2,588 sq. ft.
First Finished	1,423 sq. ft.
Second Finished	1,165 sq. ft.
Bonus Unfinished	250 sq. ft.
Basement Unfinished	1,423 sq. ft.
Dimensions	60'4"x46'
Foundation	Basement
Bedrooms	3
Full Baths	2
Half Baths	1
Max Ridge Height	30'5"
Roof Framing	Truss
Exterior Walls	2x6

SECOND FLOOR

To order your Blueprints, call 1-800-235-5700

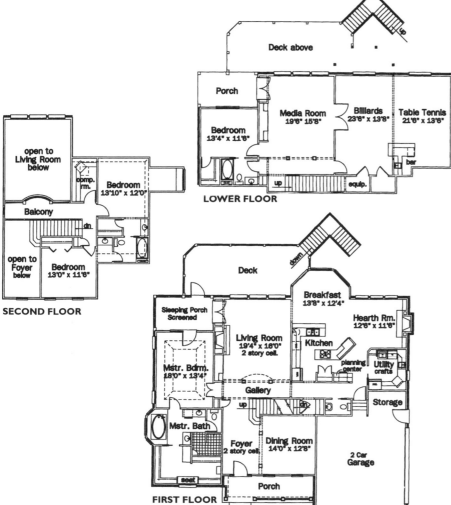

LOWER FLOOR

Deck above

Porch

Bedroom
13'4" x 11'6"

Media Room
19'6" 15'8"

Billiards
23'6" x 13'8"

Table Tennis
21'6" x 13'6"

bar

up

equip.

SECOND FLOOR

open to
Living Room
below

comp.
rm.

Bedroom
13'10" x 12'0"

Balcony

dn

open to
Foyer
below

Bedroom
13'0" x 11'6"

FIRST FLOOR

Deck

down

Breakfast
13'8" x 12'4"

Sleeping Porch
Screened

Living Room
19'4" x 16'0"
2 story ceil.

Kitchen

Hearth Rm.
12'6" x 11'6"

Mstr. Bdrm.
18'0" x 13'4"

planning
center

Utility
crafts

Gallery

up

Storage

Mstr. Bath

dn

Foyer
2 story ceil.

Dining Room
14'0" x 12'8"

2 Car
Garage

seat

Porch

Units	Single
Price Code	L
Total Finished	4,224 sq. ft.
First Finished	2,180 sq. ft.
Second Finished	672 sq. ft.
Lower Finished	1,372 sq. ft.
Garage Unfinished	578 sq. ft.
Porch Unfinished	357 sq. ft.
Dimensions	60'10''×58'2''
Foundation	Basement
Bedrooms	4
Full Baths	3
Half Baths	1
Roof Framing	Stick
Exterior Walls	2x4

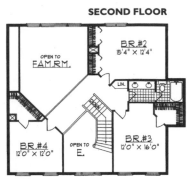

SECOND FLOOR

Units	Single
Price Code	G
Total Finished	2,751 sq. ft.
First Finished	1,888 sq. ft.
Second Finished	863 sq. ft.
Basement Unfinished	1,888 sq. ft.
Dimensions	86'x39'
Foundation	Basement
Bedrooms	4
Full Baths	2
Half Baths	1
First Ceiling	9'
Second Ceiling	8'
Max Ridge Height	32'6''
Roof Framing	Truss
Exterior Walls	2x6

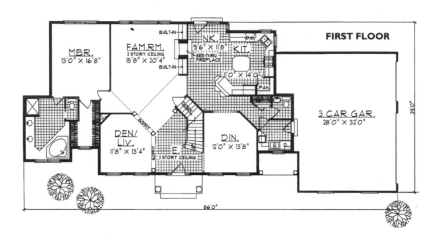

FIRST FLOOR

Units	Single
Price Code	F
Total Finished	2,513 sq. ft.
First Finished	1,887 sq. ft.
Second Finished	626 sq. ft.
Dimensions	69'4''x53'
Foundation	Basement
Bedrooms	3
Full Baths	2
Half Baths	1
Max Ridge Height	30'
Roof Framing	Truss
Exterior Walls	2x6

FIRST FLOOR

SECOND FLOOR

Units	Single
Price Code	B
Total Finished	1,564 sq. ft.
Garage Unfinished	336 sq. ft.
Dimensions	50'×39'
Foundation	Basement
Bedrooms	2
Full Baths	2

SECOND FLOOR

3,30 X 3,60
11'-0" X 12'-0"

4,30 X 3,50
14'-4" X 11'-8"

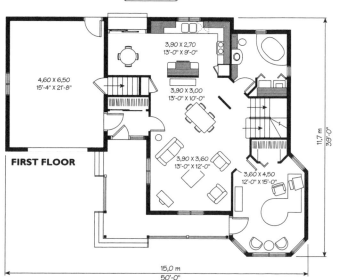

FIRST FLOOR

4,60 X 6,50
15'-4" X 21'-8"

3,90 X 2,70
13'-0" X 9'-0"

3,90 X 3,00
13'-0" X 10'-0"

3,90 X 3,60
13'-0" X 12'-0"

3,60 X 4,50
12'-0" X 15'-0"

11,7 m
39'-0"

15,0 m
50'-0"

To order your Blueprints, call 1-800-235-5700

PLAN NO. 97219

Units	Single
Price Code	D
Total Finished	2,128 sq. ft.
First Finished	1,257 sq. ft.
Second Finished	871 sq. ft.
Bonus Unfinished	444 sq. ft.
Basement Unfinished	1,275 sq. ft.
Garage Unfinished	462 sq. ft.
Dimensions	61'x40'6''
Foundation	Basement Crawlspace
Bedrooms	4
Full Baths	3
Half Baths	1
Max Ridge Height	32'
Roof Framing	Stick
Exterior Walls	2x4

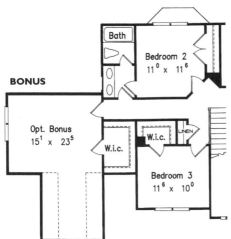

To order your Blueprints, call 1-800-235-5700

242

FIRST FLOOR

Garage 21'-8" X 23'-4"

Patio

Bath

Porch

Util

Living 19'-6" X 20'-6"

Bedroom 17'-4" X 17'

Kit

Breakfast 10' X 13'-6"

Ba

Bedroom 11'-10" X 15'

Dining 14' X 11'-8"

Foyer

Bedroom 12'-4" X 13'-6"

Porch 40' X 6'

SECOND FLOOR

Bath

Bedroom 13'-2" X 15'-9"

Units	Single
Price Code	F
Total Finished	2,732 sq. ft.
First Finished	2,346 sq. ft.
Second Finished	386 sq. ft.
Garage Unfinished	530 sq. ft.
Porch Unfinished	436 sq. ft.
Dimensions	60'10"x73'5"
Foundation	Crawlspace
	Slab
Bedrooms	4
Full Baths	3
First Ceiling	9'
Second Ceiling	8'
Max Ridge Height	26'
Roof Framing	Stick
Exterior Walls	2x4

Units	Single
Price Code	E
Total Finished	2,427 sq. ft.
First Finished	1,292 sq. ft.
Second Finished	1,135 sq. ft.
Bonus Unfinished	316 sq. ft.
Basement Unfinished	1,292 sq. ft.
Garage Unfinished	470 sq. ft.
Dimensions	65'x41'8"
Foundation	Basement
	Crawlspace
	Slab
Bedrooms	4
Full Baths	2
Half Baths	1
First Ceiling	9'
Max Ridge Height	30'
Roof Framing	Stick
Exterior Walls	2x8

OPT. STUDIO 21' X 12'

BEDRM-2 12'-6" X 11'-4"

BEDRM-4 10' X 12'

BALC.

BEDRM-3 11'-2" X 11'-8"

W. I. C.

W. I. C.

WHIRLPOOL TUB

ROOF BELOW

MASTER SUITE 18' X 12' TRAY CLG.

SECOND FLOOR

TERRACE

2-CAR GARAGE 20'-8" X 20'-8"

FAMILY RM 15' X 12'

BRKFST RM 10' X 11'-6"

KIT. 10' X 12'

PASS-THRU

LNDRY. RM

LAV.

FOYER

DINING RM 14' X 11'

PORCH

LIVING RM 18' X 14'

FIRST FLOOR

To order your Blueprints, call 1-800-235-5700

Units	Single
Price Code	E
Total Finished	2,375 sq. ft.
First Finished	1,770 sq. ft.
Second Finished	605 sq. ft.
Basement Unfinished	1,770 sq. ft.
Garage Unfinished	460 sq. ft.
Dimensions	78'x37'
Foundation	Basement
Bedrooms	3
Full Baths	2
Half Baths	1
Max Ridge Height	25'
Roof Framing	Stick
Exterior Walls	2x4

SECOND FLOOR

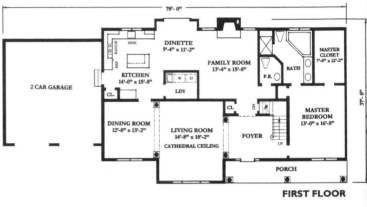

FIRST FLOOR

FIRST FLOOR

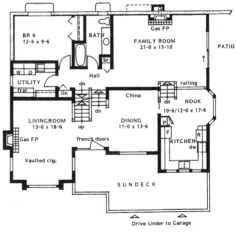

Units	Single
Price Code	H
Total Finished	2,630 sq. ft.
First Finished	739 sq. ft.
Second Finished	785 sq. ft.
Lower Finished	1,106 sq. ft.
Garage Unfinished	528 sq. ft.
Porch Unfinished	63 sq. ft.
Dimensions	44'x43'
Foundation	Basement
Bedrooms	3
Full Baths	3
First Ceiling	8'
Second Ceiling	8'
Vaulted Ceiling	13'6''
Max Ridge Height	28'
Roof Framing	Truss
Exterior Walls	2x4

SECOND FLOOR

To order your Blueprints, call 1-800-235-5700

SECOND FLOOR

- Mbr. 13⁰ x 13⁰ — 9'-0" CLG.
- WHIRLPOOL
- LIN
- DN
- Br. 2 10⁰ x 10⁰
- Br. 3 10⁰ x 10⁰

FIRST FLOOR

- Bfst. 10⁰ x 14⁰
- Kit. 9⁴ x 10⁰
- SNACK BAR
- Din. 10⁰ x 10⁴ — 10'-0" CLG.
- TRANSOMS
- Fam. rm. 14³ x 14³
- BOOKS
- W. D.
- Liv. rm. 13⁰ x 15⁰ — 10'-0" CEILING
- UP
- Gar. 19³ x 22³
- COVERED STOOP
- TRANSOMS
- 46'-0"
- 40'-0"
- © Design Basics, Inc.

Units	Single
Price Code	B
Total Finished	1,699 sq. ft.
First Finished	964 sq. ft.
Second Finished	735 sq. ft.
Basement Unfinished	964 sq. ft.
Garage Unfinished	452 sq. ft.
Dimensions	40'x46'
Foundation	Basement Crawlspace Slab
Bedrooms	3
Full Baths	2
Half Baths	I
First Ceiling	8'
Max Ridge Height	25'
Roof Framing	Stick
Exterior Walls	2x4,2x6

* Alternate foundation options available at an additional charge.
Please call 1-800-235-5700 for more information.

FIRST FLOOR

- BR 4 10-10 x 10-8
- Patio
- FAMILY ROOM 15-10 x 14-4
- up
- lin
- Bath
- Storage
- brm hw furn
- GARAGE 12-0 x 22-4
- railing
- up
- Foyer
- STUDY 10-0 x 12-2
- Porch

SECOND FLOOR

- MBR 12-0 x 13-0
- ENS.
- BR 2 9-4 x 10-0/13-0
- lin brm
- W.I.C.
- W D
- dn
- Bath
- BR 3 10-6 x 10-0
- Utility
- railing
- P F R
- KITCHEN 10-0x10-6
- dw
- dn
- Gas FP
- ½ wall
- LIVINGROOM 12-0 x 16-0
- DINING 10-0 x 11-0
- NOOK 8-6 x 9-0
- SUNDECK

Units	Single
Price Code	D
Total Finished	2,244 sq. ft.
First Finished	972 sq. ft.
Second Finished	1,272 sq. ft.
Garage Unfinished	270 sq. ft.
Porch Unfinished	80 sq. ft.
Dimensions	32'x45'6''
Foundation	Slab
Bedrooms	3
Full Baths	2
First Ceiling	8'
Second Ceiling	8'
Max Ridge Height	36'
Roof Framing	Truss
Exterior Walls	2x6

To order your Blueprints, call 1-800-235-5700

Units	Single
Price Code	H
Total Finished	3,094 sq. ft.
First Finished	2,112 sq. ft.
Second Finished	982 sq. ft.
Basement Unfinished	2,112 sq. ft.
Garage Unfinished	650 sq. ft.
Dimensions	67'1"x65'10.1"
Foundation	Basement
	Slab
Bedrooms	4
Full Baths	3
Half Baths	1
First Ceiling	9'
Max Ridge Height	30'4"
Roof Framing	Stick
Exterior Walls	2x4

* Alternate foundation options available at an additional charge.
  Please call 1-800-235-5700 for more information.

To order your Blueprints, call 1-800-235-5700

Everything you need...to Make Your Dream Come True!

Exterior Elevations

Scaled drawings of the front, rear, sides of the home. Information pertaining to the exterior finish materials, roof pitches and exterior height dimensions.

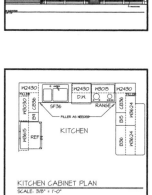

Cabinet Plans

These plans, or in some cases elevations, will detail the layout of the kitchen and bathroom cabinets at a larger scale. Available for most plans.

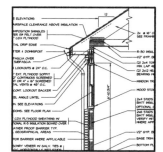

Typical Wall Section

This section will address insulation, roof components and interior and exterior wall finishes. Your plans will be designed with either 2x4 or 2x6 exterior walls, but most professional contractors can easily adapt the plans to the wall thickness you require.

Fireplace Details

If the home you have chosen includes a fireplace, the fireplace detail will show typical methods to construct the firebox, hearth and flue chase for masonry units, or a wood frame chase for a zero-clearance unit. Available for most plans.

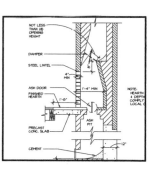

Foundation Plan

These plans will accurately dimension the footprint of your home including load bearing points and beam placement if applicable. The foundation style will vary from plan to plan.

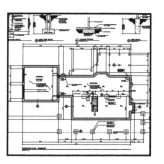

Roof Plan

The information necessary to construct the roof will be included with your home plans. Some plans will reference roof trusses, while many others contain schematic framing plans. These framing plans will indicate the lumber sizes necessary for the rafters and ridgeboards based on the designated roof loads.

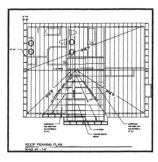

Typical Cross-Section

A cut-away cross-section through the entire home shows your building contractor the exact correlation of construction components at all levels of the house. It will help to clarify the load bearing points from the roof all the way down to the basement. Available for most plans.

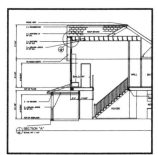

Detailed Floor Plans

The floor plans of your home accurately dimension the positioning of all walls, doors, windows, stairs and permanent fixtures. They will show you the relationship and dimensions of rooms, closets and traffic patterns. The schematic of the electrical layout may be included in the plan.

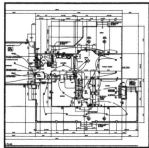

Stair Details

If stairs are an element of the design you have chosen, the plans will show the necessary information to build these, either through a stair cross-section or on the floor plans.

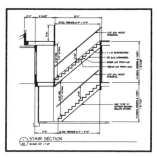

Garlinghouse Options & Extras

Reversed Plans Can Make Your Dream Home Just Right!

You could have exactly the home you want by flipping it end-for-end. Simply order your plans "reversed." We'll send you one full set of mirror-image plans (with the writing backwards) as a master guide for you and your builder.

The remaining sets of your order will come as shown in this book so the dimensions and specifications are easily read on the job site...but most plans in our collection come stamped "reversed" so there is no confusion.

As Shown   Reversed

We can only send reversed plans with multiple-set orders. There is a $50 charge for this service.

Some plans in our collection are available in Right Reading Reverse. Right Reading Reverse plans will show your home in reverse, with the writing on the plan being readable. This easy-to-read format will save you valuable time and money. Please contact our Customer Service Department to check for Right Reading Reverse availability. There is a $135 charge for Right Reading Reverse. **RRR**

Remember To Order Your Materials List

Available at a modest additional charge, the Materials List gives the quantity, dimensions, and specifications for the major materials needed to build your home. You will get faster, more accurate bids from your contractors and building suppliers — and avoid paying for unused materials and waste. Materials Lists are available for all home plans except as otherwise indicated, but can only be ordered with a set of home plans. Due to differences in regional requirements and homeowner or builder preferences... electrical, plumbing and heating/air conditioning equipment specifications are not designed specifically for each plan. **ML**

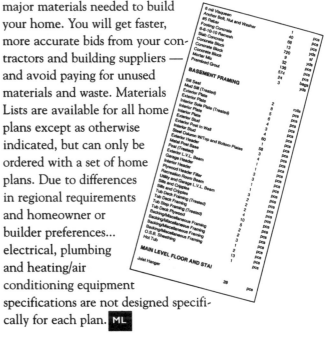

What Garlinghouse Offers

Home Plan Blueprint Package

By purchasing a multiple set package of blueprints or a vellum from Garlinghouse, you not only receive the physical blueprint documents necessary for construction, but you are also granted a license to build one, and only one, home. You can also make simple modifications, including minor non-structural changes and material substitutions to our design, as long as these changes are made directly on the blueprints purchased from Garlinghouse and no additional copies are made.

Home Plan Vellums

By purchasing vellums for one of our home plans, you receive the same construction drawings found in the blueprints, but printed on vellum paper. Vellums can be erased and are perfect for making design changes. They are also semi-transparent making them easy to duplicate. But most importantly, the purchase of home plan vellums comes with a broader license that allows you to make changes to the design (ie, create a hand drawn or CAD derivative work), to make copies of the plan and to build one home from the plan.

License To Build Additional Homes

With the purchase of a blueprint package or vellums you automatically receive a license to build one home and only one home, respectively. If you want to build more homes than you are licensed to build through your purchase of a plan, then additional licenses may be purchased at reasonable costs from Garlinghouse. Inquire for more information.

Modify Your Favorite Design, Made Easy

#1 Modifying Your Garlinghouse Home Plan

Simple modifications to your dream home, including minor non-structural changes and material substitutions, can be made between you and your builder by marking the changes directly on your blueprints. However, if you are considering making significant changes to your chosen design, we recommend that you use the services of The Garlinghouse Design Staff. We will help take your ideas and turn them into a reality, just the way you want. Here's our procedure!

When you place your Vellum order, you may also request a free Garlinghouse Modification Kit. In this kit, you will receive a red marking pencil, furniture cut-out sheet, ruler, a self addressed mailing label and a form for specifying any additional notes or drawings that will help us understand your design ideas. Mark your desired changes directly on the Vellum drawings. NOTE: Please use only a **red pencil** to mark your desired changes on the Vellum. Then, return the redlined Vellum set in the original box to us.

Important: Please roll the Vellums for shipping, ***do not fold***.

We also offer modification estimates. We will provide you with an estimate to draft your changes based on your specific modifications before you purchase the vellums, for a $50 fee. After you receive your estimate, if you decide to have us do the changes, the $50 estimate fee will be deducted from the cost of your modifications. If, however, you choose to use a different service, the $50 estimate fee is non-refundable. (Note: Personal checks cannot be accepted for the estimate.)

Within 5 days of receipt of your plans, you will be contacted by a member of the design staff with an estimate for the design services to draw those changes. A 50% deposit is required before we begin making the actual modifications to your plans.

Once the design changes have been completed to your vellum plan, a representative will call to inform you that your modified Vellum plan is complete and will be shipped as soon as the final payment has been made. For additional information call us at 1-860-659-5667. Please refer to the Modification Pricing Guide for estimated modification costs.

#2 Reproducible Vellums for Local Modification Ease

If you decide not to use Garlinghouse for your modifications, we recommend that you follow our same procedure of purchasing Vellums. You then have the option of using the services of the original designer of the plan, a local professional designer, or architect to make the modifications.

With a Vellum copy of our plans, a design professional can alter the drawings just the way you want, then you can print as many copies of the modified plans as you need to build your house. And, since you have already started with our complete detailed plans, the cost of those expensive professional services will be significantly less than starting from scratch. Refer to the price schedule for Vellum costs.

Ignoring Copyright Laws Can Be A $100,000 Mistake

"How to obtain a construction cost calculation based on labor rates and building material costs in your Zip Code area!"

Why? Do you wish you could quickly find out the building cost for your new home without waiting for a contractor to compile hundreds of bids? Would you like to have a benchmark to compare your contractor(s) bids against? Well, Now You Can!, with Zip-Quote Home Cost Calculator. Zip-Quote is only available for zip code areas within the United States.

How? Our Zip-Quote Home Cost Calculator will enable you to obtain the calculated building cost to construct your new home, based on labor rates and building material costs within your zip code area without the normal delays or hassles usually associated with the bidding process. Zip-Quote can be purchased in two separate formats, an itemized or a bottom line format.

"How does Zip-Quote actually work?" When you call to order, you must choose from the options available for your specific home, in order for us to process your order. Once we receive your Zip-Quote order, we process your specific home plan building materials list through our Home Cost Calculator which contains up-to-date rates for all residential labor trades and building material costs in your zip code area. "The result?" A calculated cost to build your dream home in your zip code area. This calculation will help you (as a consumer or a builder) evaluate your building budget.

All database information for our calculations is furnished by Marshall & Swift L.P. For over 60 years, Marshall & Swift L.P. has been a leading provider of cost data to professionals in all aspects of the construction and remodeling industries.

Option 1- The **Itemized Zip-Quote** is a detailed building material list. Each building material list line item will separately state the labor cost, material cost and equipment cost (if applicable) for the use of that building material in the construction process. This building materials list will be summarized by the individual building categories and will have additional columns where you can enter data from your contractor's estimates for a cost comparison between the different suppliers and contractors who will actually quote you their products and services.

Option 2- The **Bottom Line Zip-Quote** is a one line summarized total cost for the home plan of your choice. This cost calculation is also based on the labor cost, material cost and equipment cost (if applicable) within your local zip code area. Bottom Line Zip-Quote is available for most plans. Please call for availability.

Cost The price of your Itemized Zip-Quote is based upon the pricing schedule of the plan you have selected, in addition to the price of the materials list. Please refer to the pricing schedule on our order form. The price of your initial Bottom Line Zip-Quote is $29.95. Each additional Bottom Line Zip-Quote ordered in conjunction with the initial order is only $14.95. Bottom Line Zip-Quote may be purchased separately and does NOT have to be purchased in conjunction with a home plan order.

FYI An Itemized Zip-Quote Home Cost Calculation can ONLY be purchased in conjunction with a Home Plan order. The Itemized Zip-Quote can not be purchased separately. If you find within 60 days of your order date that you will be unable to build this home, you may then exchange the plans and the materials list towards the price of a new set of plans (see order info pages for plan exchange policy). The Itemized Zip-Quote and the Bottom Line Zip-Quote are NOT returnable. The price of the initial Bottom Line Zip-Quote order can be credited towards the purchase of an Itemized Zip-Quote order, only if available. Additional Bottom Line Zip-Quote orders, within the same order can not be credited. Please call our Customer Service Department for more information. **ZIP**

An Itemized Zip-Quote is available for plans where you see this symbol. **BL**

A Bottom-line Zip-Quote is available for all plans under 4,000 sq. ft. or where you see this symbol.

Please call for current availability.

Some More Information The Itemized and Bottom Line Zip-Quotes give you approximated costs for constructing the particular house in your area. These costs are not exact and are only intended to be used as a preliminary estimate to help determine the affordability of a new home and/or as a guide to evaluate the general competitiveness of actual price quotes obtained through local suppliers and contractors. However, Zip-Quote cost figures should never be relied upon as the only source of information in either case. **Land, landscaping, sewer systems, site work, contractor overhead and profit and other expenses are not included in our building cost figures. Excluding land and landscaping, you may incur an additional 20% to 40% in costs from the original estimate.** Garlinghouse and Marshall & Swift L.P. can not guarantee any level of data accuracy or correctness in a Zip-Quote and disclaim all liability for loss with respect to the same, in excess of the original purchase price of the Zip-Quote product. All Zip-Quote calculations are based upon the actual blueprints and do not reflect any differences or options that may be shown on the published house renderings, floor plans or photographs.

the Garlinghouse company

Order Form

BEST PLAN VALUE IN THE INDUSTRY!

Plan prices guaranteed until 2/2/03 After this date call for updated pricing

_____ foundation

_____ set(s) of blueprints for plan #_____ $_____

_____ Vellum & Modification kit for plan #_____ $_____

_____ Additional set(s) @ $50 each for plan #_____ $_____

_____ Mirror Image Reverse @ $50 each $_____

_____ Right Reading Reverse @ $135 each $_____

_____ Materials list for plan #_____ $_____

_____ Detail Plans @ $19.95 each

    ❑ Construction ❑ Plumbing ❑ Electrical $_____

_____ Bottom line ZIP Quote@$29.95 for plan #_____ $_____

_____ Additional Bottom Line Zip Quote

    @ $14.95 for plan(s) #_____ $_____

Zip Code where building _____

_____ Itemized ZIP Quote for plan(s) #_____ $_____

Shipping $_____

Subtotal $_____

Sales Tax *(CT residents add 6% sales tax)* $_____

TOTAL AMOUNT ENCLOSED $_____

Send your check, money order or credit card information to:
(No C.O.D.'s Please)

Please submit all United States & Other Nations orders to:
Garlinghouse Company
174 Oakwood Drive
Glastonbury, CT. 06033
CALL: (800) 235-5700   FAX: (860) 659-5692

Please Submit all Canadian plan orders to:
Garlinghouse Company
102 Ellis Street
Penticton, BC V2A 4L5
CALL: (800) 361-7526   FAX: (250) 493-7526

ADDRESS INFORMATION:

NAME: _____

STREET: _____

CITY: _____

STATE: _____ **ZIP:** _____

DAYTIME PHONE: _____

EMAIL ADDRESS: _____

Credit Card Information

Charge To:	❑ Visa	❑ Mastercard

Card # | | | | | | | | | | | | | | | | |

Signature _____ Exp. _____ / _____

Privacy Statement (please read)

Dear Valued Garlinghouse Customer,

Your privacy is extremely important to us. We'd like to take a little of your time to explain our privacy policy.

As a service to you, we would like to provide your name to companies such as the following:

- Building material manufacturers that we are affiliated with. Who would like to keep you current with their product line and specials.
- Building material retailers who would like to offer you competitive prices to help you save money.
- Financing companies who would like to offer you competitive mortgage rates.

In addition, as our valued customer, we would like to send you newsletters to assist your building experience. *We* would appreciate your feedback with a customer service survey to improve our operations.

You have total control over the use of your contact information. You can let us know exactly how you want to be contacted. Please check all boxes that apply. Thank you.

  ❑ Don't mail
  ❑ Don't call
  ❑ Don't email
  ❑ Only send Garlinghouse newsletters and customer
  ❑ service surveys

In closing, Garlinghouse is committed to providing superior customer service and protection of your privacy. We thank you for your time and consideration.

Sincerely,

James D. McNair III
CEO

VISA

For Our USA Customers:
Order Toll Free — 1-800-235-5700
Monday-Friday 8:00 a.m. to 8:00 p.m. Eastern Time
or FAX your Credit Card order to 1-860-659-5692
All foreign residents call 1-860-659-5667

For Our Canadian Customers:
Order Toll Free — 1-800-361-7526
Monday-Friday 8:00 a.m. to 5:00 p.m. Pacific Time
or FAX your Credit Card order to 1-250-493-7526
Customer Service: 1-250-493-0942

Please have ready: 1. Your credit card number   2. The plan number   3. The order code number   ➪ **H22S4**

Garlinghouse 2002 Blueprint Price Code Schedule

	1 Set	4 Sets	8 Sets	Vellums	ML	Itemized ZIP Quote
A	$345	$385	$435	$525	$60	$50
B	$375	$415	$465	$555	$60	$50
C	$410	$450	$500	$590	$60	$50
D	$450	$490	$540	$630	$60	$50
E	$495	$535	$585	$675	$70	$60
F	$545	$585	$635	$725	$70	$60
G	$595	$635	$685	$775	$70	$60
H	$640	$680	$730	$820	$70	$60
I	$685	$725	$775	$865	$80	$70
J	$725	$765	$815	$905	$80	$70
K	$765	$805	$855	$945	$80	$70
L	$800	$840	$890	$980	$80	$70

Shipping — (Plans 1-59999)	1-3 Sets	4-6 Sets	7+ & Vellums
Standard Delivery (UPS 2-Day)	$25.00	$30.00	$35.00
Overnight Delivery	$35.00	$40.00	$45.00

Shipping — (Plans 60000-99999)	1-3 Sets	4-6 Sets	7+ & Vellums
Ground Delivery (7-10 Days)	$15.00	$20.00	$25.00
Express Delivery (3-5 Days)	$20.00	$25.00	$30.00

International Shipping & Handling	1-3 Sets	4-6 Sets	7+ & Vellums
Regular Delivery Canada (7-10 Days)	$25.00	$30.00	$35.00
Express Delivery Canada (5-6 Days)	$40.00	$45.00	$50.00
Overseas Delivery Airmail (2-3 Weeks)	$50.00	$60.00	$65.00

Additional sets with original order $50

IMPORTANT INFORMATION TO READ BEFORE YOU PLACE YOUR ORDER

How Many Sets Of Plans Will You Need?

The Standard 8-Set Construction Package

Our experience shows that you'll speed every step of construction and avoid costly building errors by ordering enough sets to go around. Each tradesperson wants a set — the general contractor and all subcontractors; foundation, electrical, plumbing, heating/air conditioning and framers. Don't forget your lending institution, building department and, of course, a set for yourself. * Recommended For Construction *

The Minimum 4-Set Construction Package

If you're comfortable with arduous follow-up, this package can save you a few dollars by giving you the option of passing down plan sets as work progresses. You might have enough copies to go around if work goes exactly as scheduled and no plans are lost or damaged by subcontractors. But for only $60 more, the 8-set package eliminates these worries. *Recommended For Bidding *

The Single Study Set

We offer this set so you can study the blueprints to plan your dream home in detail. They are stamped "study set only-not for construction", and you cannot build a home from them. In pursuant to copyright laws, it is illegal to reproduce any blueprint.

Our Reorder and Exchange Policies:

If you find after your initial purchase that you require additional sets of plans you may purchase them from us at special reorder prices (please call for pricing details) provided that you reorder within 6 months of your original order date. There is a $28 reorder processing fee that is charged on all reorders. For more information on reordering plans please contact our Customer Service Department. Your plans are custom printed especially for you once you place your order. For that reason we cannot accept any returns. If for some reason you find that the plan you have purchased from us does not meet your needs, then you may exchange that plan for any other plan in our collection. We allow you sixty days from your original invoice date to make an exchange. At the time of the exchange you will be charged a processing fee of 20% of the total amount of your original order plus the difference in price between the plans (if applicable) plus the cost to ship the new plans to you. Call our Customer Service Department for more information. Please Note: Reproducible vellums can only be exchanged if they are unopened.

Important Shipping Information

Please refer to the shipping charts on the order form for service availability for your specific plan number. Our delivery service must have a street address or Rural Route Box number — never a post office box. (PLEASE NOTE: Supplying a P.O. Box number only will delay the shipping of your order.) Use a work address if no one is home during the day. Orders being shipped to APO or FPO must go via First Class Mail. Please include the proper postage.

For our International Customers, only Certified bank checks and money orders are accepted and must be payable in U.S. currency. For speed, we ship international orders Air Parcel Post. Please refer to the chart for the correct shipping cost.

Important Canadian Shipping Information

To our friends in Canada, we have a plan design affiliate in Penticton, BC. This relationship will help you avoid the delays and charges associated with shipments from the United States. Moreover, our affiliate is familiar with the building requirements in your community and country. We prefer payments in U.S. Currency. If you, however, are sending Canadian funds please add 45% to the prices of the plans and shipping fees.

An Important Note About Building Code Requirements:

All plans are drawn to conform to one or more of the industry's major national building standards. However, due to the variety of local building regulations, your plan may need to be modified to comply with local requirements — snow loads, energy loads, seismic zones, etc. Do check them fully and consult your local building officials.

A few states require that all building plans used be drawn by an architect registered in that state. While having your plans reviewed and stamped by such an architect may be prudent, laws requiring non-conforming plans like ours to be completely redrawn forces you to unnecessarily pay very large fees. If your state has such a law, we strongly recommend you contact your state representative to protest.

The rendering, floor plans and technical information contained within this publication are not guaranteed to be totally accurate. Consequently, no information from this publication should be used either as a guide to constructing a home or for estimating the cost of building a home. Complete blueprints must be purchased for such purposes.

Index

Option Key

BL Bottom-line Zip Quote **ML** Materials List Available **ZIP** Itemized Zip Quote **RRR** Right Reading Reverse **DUP** Duplex Plan

TOP SELLING
GARAGE PLANS

Save money by Doing-It-Yourself using our Easy-To-Follow plans. Whether you intend to build your own garage or contract it out to a building professional, the Garlinghouse garage plans provide you with everything you need to price out your project and get started. Put our 90+ years of experience to work for you. Order now!!

No. 06016C   **$86.00**

Apartment Garage With One Bedroom

No. 06015C   **$86.00**

Apartment Garage With Two Bedrooms

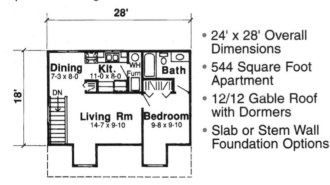

- 24' x 28' Overall Dimensions
- 544 Square Foot Apartment
- 12/12 Gable Roof with Dormers
- Slab or Stem Wall Foundation Options

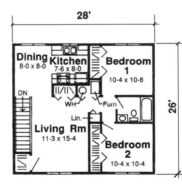

- 26' x 28' Overall Dimensions
- 728 Square Foot Apartment
- 4/12 Pitch Gable Roof
- Slab or Stem Wall Foundation Options

No. 06012C   **$54.00**

30' Deep Gable &/or Eave Jumbo Garages

- 4/12 Pitch Gable Roof
- Available Options for Extra Tall Walls, Garage & Personnel Doors, Foundation, Window, & Sidings
- Package contains 4 Different Sizes
- 30' x 28' • 30' x 32' • 30' x 36' • 30' x 40'

No. 06013C   **$68.00**

Two-Car Garage With Mudroom/Breezeway

- Attaches to Any House
- 24' x 24' Eave Entry
- Available Options for Utility Room with Bath, Mudroom, Screened-In Breezeway, Roof, Foundation, Garage & Personnel Doors, Window, & Sidings

No. 06001C   **$48.00**

12', 14' & 16' Wide-Gable 1-Car Garages

- Available Options for Roof, Foundation, Window, Door, & Sidings
- Package contains 8 Different Sizes
- 12' x 20' Mini-Garage   • 14' x 22'   • 16' x 20'   • 16' x 24'
- 14' x 20'   • 14' x 24'   • 16' x 22'   º• 16' x 26'

No. 06003C   **$48.00**

24' Wide-Gable 2-Car Garages

- Available Options for Side Shed, Roof, Foundation, Garage & Personnel Doors, Window, & Sidings
- Package contains 5 Different Sizes
- 24' x 22'   • 24' x 24'   • 24' x 26'
- 24' x 28'   • 24' x 32'

No. 06007C   **$60.00**

Gable 2-Car Gambrel Roof Garages

- Interior Rear Stairs to Loft Workshop
- Front Loft Cargo Door With Pulley Lift
- Available Options for Foundation, Garage & Personnel Doors, Window, & Sidings
- Package contains 5 Different Sizes
- 22' x 26' • 22' x 28' • 24' x 28' • 24' x 30' • 24' x 32'

No. 06006C   **$48.00**

22' & 24' Deep Eave 2 & 3-Car Garages

- Can Be Built Stand-Alone or Attached to House
- Available Options for Roof, Foundation, Garage & Personnel Doors, Window, & Sidings
- Package contains 6 Different Sizes
- 22' x 28'   • 22' x 32'   • 24' x 32'
- 22' x 30'   • 24' x 30'   • 24' x 36'

No. 06002C   **$48.00**

20' & 22' Wide-Gable 2-Car Garages

- Available Options for Roof, Foundation, Garage & Personnel Doors, Window, & Sidings
- Package contains 7 Different Sizes
- 20' x 20'   • 20' x 24'   • 22' x 22'   • 22' x 28'
- 20' x 22'   • 20' x 28'   • 22' x 24'

No. 06008C   **$60.00**

Eave 2 & 3-Car Clerestory Roof Garages

- Interior Side Stairs to Loft Workshop
- Available Options for Engine Lift, Foundation, Garage & Personnel Doors, Window, & Sidings
- Package contains 4 Different Sizes
- 24' x 26'   • 24' x 28'   • 24' x 32'   • 24' x 36'

Order Code No: **G22S4**

Garage Order Form

Please send me 3 complete sets of the following GARAGE PLANS:

Item no. & description		Price
Additional Sets	$	_____
(@ $10.00 EACH)	$	_____
Shipping Charges: UPS-$3.75, First Class-$4.50	$	_____
Subtotal:	$	_____
Resident sales tax: KS-6.15%, CT-6% (NOT REQUIRED FOR OTHER STATES)	$	_____

Total Enclosed: $ _____

My Billing Address is:

Name: _____

Address: _____

City: _____

State: _____ Zip: _____

Daytime Phone No. (_____) _____

My Shipping Address is:

Name: _____

Address: _____
(UPS will not ship to P.O. Boxes)

City: _____

State: _____ Zip: _____

For Faster Service...Charge It!
U.S. & Canada Call
1(800)235-5700

All foreign residents call 1(860)343-5977

MASTERCARD, VISA

Card # | | | | | | | | | | | | | | |

Signature _____ Exp. _____/_____

If paying by credit card, to avoid delays:
billing address must be as it appears on credit card statement

or FAX us at (860) 343-5984

Here's What You Get

- Three complete sets of drawings for each plan ordered.
- Detailed step-by-step instructions with easy-to-follow diagrams on how to build your garage (not available with apartment garages)
- For each garage style, a variety of size and garage door configuration options
- Variety of roof styles and/or pitch options for most garages
- Complete materials list
- Choice between three foundation options: Monolithic Slab, Concrete Stem Wall or Concrete Block Stem Wall
- Full framing plans, elevations and cross-sectionals for each garage size and configuration

Build-It-Yourself PROJECT PLAN

Order Information For Garage Plans:
All garage plan orders contain three complete sets of drawings with instructions and are priced as listed next to the illustration. Additional sets of plans may be obtained for $10.00 each with your original order. UPS shipping is used unless otherwise requested. Please include the proper amount for shipping.

Send your order to:
(With check or money order payable in U.S. funds only)
The Garlinghouse Company
174 Oakwood Drive
Glastonbury, CT 06033

No C.O.D. orders accepted; U.S. funds only. UPS will not ship to Post Office boxes, FPO boxes, APO boxes, Alaska or Hawaii. Canadian orders must be shipped First Class.

Prices subject to change without notice.